Making Stewardship
A Way of Life

A Complete Guide for Catholic Parishes

Making Stewardship
A Way of Life

Andrew Kemberling and Mila Glodava

Our Sunday Visitor Publishing Division
Our Sunday Visitor, Inc.
Huntington, Indiana 46750

Published 2009.

14 13 12 11 10 09 1 2 3 4 5 6 7 8 9

Our Sunday Visitor Publishing Division
Our Sunday Visitor, Inc.
200 Noll Plaza
Huntington, IN 46750

bookpermissions@osv.com
1-800-348-2440

ISBN 978-1-59276-577-5 (Inventory No. X861)

Interior design by Sherri L. Hoffman
Cover design by Lindsey Luken
Cover photos by Shutterstock
Interior photos courtesy of the authors

PRINTED IN THE UNITED STATES OF AMERICA

CONTENTS

ACKNOWLEDGMENTS

This book is a work of love and many people gave their support to make it happen. We want to thank them for their assistance and advice. Our thanks go to the staff in the office of communications and stewardship, especially Gary Olmsted, Jerry Nix, Michael Angell, Cindy Shinners, and Irene Lindemer, for their assistance in finishing this book.

Special thanks to Barb Markulik, assistant principal of the St. Thomas More Parish School; and Kitty Kolody, editor of the More Informed parish newsletter; Dick Rapp, business manager; Joe Zimmerman and Donna Rood in the accounting office; and Vicki Turner, Father Kemberling's secretary. Without their help this book could not have been completed.

We would also like to thank the STM stewardship committee members: Jim O'Brien, Therese Beaudette, John Christian, Phil and Irene Lindemer, and Pat Corder; the finance council liaison, Don Smith; and pastoral council liaisons: Michelle Thomas, Bob Moenster, and Joanne Horne for their encouragement and support. Our thanks to all our countless volunteers and committees, especially Bob and Joe Pristera and their family, our volunteer Refreshment Committee coordinators for Ministry Fair since 1998.

Our thanks go to all the commissions for helping us promote stewardship in their sphere of influence, especially the three branches of the parish's faith and academic formation commission: office of catechesis; parish school; and youth and young adults ministry. Their active participation is invaluable in making stewardship a way of life at St. Thomas More.

Sincere thanks, too, to the liturgy office for the beautiful liturgies during the season of stewardship. Special thanks to all the lay witness speakers who have inspired our parishioners to become good stewards.

Our thanks, too, to Rory Reilly and his staff at Cavan Corporation, especially Doug Bryan and Nicki Crook for their attention to detail. Special thanks to Cathi Politano and Janette Fayhoe, of Spirit of Christ Parish, for helping us introduce stewardship to St. Thomas More in 1989.

There are many more people who have helped us along the way but our limited space does not allow us to mention them all. To all of you, "Thank you." All of you are an important part of our success at St. Thomas More.

(And, on a personal note from Mila: My special thanks to my husband, Mark, for his patience and for giving me the space so I could actually work on the book, even on our vacation. Specials thanks, too, to my children, Kirsten Angela and Kevin Marc and his wife Trish for their encouragement.)

All for God's glory!

INTRODUCTION

Who We Are and How We Became Stewardship "Converts"

FATHER ANDREW KEMBERLING

The story of the millionaire at the church meeting is a good example of how stewardship is often associated with money. Talking about a turning point in his faith, a wealthy man told the others that just after he had earned his first dollar he went to church to worship. A visiting missionary happened to be giving a fund-raising talk that morning and the man came to the momentous decision to drop the bill into the collection basket. Now, looking back, he said, "Yes, I chose to give all my money to God. I believe he has blessed me for that and it's why I'm a rich man today."

There was a respectful silence until one elderly woman piped up, "I dare you to do it again!"

Again and again God asks us to renew our stewardship commitment. Time, talent, and treasure are spoken about but sadly people often hear, "treasure, treasure and treasure." The spirituality of stewardship has roots deeper than time, talent, and treasure. There are underlying values that dare us to give all of ourselves in our relationship with God. These values are identity, trust, gratitude and love. As we examine these essential stewardship values, we naturally go to the core of the Christian message.

When I was first ordained as a priest in 1988 I was assigned to Sacred Heart of Mary Parish in Boulder, Colorado. Its pastor then was the legendary Benedictine Abbot Edward Volmer who had been teaching stewardship for more than twenty years. He decided that my learning to do stewardship was one of his main goals. After I left Sacred Heart of Mary, I went off to Grand Junction, and lo and behold, they had a stewardship program there, too. And where did it come from? Abbot Edward Volmer, O.S.B. So I said, "I know how to do that!" and began my teaching stewardship there.

For a short period I was assigned to St. Francis Xavier Parish in Pueblo — where Abbot Volmer's stewardship program was also in use. I continued teaching and preaching about stewardship there until I was reassigned to Sacred Heart of Mary to take over for Abbot Volmer who had retired. In the six and a half years that followed, I learned to develop stewardship even more. I was on the archdiocese's stewardship committee with others already practicing stewardship, including my co-author Mila Glodava, who is the director of Communications and Stewardship at St. Thomas More Parish in Centennial.

What I learned from Abbot Volmer and all the years in various parishes worked well at Sacred Heart of Mary in Boulder. I also was discovering many more avenues of implementing and practicing stewardship. I learned there are more ways of doing stewardship than what I had originally thought. In subsequent years I've seen and tested even more ideas about stewardship and how to make it a process that really changes people's lives. The important difference right at the starting point is to realize that stewardship is not fund-raising: It is a way of life.

People have used "stewardship" as a catch phrase to describe fund-raising or regarding a development office. They would say they are using "the stewardship approach." Yet it has very little to do with stewardship. Rather, what they are talking about is how to raise money. I imagine that is very helpful to them because they look for whatever avenue they can use to raise money.

Nevertheless, stewardship is not just about money. Does it involve money? Of course it does, as do a lot of other things. Stewardship, however, is a means to an end: evangelization.

Stewardship is a way of life, whereas fund-raising is all about raising money. Moreover, stewardship is spirituality rather than theology. This should be of special interest for the priests and deacons who are trained in theology. I am not presenting *a* theology in this book.

A theology is like an order of ideas that you can keep in your head but in spirituality there is a group of actions that are generated from your heart. Theology is something that you can think your way through. Spirituality is something you have to act your way through. With this in mind, what we're going to share with you in this book are collective and time-tested experiences to make this spirituality happen.

A Note for Priests: I must admit that one of the hardest groups for me to convince regarding this spirituality is my fellow pastors and clergy. So if the laity finds some frustrations trying to convert their pastor, please know I have the same problem. I have been wondering why this is true. When I was in the Philippines I had a chance to talk to quite a few priests, several bishops and a cardinal. I said the same thing to them. So don't feel offended. I tell priests, "You are my toughest customers."

I have given a lot of thought on this problem of convincing fellow priests about the spirituality of stewardship. I realized that the clergy feel that they already have some kind of spirituality. They already are spiritual men who are comfortable with a spirituality that's working for them. Why add another kind of spirituality? After all, they have dedicated themselves to God as priests. They are consecrated and ordained. "The last thing we need is one more thing." It's true! We're constantly asked to do another thing or another program.

Well, another way to explain the difference between spirituality and theology is that it is born out of necessity. People need spirituality. They are usually in pain or they are hurting. Something has happened in their lives and now they need God. Whereas when people are doing really well, in some sense they think about God, but they don't really feel the need for God.

One way to look at spirituality and theology is a practical one. Theology teaches you that there is a hell. Those who have spirituality are those who have visited there and don't want to go back! So out of pain and suffering you will realize you cannot think your way out of this. You have to act your way out. That's what stewardship spirituality does.

I would ask you, therefore, to identify with those people who are struggling in your parish, perhaps financially. Yet, you know your answer to the problem cannot be a quick-fix. Perhaps looking into the spirituality of stewardship may just be the key to sustaining your parish. This would give you a reason to add one more form of spirituality to the spirituality you already have.

I was a Benedictine priest for twenty years before leaving the order and becoming a priest for the Archdiocese of Denver. When I first heard of stewardship I said, "I don't need another kind of spirituality. I'm a Benedictine, therefore, I have a Benedictine spirituality." Well, I found out that stewardship spirituality is like a glove that fits over the spirituality I already had. It gave meaning to the spirituality that I already had. I invite those of you who have already adopted some other kind of spirituality to consider that. Stewardship spirituality does not *replace* the spirituality you already have. In fact, it deepens your own spirituality.

Another contrast between theology and spirituality is that theology is very mind-oriented, while spirituality is very emotion-oriented. It deals with how you feel. There are certain things that change the way you feel when you change your thinking. Those are some of the things that I identify in this book.

At the back of this book are examples of homilies that further expound on the themes that are presented here.

MILA GLODAVA

Why did Father Andrew Kemberling and I write this book? It's all about sharing a good thing! It's like the Good News: You cannot keep it to yourself. It's true. As director of communications and stewardship of St. Thomas More Catholic Church in Centennial, Colorado, I have learned some tried and true ways to make the parish self-sustaining through the embrace and practice of stewardship as a way of life. This means teaching a life of thanksgiving for all of God's blessings that result in a spirit-filled, vibrant parish.

Indeed, with this way of life, St. Thomas More is blessed with sufficient human and financial resources to carry out its mission "to go and make disciples." Many times when I attend meetings with other parishes, I hear of concerns over the lack of volunteers and funds to carry out parish work and I ask myself, "What are we doing right?" The answer always goes back to our practice of stewardship as a way of life in the parish. That's why, to me, it makes sense to promote making stewardship a way of life in the parish.

St. Thomas More's pastor, Father Andrew Kemberling, and I started sharing the St. Thomas More model of stewardship with other parishes in the Archdiocese of Denver, after we had introduced it in 2003 to some seventy bishops, clergy and laity in the Philippines.

Honestly, I did not plan this. All I wanted was to help my own home diocese, the Prelature of Infanta in the Philippines, become self-sustaining. I thought stewardship could help. Fortunately, Carmelite Bishop Julio X. Labayen, then bishop of Infanta, arranged for me to introduce stewardship in 2002 to all his clergy. It was then he realized that stewardship was a grace he needed to share with others, including Cardinal Ricardo Vidal, Archbishop of Cebu, and several other bishops. In 2005, Father Andrew and I gave a day-long conference to the entire Catholic Bishops' Conference of the Philippines (CBCP).

After our 2003 stewardship conference in the Philippines, Father Andrew and I realized that we could just as easily share our stewardship program with other parishes in the Archdiocese of Denver. Since then we have given dozens of workshops and conferences to hundreds of bishops, clergy and laity, not only in the Archdiocese of Denver but in other parts of the country as well.

In fact, we have received so many requests that we soon realized that it would be impossible to accommodate them all. That's why we decided to write this book, so we could share our program with others while keeping our top priority — our work at St. Thomas More.

Update on Stewardship in the Philippines: Since planting the seeds of stewardship in the Philippines in 2002, I have seen some growth and some fruits of it there. Several parishes which can be described as among the poorest of the poor are showing how stewardship is helping them renew and enliven their parish life. Stewardship is also changing how they view the Church. While in the past, the Church was there to help them in their daily struggle, now they *are* the Church. They take care of the Church. With this new mindset, giving has become a part of their ownership of the Church.

Speaking to the executive secretaries of the Episcopal Commissions of the Catholic Bishops' Conference of the Philippines at a recent stewardship conference, Archbishop Angel Lagdameo, president, said, "It is hoped that through your group one of the decrees of PCP II (Second Plenary Council of the Philippines) will come to life, which says 'The Church through the initiative of the CBCP should develop a comprehensive theology of Stewardship…' (Art. 31, sec. 1). It has never been done. Will it be done this year? Through you? That is the challenge I am putting to you. It will not, it cannot, be done today. But it will be a reason for your group or commission to come together again and again with a vision of articulating for the CBCP, whose secretaries you are, a comprehensive theology of stewardship."

I saw the message of stewardship lived in several parishes. In General Nakar, in the Prelature of Infanta, in the Province of Quezon, and in West Solana, in the Province of Tuguegarao, parishioners began embracing stewardship after their pastors began teaching its message of thanksgiving for all of God's blessings. Working with the Basic Ecclesial Communities and using catechesis as their principal method of teaching, even the poorest of the poor have embraced stewardship as a way of life in their respective parishes.

Father Andrew and I have continued our efforts to promote stewardship in the Philippines with the help of our mission partner, the Socio Pastoral Institute. I am, therefore, grateful to Father Andrew and St. Thomas More for their continued commitment to the Philippine mission and its goal to become a self-sustaining church.

PART I

The Spirituality of Stewardship

By Father Andrew Kemberling

SECTION 1: CORE VALUES

Most people think of stewardship as time, talent, and treasure. Yet there's more to stewardship than the commonly known "three T's." Underneath the time, talent, and treasure are four underlying core values: identity, trust, gratitude, and love. These are fundamental in developing the importance of time, talent, and treasure. Once you understand the four values, the three T's take on an even greater importance.

Identity

"God created man in his image; in the divine image he created him; male and female he created them" (Gn 1:27).

Our Christian identity is founded upon the basic idea of God as Creator. God created us in His image and likeness. This means that we have human dignity, but don't stop there. We are created *by* God *for* God. In a very real way, we are not our own. We belong to God. Thus, we can truly profess, "I am a child of God. I belong to God."

Scripture says this well. In Psalm 95:6-7 we hear: "Enter, let us bow down in worship; let us kneel before the Lord who made us. For this is our God, whose people we are, God's well-tended flock." Psalm 100:1-3 says it even better: "Shout joyfully to the Lord, all you lands; worship the Lord with cries of gladness; come before him with joyful song. Know that the Lord is God, our maker to whom we belong, whose people we are, God's well-tended flock." And in the New Testament, St. Paul says: "Do you not know that your body is a temple of the holy Spirit within you, whom you have from God, and that you are not your own? For you have been purchased at a price. Therefore, glorify God in your body" (1 Cor 6:19-20).

Not only do these passages tell us of our identity, but they remind us of the primacy of God in our lives. The fact remains, if we are not our own, then the things we have are not our own either. We really do not own them. We steward them. God lets us have these things and asks us to be good stewards. Even our talents are not our own. They, too, belong to God.

A good illustration of this is the Parable of the Talents (Mt 25:14-30). (The word "talent" is a unit of coinage. The English word we use is derived directly from this biblical passage.) In the story, before a man went on a journey, he called in his servants and entrusted his possessions to them. To one he gave five talents, to another two and to a third, one — each according to the servant's ability. Then he went away. Immediately, the one who received the five talents went and traded with them, and made another five. Likewise, the one who received two made another two. But the man who received one went out and dug a hole in the ground and buried his master's money.

Please notice that the man did not bury his *own* money, but his master's money. The "talents" did not belong to the servant. They were given to the servant by the master. They were given to be used, not wasted. The same is true of us. Our talents are not our own, because we are not our own. We belong to God and everything we have is from God.

It's important to remember this value of identity because as you look at your identity you begin to realize that "I am a steward." What does it mean to be a steward, a good steward? To be a good steward, you have to go back to the relationship between God and us. God is the Creator. He made us in his image and likeness.

"We are created by God" is what most people would agree upon. Of course, God created me! But what most of us Christians have a hard time accepting is "I am not only created *by* God; I am created *for* God." I am created for God, not for myself. This is not what much of the world tells us, however. The trend nowadays is towards individualism, which emphasizes, "I was created for myself so that I could satisfy all my needs and wants." No. This is not the case. Nowhere in Christianity do you find that concept. Rather, we are created by God for God.

The *Catechism of the Catholic Church* (like the Baltimore catechism) teaches us of our universal longing for God. It says, "The desire for

God is written in the human heart, because man is created by God for God" (CCC 27). Thus I can truly say, "I am created by God and for God, to serve him in this world and to be happy with him in the next." The *for* God part is an essential part of stewardship spirituality. It is something we need to inculcate in the programs, in our talks, and in what we believe about stewardship. It begins to create a detachment from things, even from ourselves. In that detachment we can see that God is the owner of everything.

In stewardship spirituality you're looking at that very basic identity issue: "Who am I?" I am created by God, for God. This is very clear in the Old Testament. The New Testament tells us we are temples of the Holy Spirit. We are not our own. We were purchased at a price, the price of the cross. It's there repeatedly. We really don't own ourselves.

I often remind people about our bodies. Our bodies are not ours. They are God's. It is God's body. He has given it to us and it is temporary. It dies. We get our permanent one at the resurrection of the dead. That's our permanent body. The one we have right now is mortal. It will pass away. And God asks us to steward it as we steward every other thing in our lives.

Recognizing our identity in its relationship to our being created for God has a lot of implications. If I am not my own, then all the things that I "own," and all that I have, are not mine either. They are lent to me by God. They are given to me by God, for a time. As his stewards, our duties include taking care of everything that he has given us. Remember, a steward is someone who manages someone else's things. And more than being responsible just for ourselves, we may also be responsible, to a degree, for the talents, time, and treasure of others. That may be the case in our roles as parents or priests, or in other positions of authority.

We are also created for God's purposes. Our mission is to love and serve him in this world and the next. God's love for us is far beyond our imagination. Our service is easily grasped when we realize that at baptism we were each called to be priest, prophet and king.

The common priesthood of believers prays to God. This may not sound important until we look into the Old Testament and realize that the ordinary worshipper had to go to a priest and have him offer prayers and sacrifices. As the manifestation of Christ's priesthood, our priesthood gives us the privilege of offering our own prayers directly to God. A certain intimacy is required which allows us to be personally close to God. Time in prayer builds the relationship. The importance of prayer and its resulting holiness should not be underestimated in stewardship spirituality.

We have been granted the honor of speaking in God's name when each of us was called to be a prophet. When taken seriously, we understand that we represent him personally. Prophets call the community to repentance but that is not a genuine exhortation unless we are repentant ourselves. Walking the talk is a consistent practice in stewardship spirituality. God the Father is "King of the Universe" and Jesus, his Son, is called the "Prince of Peace." Jesus is our brother, because we share our blood with him. He certainly shares his blood with us. The groundwork for establishing that we are a kingly people lies in the fact that we share the same blood with Jesus. The kingship of Jesus is part and parcel of our kingly role, and governance is the function of a king. Therefore we work for justice and peace. Goodness and the common good are goals that guide our objectives. That means that all of our behaviors, especially our talents, are gifts that we share to build up the Church as God intends. Evangelization challenges us to live up to our kingly role.

When stewardship is practiced well, we are changed into the people that God intends us to be. When Jesus says "Go and make disciples," it means we have to be disciples ourselves. We cannot give away what we don't have. When we ask the question "How do we grow closer to God?" we realize that we have to know God in a personal way. All the theology and all the ideas we have about God cannot interfere with our personal relationship with God. We can know God intellectually, but that cannot substitute for the obligation we have to personally serve him in our roles as priest, prophet, and king. We have to put these roles into practice. This brings us back to our original mission to love and to serve him. To love him is to serve him. Love motivates us to give ourselves completely to God. The spirituality of stewardship sees love in terms of giving. Giving and receiving are behaviors of the good steward. The experience of giving ourselves personally to God helps us to become the disciple he has called us to be. Once we become a disciple, we can go and make other disciples. We don't have to go far, as the parish is a place to seek out others who have not yet discovered God. The parish becomes alive in stewardship spirituality. We truly discover that God is personal and can be known personally.

Trust

"Many shall look on in awe and they shall trust in the LORD" (Ps 40:4).

THE UNDERLYING VALUE OF TRUST builds upon the value of identity. Since everything we have is from God, it is God who is in charge of our lives, not us. As we live our lives, we are caught up in something much bigger than ourselves. The value of trust allows us to let go of what seemingly is in our control and to "let God" do what he is already doing for us. Thus the saying "Let go and let God."

As hard as it is to believe, everything is just the way God would have it at this very moment. Yes, evil is real and causes pain, suffering, and death. But God has a plan to bring about life, and it's happening right now. Mysteriously, God brings about good even from evil. All we have to do is trust. For the good stewards, God provides everything we have. Our ability to be a provider is in itself a gift from God. He gives us everything we need.

Stewardship becomes a way of life by activating the trust that we have. Acceptance comes from letting go of control. Our control is self centeredness. It is the false belief that the world is created in our own image, and that somehow we are in charge. When things don't go "our" way, anger and resentment fuel a cynical view of life that is full of frustration. Trusting in God is based upon the belief in our own powerlessness. We realign our belief in God's almighty power and his total but hidden control to bring about what's best for us in the midst of a struggling world. We "let go" and we "let God." Acceptance only comes when we come to the realization that we pray for God's will in our life, not our own. God does not let us down either. He sends his calming grace that says, "Everything is all right, don't worry. You'll be OK." Peace of mind is the end result of trust brought about by acceptance.

This trust level comes out of our sense of identity: "I don't create all this stuff, God does, and he provides it to me." We develop an understanding that we're not making it happen, God is. But even then, our free will — another God-given gift — can confuse us. We can think that *we're* causing things to happen and trust in ourselves instead of realizing that when we surrender our wills, it is God who does for us what we cannot do for ourselves. That's the basic understanding of trust. We trust in God that there is something greater than ourselves going on here — and it does take faith to believe that God really will provide for us!

People generally believe that, even if only in some sort of nebulous way, but when it's time to head off to work to make money to pay the bills, they might think, "*I'm* the one doing this all by myself." Don't be fooled! God is really the one providing for you and your family. All you need to do is to trust him and do what he asks you to do.

If you really believe and trust that God will provide for all your needs, then you must be trustworthy also. You must grow in your being worthy of his trust. You must be honest in all your dealings. You can't just declare that you're trustworthy. You must actually *be* trustworthy in your words and deeds.

This is particularly true in your relationships with your families and your parish and diocese. If you're not trustworthy in reporting things properly and in doing what you're obliged to do, then stewardship becomes a sham. It becomes an outward show with internal corruption. The internal issue of trust has to be established firmly within good stewardship. You miss the point of identity, if you don't understand the trust part. The trust comes from the fact that "I am not my own. I am God's and God trusts me to take care of what he has given me." This trust is shown in the way you handle all of your material possessions. (As Our Lord says, if a person can be trustworthy in a small matter, he or she can be trustworthy in larger matters — see Mt 25:21.) It means you have to put your spirituality into action. It means you have to be trustworthy in your own parish.

How do you behave with others? Do you misuse them? Are you honest with them? How do you deal with people's money? Are you trustworthy? Are you totally honest with the church, with the government, and with all?

The value of trust must not be sacrificed. It is easy to come up with excuses like, "Well, you know, it's really an unfair system, so I'm holding a little something back because in justice we've really got it coming to us." Folks, you would be fooling yourselves. You would undermine the very grace that comes from God as part of the spirituality. Trust God. You don't have to cheat your way into being a good steward.

That's exactly why Jesus criticized the Pharisees. They were excellent "tithers," yet they were crooked and that was what upset him. Outwardly, they would really tithe. They tithed on everything, even on their garden at the back of the house, and even on the littlest plants they would tithe ten percent. Still…

> *"Woe to you, scribes and Pharisees, you hypocrites. You pay tithes of mint and dill and cummin, and have neglected the weightier things of the law: judgment and mercy and fidelity. (But) these you should have done, without neglecting the others" (Mt 23:23).*

Justice is based upon truth. You cannot be cheating. Truth and being trustworthy are an essential part of stewardship spirituality.

This is a hard pill to swallow for some people. Nevertheless, everything has to be as forthright as possible. Believe it. You cannot cheat and get ahead on stewardship. God has *all* the money in the world. To priests, I say, "Don't worry about paying your full amount to the archdiocese. Don't worry about a full assessment. *Just pay it.* God will give you more. In fact, that's what he's counting on. How is the diocese going to get funding for its services? It's going to get it from you. God's going to give you more than you've ever had.

You cannot cheat the poor, either. In the words of the *Catechism of the Catholic Church*: "Trust in God is a preparation for the blessedness of the poor. They shall see God" (CCC 2457).

Again, we are not our own. We belong to God. We are created by God and for God. Our identity helps us to trust that God will provide for us. On our part, we need to be trustworthy in all our dealings. That's the underpinning of what it is to be a steward. A steward is first and foremost honest and full of integrity.

Gratitude

"Give thanks to the LORD who is good, whose love endures forever!" (Ps 107:1).

TRUST AND ACCEPTANCE naturally lead to the next core value: gratitude. Coming to the realization that enough is enough is fueled by acceptance. It is an attitude shift of looking at what we have, not at what we don't have.

The greatest gift is our relationship with loved ones. People are more important than things. We come to accept that God has given us just what we need. We come to believe that God does for us what we cannot do for ourselves. God's way of providing is for our own good. Our detachment from material goods places them in their proper perspective. We appreciate them for what they are: gifts.

Gratitude fills our heart as we realize the wisdom and forethought God has in giving us what we need. If we don't have it, perhaps we don't need it. If God wants us to have something, we remember that nothing is impossible with God (see Lk 1:37). What we have is shared with us by God and we appreciate his trust in us to be stewards of the good things of life. Our thanks to God is an offering in itself. It is our way of responding to the relationship founded upon God's love.

Gratitude is like the fruit of identity and trust because as you start losing yourself, you start focusing on the things that you have been given. All of stewardship sees everything as a gift, a gift from God. Listen for the gift language in the Eucharistic prayer: "Oh God, we present these gifts to you and all the gifts that you've given us." ("In the *preface*, the Church gives thanks to the Father, through Christ, in the Holy Spirit, for all his works: creation, redemption, and sanctification" (CCC 1352).) Indeed, God has given you every single thing in your life. Thus you won't take anything for granted. You realize how God's action and control has made everything happen in your life.

Gratitude is born out of trust because the ultimate trust is letting go of the control. God is in control. When you realize that God is in control and he has given everything as a gift, gratitude is born.

The opposites of gratitude are greed and envy. Greed and envy are qualities in our world that are destructive to gratitude because greed and envy want more, more, *more!* With gratitude we say, "I am not trying to seek what I don't have. Rather, I appreciate what I already have." It changes the focus. It's like taking a 180-degree turn. You start seeing a different picture.

The result is you say, "I have this and I have that." You begin to realize what you do have instead of being filled with covetousness, with avarice or with wanting more. You appreciate what you have. You begin to say, "I don't need so much. I can live with less." That's what gratitude does. It helps you realize you can have less. You don't have to have all that you want. Instead, you say, "I have enough. In fact, I have too much already. Look at all God's given me!" You start to take an inventory of everything you have and you say, "I have more than I've ever needed!" Then you begin to realize, when you compare what you have to what other people have, that: "I am blessed. I am truly blessed."

This is especially true for travelers from First World countries to developing countries. They can be real wimps when it comes to getting ready in the morning without hot water and a shower readily available. It can be a very hard experience for some and you can bet when they go home they'll be thanking God for hot water!

When was the last time you thanked God for things as simple as hot water and a shower? We have so much, yet we take them for granted — even the most basic creature comforts of life: indoor plumbing, drinkable water. Imagine not having ready access to drinkable water!

Gratitude is a quality of humility. We need to lose our selfishness and, perhaps, some sense of control. We need to become humble. Humility does not focus on oneself. Rather, it focuses upon the ultimate. The ultimate is that God is God and he gives us everything we have. Then we realize we don't need anything more because we already have so much now.

Everything we have is a gift. That means there's this relationship of giving and receiving that's very important to stewardship spirituality. God gives and we receive. Then on our part we learn how to give. Just as God gives us everything, we too, need to learn to give as part of this spirituality. This is not an intellectual process. These are actions that come from your heart. This is very moral. So in this spirituality, gratitude means you need to be thankful. You cannot just think thankfulness. You have to act out being thankful.

Love

"So faith, hope, love remain, these three; but the greatest of these is love" (1 Cor 13:13).

We have identified the first three core values of identity, trust, and gratitude, and now we come to the last one: love. As God loves us, we love God. Love is *the* requirement of the Christian. It is *not* optional.

I often remind people that love is also in our language as another word. It's called charity! When people hear charity they immediately think money but not so when they think of love. But we say faith, hope, and *love*, or faith, hope, and *charity*. Charity and love are the same thing. They are interchangeable. We use them all the time in theological context. If you're going to move it into a spiritual context that means you *are* going to love. You *are* going to have to give.

Charity, therefore, is the requirement of a Christian. Love is not self-seeking. Love itself requires one to give. One cannot love if all one does is receive, receive, receive. Think about it. If in our family relationships all we do is receive, would we call that love? No. Love, therefore, requires us to give and to give of ourselves. To give time to God in prayer is an exceptional sign of our love.

The good steward understands that our charitable giving is based on the key idea that *we have a need to give before we give to a need.* Our need to give is our response in love. We give back what is not really ours. God does not want all of it back — not yet. He will when we die. He does not want half of it back. No. God asks a tithe back in thanksgiving for what he has done. He asks us to give of our time, talent, and treasure. As God loves us we love God. When God sees our response in love, God gives us even more. God cannot be outdone in generosity.

The love we have for God is manifested in setting nothing before our relationship with him. Out of love, our first priority is God. We don't let things get in the way. Remember, God made us. We don't belong to ourselves. If we don't belong to ourselves, then the things we have are not even ours. They are lent to us.

Just as when we rent something, there is a real owner, and that owner is God. (This is particularly true when it comes to spending money entrusted to us. Put God first before paying any bills or setting any money aside.) When we rent something, we have to return it and give it back. Renters can be careless, which shows lack of respect for the owner. An even greater insult is for the renter to use an item and never to return it. That's stealing from the owner. God is the owner, and we are the managers of his treasure. God, however, says, "Keep ninety percent; use it even though it is not yours. Give back only ten percent — a tithe." A tithe is not what's leftover or the table droppings. It is the best portion, the first portion. It is a sign of our love to give the very best.

I ask married couples, would it be love if all your spouse ever did was receive, receive, receive? No. That's not love. Plus, you need to give. It must be mutual giving. That's what we believe marriage is. It's a covenant of mutuality. It means you give and you receive. You receive and you give. You learn how to give back and forth. In the same way, the requirement of the Christian is to love, is to give.

What do you give? Well, we believe there are a number of things you can give but we have categorized these as time, talent, and treasure. Often, we think that giving is optional. It's not. Love requires us to give; it's part of loving. You can think your way through love, but when you act your way through love you have to give of yourself. Again, marriage is a good example because it's a covenant of giving and receiving. You love each other. You know how to give. You give of yourself. You don't give 50/50. You give 100/100. You give your whole self. By giving yourself, you hold nothing back and you become even greater because you're giving yourself away. That's what the sacrament of marriage is about. It's a beautiful image. It is born out of this image of love.

Love is important in stewardship spirituality. It is expressed in giving. If we say we love God, why is it hard to give to the collection basket at church? Why do so many make excuses for not giving? This, to me, diminishes the value of love. If people give, even in small amounts, it teaches them to focus on someone else rather than on themselves. It focuses on a relationship, a deep and loving relationship with God. Remember the first core value of identity? God created us for him.

One way to look at love as a requirement of the Christian is written in the Old Testament: "Do not come empty handed when you come to the altar." In biblical times, there were the three times a year when they were required to "keep a feast to me" (see Ex 23:14). They didn't come empty-handed: "The choicest first fruits of your soil you shall bring to the house of the Lord, your God" (Ex 23:19).

It was a way of life then in the Old Testament, and it's a way of life for us now. To explain this further, I would like to go back to that identity issue. One of the images we came across while promoting stewardship as a way of life in the Philippines was this idea of the spousal image of identity. Remember what Scripture teaches us: God has married us. We are married to God. We are his spouse. In addition, Jesus calls himself the "bridegroom" and the Church is his bride. The Church is our spouse. That's a beautiful image.

Of course, we also have another image which is more accepted within the Church and that is the Church is "our mother." It's a beautiful image, a very beautiful image. Indeed, the Church provides for, feeds and looks after us just as a mother does for her child. It's very tender. There's trust and the sense of security.

Let's face it though, little children grow up. When you grow up, you don't marry your mother. You don't marry your father. You marry your spouse. You marry your husband. You marry your wife. If you can see the Church not as just your mother, but as your husband or as your wife, then you also see an obligation that comes with loving a spouse. It is in that spousal relationship that we challenge a poor parish to ask: "How would you treat your wife? Would you treat your wife this way by giving her nothing? You would go out of your way to make sure she had everything she needed."

Remember, that's what spirituality is — applying it — asking people to take seriously that the Church is their spouse. Are you in love with your spouse? Look at her. Look at him. Are you only *thinking* your love or are you *showing* your love.

Even the poorest people know about marriage. They know that image. You don't have to explain it too hard. They get that one real fast because they know what it is to have a husband and a wife. They know how to be good to their spouses. When they think of the Church as their spouse, they learn to treat the Church with that same understanding.

Remember, love is a requirement of the Christian. We love, and then we know how to love. Those who are married know what's required of love. They know how to love. If they can understand the kind of love there is between husband and wife, they can transfer that to the Church. That's an important start, but it's just a start.

SECTION 2: TIME, TALENT, AND TREASURE

The spirituality of stewardship deals with time, talent, and treasure. As we look into the core values of identity, trust, gratitude and love, we understand how to be good stewards. We remember who we are. We trust enough to let go and let God. It is a sign of our love to give the best by putting God first in our lives and in our spending. We love God as he loves us. We express our love of God by giving of our time, talent, and treasure.

As St. Peter said, "As each one has received a gift, use it to serve one another as good stewards of God's varied grace" (1 Pt 4:10).

Time

Glory be to the Father and to the Son and to the Holy Spirit. As it was in the beginning, is now and ever shall be, world without end. Amen

Time is a gift from God. In stewardship spirituality, we think of time and talent as connected. One has to spend time giving of one's talent so the two are obviously linked. But reflecting upon time alone gives further insights into the spirituality of stewardship.

The timelessness of God is found in the "Glory Be" prayer. Yes, God's world is not like our world. Time is a creation of God. Time is for our created world. It's limited, and it will have an end. We clearly hear in Scripture that Jesus will return at "the end of time." Since time is a creation for our world, perhaps time has been created solely for our human benefit. This is a staggering thought in light of the millions and billions of years that have passed before human existence. Perhaps time was created so that the phrase "in the fullness of time, God sent his only Son to be our redeemer" would take on greater meaning. In comparison to the vast amount of time that has passed before us, a relatively short time has passed since Jesus made the announcement, "This is the time of fulfillment; the kingdom of God is at hand" (Mk 1:5).

We have learned from science that time and space are intricately connected since they are a function of each other. Since God is timeless, he is also spaceless. The world of the afterlife, where God lives, has no time. It has no space. God's world is not like our world. These are qualities of our world that need to be appreciated for the gifts that they are.

I believe that when we no longer have them, we will appreciate them for the gifts that they are. I think we will be able to look upon all of our time and how we spent it. How we prioritized our time will reveal our motives and intentions. We will remember the hours we spent watching movies or television. Time spent with family will be compared with time spent working. The time spent with God will stand out in a special way. Will this review of our time betray us and reveal us to be hypocrites?

Time spent in prayer is time well spent. In the beginning God took six days to create and on the seventh day he rested. As a reminder, these are divine days, since an earthly day was not created until the fourth day when God created the sun and the moon. Time operates differently for God. Scripture tells us in Psalm 90 that a thousand years are like a day, and a day is like a thousand years. Whatever these divine days mean to God, who has no time, he took the seventh day and made it holy.

We imitate God since we have seven days in our week, with Sunday the day set aside for rest. Six days may be considered ours but the seventh day belongs to God. That is why Sunday is called the "Lord's Day." The main reason for the prohibition of work is so we will have the time to pray. I like to say, "Remember when missing Mass on Sunday was a sin? Well, *it still is*." Yes, the primacy of Sunday being a day of prayer is important in stewardship spirituality. (And, of course, "Sunday Mass" includes the vigil Mass on Saturday evening.)

In stewardship spirituality we fulfill an obligation of being thankful for this gift of time by giving a portion back to God in prayer. The portion that is given back to God is called the tithe. The first ten percent of this gift is to be given back to God in thanksgiving. In respect to time, we would be asked to give the first and the best of it. Sunday being the first day of the week has a special place in our time marked out for prayer. The one-tenth portion of a day is two hours and twenty-four minutes. Being conscious of the amount of time we spend in prayer will allow us to pass the best of our time ever mindful of it being a gift to us.

Well, that's what many people in religious orders do. For those who already have a dedication to a prayer life, wouldn't it be wonderful if added to that spirituality was the understanding that the time spent in prayer is that of being a good steward: accepting, receiving, and giving back the gift of time that God has given to us? It gives greater meaning to a prayer life. You might say, "I'm doing this as a gift back to God."

This is particularly true for me as a priest. There may be two or three days a week when I get to tithe two hours and twenty-four minutes of time back to God. I'm celebrating Mass. I'm hearing confessions. I'm praying the rosary. I'm leading a group in prayer. When I do that and it starts to seem burdensome to me I remind myself, "Wait a minute, this is my opportunity to tithe this time back to God in thanksgiving for what God has done." I'm being a good steward of time when I realize that I'm saying, "Wait a minute. Where is the present moment in this?" Then it gets me deeper into the prayer that I'm praying. The distractions become something further away. When we become aware that distractions are part of interfering with the present moment, then we deepen our prayer life.

Making time to pray can be seen in this story:

> During the lunch hour the president of a large factory wanted to talk to his company's manager about an urgent matter, but the manager's secretary said, "He is in conference as he is every day at this time." "But," said the impatient official, "tell him the company president wants to see him." The secretary firmly replied, "I have strict orders not to disturb him when he is in conference." Angrily, he brushed the secretary aside and opened the door to the manager's private office. After one look, he backed out slowly, gently closed the door, and said, "I'm sorry. Is this a daily occurrence?" "Yes, every day he spends fifteen minutes in such a conference," said the secretary. The president had found the manager on his knees before an open Bible. Of course, the fifteen-minute daily conference was with God.

Sometimes people feel distracted when they pray. Understanding the relationship of prayer to time can be helpful in this matter. Experiencing time in relation to the present moment is a critical idea in understanding time as a gift. It is even more important when we see the link of time to prayer. Time can seem elusive because we view time as being past, present, and future. As hard as it may seem, time is only experienced in the here and now. There is the constant temptation to live time as if it were either in the future or the past. When we begin to think like this, we rob ourselves of the present moment and we lose peace and serenity. By living in the future, we may experience worry and fear. By living in the past, we can be plagued by guilt and shame. Only in the present moment is there any relief. Finding that present moment is where we also find the presence of God.

When we try to seek to live in the past without the involvement of God in the present moment, we fail miserably. Historians have a noble profession but have always found their efforts ultimately take on meaning in relation to the present. Planners and developers dream dreams that ultimately have their meaning also in the present. Living in the here and now means adopting spiritual principles that recognize time as a gift.

In our modern society, we have many timesaving devices, yet less time than ever! Over-activity and the pursuit of leisure activities rob us of the present moment. Being busy has us scurrying about, causing a lack of focus and priorities. We become too busy to pray. Some are too busy to attend Sunday Mass. Time gets hijacked by the business world. Time is money, and no losses will be recorded by the industrious. This kind of utilitarian way of thinking wickedly transforms time into being a measure of production and efficiency. Time becomes a curse and not a blessing. The pursuit of pleasure also makes time into a commod ity. Our hedonistic tendency needs time to experience gratification. Of course, one can never get enough, as temperance is a casualty in the pursuit of pleasure. God is lost, or forgotten, because the gift of the present moment becomes irrelevant.

These threats need to be consciously addressed as we reclaim the present moment out of respect for God. Time is a gift, a gift from God. True peace and serenity will not be found in greed or gratification, but in God. The spiritual principle of stewardship resets our priority upon the primacy of God as creator. We are creatures of his created order, an order of time and space. Past and future have their places as do fear and shame. Emotional freedom is found in the here and now and recognizes life as being lived in the present moment.

Stewards of all that God gives us, we are ever conscious of the gift of time. We don't *find* time to pray, we *make* time to pray. Time spent in prayer is balanced with the time experienced each moment of our lives. When we are too far ahead of ourselves, we know that we will experience fear and worry. When we are too far behind ourselves, we will experience guilt and shame. The good steward acts rightly, loves goodness, and walks humbly with his God. (*See Micah 6:8.*) First things are done first and one thing is done at a time. We stay focused on the primacy of God and see every moment as a gift. In all things may God be glorified.

Time, in stewardship spirituality, is more than time spent in giving of our talents. It is an attitude that stays focused and unafraid. Being God-conscious in all that we do keeps us ever linked to the present because only God is found in the here and now. This spiritual understanding of time is important to understanding and embracing the spirituality of stewardship.

Talent

"Since we have gifts that differ according to the grace given to us, let us exercise them: if prophecy, in proportion to the faith; if ministry, in ministering; if one is a teacher, in teaching; if one exhorts, in exhortation; if one contributes, in generosity; if one is over others, with diligence; if one does acts of mercy, with cheerfulness" (Rom 12:6-8).

As we mentioned in the section on "Identity," the English word "talent" originated in the Bible which describes talent as a unit of money. It's a coin representing a specific amount. And, as we talked about there, the Parable of the Talents (Mt 25:14-30) is a reminder that a talent is something that is not our own.

I have to convince myself of that sometimes. I'm trained as an artist but right now a lot of my art training is on hold. Most parishioners don't know that I'm an artist. They have never seen me do any artwork, so they have no clue. Although I was able to leave behind a work of art in my previous parish, I still ask: "God, what about the talent you gave me in art? How am I going to use that?" My mind tells me, "It's coming. It will have a way of coming out."

It's not mine. It's God's gift to me and it's how well I use it that counts. I have other talents. I use those in a way that I believe God is directing me to. As with yourself, every one of us is given talents, some more, some less. With each of the talents we received, we are asked first of all to appreciate them, to be grateful for God's gifts. Remember how we were being grateful for the gift of time? We need to see everything as gift, and that's why gratitude is an underlying value. We begin to understand that we are not our own. We need to identify with our Master. We need to be trustworthy and to trust that God gives us talent to use well and to use it honestly and with integrity.

Again, the talent is a reflection of God the creator. God has created us in his image and likeness. The abilities that we have are in some sense a reflection of who God is in us. We all reflect God a little differently in the talents that we have. Our talents reflect the goodness and creativity of God as well as the activity of God in one another.

As we see that our talent is not our own and that we should use it for God and for the benefit of God, we realize that part of this gift of our talent needs to be given back to God in thanksgiving for what he has done. Tithing of one's talent is a difficult quantity to put together, so giving a tenth of one's talent is something I don't know how to tell you to do. I have yet to hear anybody really explain that one, and I'm open for suggestions. I do know that at least making a commitment of one's time and talent together has been the way most people see time, because you have to give of your time to be able to give of your talent. So that's how the two were put together in discussing stewardship.

I like to separate out our time in prayer because that's an important one for all of us Christians. Everybody says prayer is important. Well then do it! Make a schedule. Set it up so that you're spending two hours and twenty-four minutes a week in prayer. At least set aside specific time for prayer throughout the week. It is the same thing with talent. Tithe your talent back to God by putting time and talent together. Tithe that back to God in thanksgiving for all that God has done.

Treasure

"For where your treasure is, there also will your heart be" (Lk 12:34).

Treasure is everything that God has given to us; it's not just the money that God provides. It's the food. It's the shelter. It's the clothing. God has given them all to us as a gift. Now in our society when we've become "self-sufficient," meaning that we're more than self-sufficient, we can start thinking: "I'm providing for myself. I'm making that money happen. I'm earning the salary. I'm paying the bills. I bought all of this stuff."

What do I mean God gave it to you? Well, God gives us our every breath. God makes everything happen to enable us to have our job, our health, and the ability to *keep* the job we have. God has created the economy and he blesses us. I believe this. God bless America! God *has* blessed America. I believe that when we get rid of our greed and look with humility and thankfulness at all that God has given us, we will realize how incredibly blessed we are in this country, and that God *keeps on* blessing us. We have so much in comparison to other countries.

When we look at treasure as a gift of all the things that God has given us, we need to remind ourselves that what God gives us is not our own. It belongs to God. He gives it all to us.

When you give ten percent back, that's tithing. What a great idea the tithe is! In the Old Testament everybody knows that you give a tithe and we've heard about that, but do we remember how it gets used? The tithe is given to the Levites. Now there were twelve tribes, and the tribe of Levi was one of them. All except the Levites got land. Well, how are they going to have a farm? How are they going to raise food to feed themselves? How will they live if they don't have any land? They are given some cities, but they are given no land. How can they survive? God told Moses that the people, the other tribes, would provide for the tribe of Levi by tithing. They would give their food to the Levites and that's how the Levites would survive.

What kind of a system would be developed to implement this? The Levite tribe provided the priests. To be a priest you had to be in "perfect" condition. You had to be male, and you had to be between the ages of twenty-five and fifty. If you had a broken finger or a bad eye, you couldn't be a priest. If a person was spotless, unblemished, male and a Levite, that person would become a priest. The priests offered sacrifices and also helped run Israel. They had the responsibility of collecting the tithe. After all, they had to feed Mom and Dad and Sister and Brother. The people would bring the tithe in so it could be used to feed everyone.

The Levites also were required to tithe and this tithe provided for the poor. In the Old Testament the poor were directly provided for in the year of jubilee. It was the time when debts were forgiven, land was returned (that is, rested: no planting crops), the prisoners and slaves were set free. There was a prohibition on interest and on taking collateral for loans from neighbors. (Foreigners, yes. Neighbors, no.) There was an obligation to tithe. Even in the fields there was a tithe; the poor were allowed by law to glean them.

The third section of the *Catechism of the Catholic Church* focuses on the "Moral Life and the Ten Commandments." The seventh commandment, "thou shall not steal," is all about stewardship and you might be surprised at what the *Catechism* has to say about private property and about having an obligation. Private property is not an absolute. The goods of creation are destined for the entire human race. We can own it. We're allowed to own what we need for ourselves, but there's also an obligation to others outside of ourselves and our privacy. It has to do with justice and charity. When we do not give our money to the poor, we are stealing from them.

That's what the *Catechism* describes. We have an obligation to the poor, and where do we find it? In the commandment "thou shall not steal." There's one other place that treasure and stewardship is mentioned in the *Catechism of the Catholic Church*. It is in the fourth section, the one on prayer. In the Our Father, we say, "Give us this day our daily bread." We have an image of God providing us everything we need. Remember, this is about treasure. God gives us everything we need.

In addressing the issue of helping the poor, the *Catechism* talks about the parable of a rich man and a poor man named Lazarus. (See Lk 16:19-31.) There he is at the gates of the rich man and he is covered with sores which are licked by the dogs. The rich man eats splendidly every day and poor Lazarus longs to eat the scraps that fall from the rich man's table. One day the poor man dies and is immediately whisked to heaven in the arms of Father Abraham. Sure enough, the rich man dies and finds himself in torment and flames. He looks up and sees Lazarus in the arms of Abraham and calls out, "Father Abraham, send Lazarus down here to give me some water." Father Abraham says, "No, Lazarus is not coming to give you any water. You were well off in your life and now you suffer, whereas Lazarus was poor and now he's found consolation." He says, "Besides, he can't come down to you and you can't come up to us. There's a chasm between the two." Then the rich man says, "Well then, send him to my family. I have five brothers. Tell them so that they don't end up in this terrible place like me." Father Abraham says, "Look. If they won't believe Moses and the prophets, they won't believe if someone rises from the dead" — a reference to Jesus, rising from the dead.

What does that story tell us? The rich man is not condemned for being rich. He is condemned for not caring for the poor. You see, God gives us everything we need to live. God even gives us the portion — the tithe — to be given back to him. People tend to think it's theirs and they tend to keep it for themselves. It isn't ours. It belongs to God. "Give us this day our daily bread" applied to Lazarus. God gave Lazarus his daily bread. The problem is he didn't get it. The rich man kept it for himself. That's the problem of poverty in the world. The rich keep the tithe for themselves and don't feed the poor. "The poor you will always have with you," Jesus tells us. (See Mt 26:11.)

So when we have poverty in our midst it's proof that we're not treating the treasure that God has given to us with the respect that God expects of us. The tithe, that ten percent, isn't ours. It is to be used to take care of the needs of the poor. The rich man would not have even noticed the scraps that fell from his table. He probably wouldn't have noticed if he had given the first and best ten percent to Lazarus. Do you think the rich man would have ended up with less? God would have given the rich man even more. You will find out that God loves a good steward because he can trust him. What happens when you are trustworthy, or you're in charge of something, and you find someone who is trustworthy? Do you give that person less or do you give that person more? You give more of course, or you take on more. God will give you more. He'll give you more to manage. You know what? You don't have to give all that increase away. He just says give ten percent of it away. So you get ninety percent more. You think, well, I'll tithe again. God will again give you more.

That's what God does. It is amazing. I've watched it happen. You will not end up with less. You'll end up with more. Lazarus would have had his stomach full. The rich man would have had just as much food on his table and would not have noticed any lack. In fact, he would have had more food on his table. In that sense, we need to talk about treasure and how the tithe worked in the Old Testament. First of all, the tithe is not leftovers. You can't look at everything you have and then say, "OK, whatever I can spare and whatever I can do without I give to God." That's not it at all. It needs to be an action of the first priority. It is the first fruits of the harvest. It's not after sweeping up the grain bins that you figure out what you're going to give to God. It is the first thing that is picked.

There's a story of a village where a missionary came and talked all about tithing. A little boy went fishing. When he returned he came and knocked on the door of the missionary and said, "Here's my fish." The missionary asked, "Where are the other nine?" The boy said, "They're still in the river. I haven't caught them yet."

He gave his first fish! This is a great story about trust. He trusted that God would provide and give him those other fish. It should be the same with us. We need to give the first tenth to God knowing that the other nine are in the river. God will give them to us. Can we do that? It was what was expected of the Israelites. They gave the first fruits to God, not knowing what the rest of the crop would bring.

When the Israelites offered a lamb for sacrifice, they didn't pick out the blind and lame one. They didn't ask, "Which lamb can I do without?" They found the prettiest, the most beautiful, and the healthiest one-year-old male lamb without blemish, the best one. That's the one that was given to God and by God as our sacrifice. So it is in stewardship spirituality; when we're looking at treasure and it's time to tithe we need an attitude change. We need to give not what's leftover but what we have now. We give to God in thanksgiving for what God has done. We give our first and our best.

My personal practice is to get ahead of my tithe. I like to give more at the beginning of the year than I do at the end of the year. A lot of people catch up at the end of the year. I front load the year. I think that if God's going to really bless me, he might really surprise me. I don't want to find out I'm behind in my tithe when he is blessing. It's an attitude change I made in myself because then I'm always looking for the blessings of God. I find out that God has already blessed me.

I don't look for some sort of extraordinary way God has blessed me. I start appreciating the ordinary blessings that I have and I'm grateful.

That's what it does for me personally when I'm ahead of my tithe. I keep giving. I keep challenging myself saying, "OK, maybe I can give more." When I just keep giving more I find out more keeps coming in. Try it. You'll find out. You cannot outdo God in generosity. You cannot. Try it. Try giving half of it away and see what happens. You'll get it all back and more. That's just how God works. It's amazing.

SECTION 3: KEEPING PARISHIONERS INFORMED, ENCOURAGED, AND MOTIVATED

The material in this section is based on articles I wrote for the St. Thomas More Parish newsletter over several years.

The Sustainability of the Church of the Poor

THERE I WAS, sitting on the edge of my bed in a Manila hotel wondering why I was in the Philippines to talk about stewardship. All of my talks had been geared to middle-class Americans. How would they be received by the poor? Regardless of my apprehensions, my first day there was filled with a wonderful visit to the town of Infanta. Mila Glodava, our director of stewardship and communications at St. Thomas More Parish [and this book's co-author!] was guiding me to her hometown.

A banner over the town square welcomed us and we promptly joined Carmelite Bishop Julio Labayen for Mass at the cathedral. St. Thomas More parish has been very generous to the Prelature of Infanta. There were many people who wanted to express their genuine appreciation. Later, at a banquet, the local youth performed songs for our entertainment and the food was delicious but our work was just beginning. A radio interview kept us busy by having us explain the importance of stewardship to a listening audience of more than one million people. Our parish had paid for the restoration of the transmitter, so they too wanted to thank us. I happily received the hospitality and gratitude of Infanta on behalf of our parish.

In a couple of days the conference was underway in the city of Cebu. Seven dioceses and ten religious congregations were represented with more than seventy people in attendance. There were many priests and we were honored to have with us three bishops, including the Cardinal Ricardo J. Vidal of the Archdiocese of Cebu. It is important to note that there were ten religious congregations there, too.

You see, the Philippines is a developing country which continues to rely on outside help to run their dioceses. Most of the religious buildings such as churches, rectories and orphanages, have been built by resources coming from outside the country. Religious orders are struggling to continue to staff the parishes as they have done in the past. As religious orders decline in the United States and Europe, the Filipino churches are struggling to make ends meet. They are facing the fact that they have to be self-sufficient for the first time. This is where stewardship comes into the picture. Different dioceses have tried a variety of fund-raising methods that resulted in failure. Sustainability is the goal, but does that happen there?

Since 1991, the Church of the Philippines has also been chasing another idea called the "Church of the Poor." This concept comes from the Second Vatican Council's preferential option for the poor. Church leaders deeply want this, but they have struggled with how to make this dream come true. They have developed an incarnation theology but have not been able to implement it. Basically, they have an idea that has been looking for a *spirituality*. Well, this is where stewardship comes in again.

To be the "Church of the Poor" they are going to have to rely on their own prosperous parishioners and not on those outside the country. But the people of prosperity there are reluctant to be called poor. Those who have left poverty bear the "shame" of having once been poor. Why go back? Stewardship has an answer. Not only does stewardship provide sustainability, but it encourages people of prosperity to detach themselves from material goods.

As Mila and I led this conference for bishops, priests, sisters, and lay people, we laid out for them the reality that stewardship is not fund raising but a way of life. We presented to them what, earlier in Part I of this book, I presented to you. (Like all effective teachers and preachers, I'll do a little recapping here.)

We started with a distinction that this was about a spirituality, not a theology. A theology deals with ideas arranged in one's mind, whereas a spirituality arranges actions that are centered in one's heart. The Filipino people were not going to *think* their way through this problem. They had to *act* their way through this problem. (It only works if you work it!) Stewardship is a practical spirituality with a set course of actions that enables parishioners to live it out. Using St. Thomas More Parish as a model, we went through a season of "Stewardship Renewal" and provided the steps needed to put into practice the spirituality of stewardship.

We said that, as a spirituality, stewardship means that we find meaning in our identity as creatures of God. We are not our own, we belong to God. God is a loving father who gives us everything that we need. The things we have are not ours either. They belong to God and he trusts us to use them wisely. This knowledge should manifest a detachment from material things and is called "evangelical poverty." Stewardship encourages us to adopt this spirit of poverty. We are not actually poor, but we are spiritually poor. It's easy to say that we are detached from things; it's another to prove it. Stewardship says that we must give ten percent away (back to God) in thanksgiving for what God has given us. The proof that we are detached is our tithe.

We showed the attendants of our conference that tithing is the way everyone becomes the "Church of the Poor." Although everyone's gift is not the same size because the gifts differ, everyone makes the *same sacrifice* of ten percent. This is the concept, not of equal gifts, but of equal sacrifice. The people of prosperity are in solidarity with those who are poor, resulting in one church: the *Church of the Poor*. There is much more to this spirituality, but its essence resides in evangelical poverty. Jesus himself says, "Blessed are the poor in spirit, for theirs is the kingdom of heaven" (Mt 5:3). If the Filipino Church is going to be the Church of the Poor, it seems that God is leading them to embrace stewardship.

Talking to people of prosperity is what is normally done in middle-class America. We cannot let ourselves be fooled into believing that things are going to make us happy. They don't, but people seem to chase foolishly this notion all their lives. I am convinced that stewardship will be the conversion of a materialistic world. It puts God first, not our things. When we give our tithe to the parish church, the church itself tithes by giving to others from an established charity account. This charity account allowed St. Thomas More Parish to assist our poor brothers and sisters in the Philippines. The Filipino Church will soon discover what it is like to be the one giving charity instead of receiving it. I'm sure that God in his goodness will bless their Church with the gifts given to good stewards.

The Laity's Invitation to Evangelical Poverty

THE VOW OF POVERTY is a Catholic idea that is practiced by many people in religious life. It's one I practiced for about twenty years as a Benedictine monk. It's not as hard as one might think. It doesn't mean that you have to be physically poor or actually poor. It means that you are poor in spirit. Jesus tells us, "Blessed are the poor in spirit, for theirs is the kingdom of heaven" (Mt 5:3).

When I entered the monastery I gave up all my earthly possessions, but I didn't feel very poor. I had a roof over my head, I had clothes to wear, and there was plenty to eat. I had the supplies to do my work and there was adequate time to sleep. We spent a lot of time in prayer by a layperson's standard, but that wasn't hard, either. The spirit of poverty was found in the way we looked at the things we used. We had to remember that everything belonged to the monastery, not to us.

The vow of poverty is rooted in evangelical poverty. There are three evangelical counsels: poverty, chastity and obedience. The *Catechism of the Catholic Church* says that these three "precepts are intended to remove whatever is incompatible with charity" (CCC 1973). The evangelical counsels are not just for priests, brothers and sisters. They are for everyone. Some people live these counsels by taking vows. Others keep them in their ordinary Catholic life. Stewardship spirituality reminds us to embrace a spirit of poverty out of love for God. Just as in the monastery, poverty is found in the way we look at the things we use. In stewardship spirituality, poverty is an attitude that sees everything as a gift from God. Everything belongs to God, not to us.

The laity's invitation to evangelical poverty is found in the detachment from things. It doesn't mean that we won't have things. It means that we will look at them differently. We learn a lesson from those who are actually poor. The detachment of those who are physically poor causes them to trust God. They look for the goodness of God by the way others are charitable to them. Those of us who are spiritually poor are also asked to trust God for everything. We recognize God's goodness in our charity to others. When we embrace evangelical poverty, we also embrace the poor. We are sensitive to the needs of the poor and recognize our need to give.

Saying that we are detached from material goods is one thing, proving it is another. The proof of our detachment from things is found in the tithe. When we set aside one-tenth of our income for God we prove to God and ourselves that we can let go. We don't have to give it all away, yet. We will, when we die. We don't have to give half of it away, unless God is challenging us to do so. In stewardship spirituality we are asked to give ten percent away. We "let go" and we "let God" do the rest.

Tithing also allows us to be in solidarity with the poor. The tithe lets us not only claim that we are spiritually poor, but be ten percent physically poor. Our poverty is modeled on trust in God. We look to each other to see God's goodness and love. Our need to give finds even deeper meaning when we see the needs of others met. We begin to understand how God uses us as his representatives. In a sense, we "stand in" for God. We are ambassadors and stewards of God's grace. Even as we trust God, God puts his trust in us. He uses us and gives us more to give on his behalf. This is the root of the belief that God doesn't give the one who tithes less, but more. The more one gives away, the more God gives to the giver. God gives us plenty so that we will share it with those who are without.

Evangelical poverty is a pathway to holiness. When we learn to let go of earthly things, we learn to cling to the things of heaven. Our purpose on earth becomes full of meaning. We learn that the true nature of love is found in God's love for us. Just as God gives, we learn to give. Just as the poor receive, we learn to receive. In the end, the ultimate gift is that God gives and we are happy to receive. We receive the good steward's reward. Let us recall again what Our Lord says, "Blessed are the poor in spirit, for theirs is the kingdom of heaven."

The Gift of Redemptive Suffering by the Church of the Poor

THE WORST THING that can be told to the poor is that they have nothing to give. The world often tells the poor that they are of no value, that they are of no good and are a drain on society. This is not true. We realize that the poor have much to give if we counteract the false premise that things are more important than people.

The truth is that people are more important than things. The greatest person in our life is God. The world is preoccupied with the acquisition of things. This makes us act as if material goods are more important than God. Materialism becomes a false god that leads us away from the one true God.

When the poor are told they have nothing to give they are led to believe that things are the focus of life. Obviously, this is not true. Stewardship spirituality teaches that God is the source and summit of our lives. God gives us everything and we have everything to give back to God in thanksgiving for what God has given us. The greatest gift we can give is the gift of ourselves. Jesus sets this example upon the cross when he says, "Father, into your hands I commend my spirit" (Lk 23:46).

Redemptive suffering sounds strange to a world preoccupied with the pursuit of pleasure. Just as the world seeks things, pleasure is held up to be the greatest good. Pleasure is good and feels good, but it is a falsehood to be tricked into believing that it is the highest good. Suffering is abhorrent to a pleasure-seeking society. Hedonism says suffering is meaningless. Stewardship spirituality upholds the Christian belief that suffering is meaningful.

The poor are very familiar with suffering, struggle, and hardship. Even as the world tells the poor they have nothing to give and that their existence is meaningless, we know this is false. The poor experience suffering in a personal way. Just as we can give the gift of ourselves to God, we can make a gift of our sufferings to God as well. Suffering will only be given as a gift if it is seen as being meaningful. Our greatest example of the value of suffering is found at the Cross. Jesus suffered and died for us so that we would receive the gift of redemption. Just as we have received, we are asked to give in return. Suffering can be given as a gift that can be used by Jesus to redeem the world. Who better to give the gift of suffering than the poor?

Who are the poor? The answer to that question comes in layers, but the answer put simply is: everybody. The phrase "We are dust and to dust we shall return" reminds all of humanity of our inherent poverty. We start with nothing and we leave with nothing. During our lives we cannot let ourselves be fooled into believing that our possessions really belong to us. They don't. Evangelical poverty is the virtue that the Church asks us to embrace as a reminder to be detached from our possessions. The Beatitudes speak to every age. "Blessed are the poor in spirit, for theirs is the kingdom of heaven" (Mt 5:3) is spoken for us to hear in the twenty-first century. Materialism is a curse that affects us all. Stewardship can be a tool for the conversion of a materialistic world. Consequently, we are all invited to be the Church of the Poor.

Stewardship empowers evangelical poverty. The good steward is converted to lead a life that involves giving gifts of time, talent, and treasure. We identify with being poor so that we can be rich in the eyes of God. Some people think that giving money is the greatest gift. It isn't. The gift of oneself is the greatest gift we can give to God. Giving monetary gifts allows the steward to start a different level of giving. This new level allows one to realize that money is not so important. In fact, God already has all the money in the world. However, giving money frees us to see that there are other gifts that can be given. The gift of our free will in redemptive suffering becomes relevant. The sufferings that we experience can be transformed into a gift.

To better understand redemptive suffering, we must first understand redemption. The gift of our redemption is accomplished with God's mercy and justice. How can we explain God's mercy and justice? Imagine that a son has stolen ten dollars from his father and blows it all by eating at a fast-food restaurant. He comes home, sick as a dog, and the dad realizes his money is gone. After a short confrontation the son asks for mercy and the dad says that he is forgiven. Is it finished? Not even close. The father has displayed mercy, but justice still needs to be enacted. The boy will have to pay back the ten dollars in restitution, but that's not all. The child still needs to be punished by being grounded for a week. Forgiveness, therefore, involves both mercy and justice. On a divine level, the same is true for God and us.

God gives us his mercy when we are sorry for our sins. Conversely, we satisfy his justice when we do penance for our sins. Both mercy and justice are found in the sacrament of penance. Confessing one's sins and receiving absolution assures the penitent of God's mercy. The penance that the priest gives the penitent is given to satisfy God's justice. Doing voluntary penance also satisfies God's justice. This is typified in receiving a plenary indulgence.

Some people have discovered that there is enjoyment in doing plenary indulgences for others, especially for the dead. One should be in a state of grace so that the penance will be used by God to satisfy justice for others. There is a great gift in offering up our sufferings for the forgiveness of sins. When we become comfortable offering our voluntary suffering to God, then the involuntary sufferings we experience can be freely offered as a gift also. Suffering is a meaningful and valuable gift that is used by God when it is united with the sacrifice of the Cross for the redemption of our sins. The good steward understands that redemptive suffering is more valuable than the gift of money.

Because the materially poor of our world are told that they have nothing to give they neglect the treasure they could give if they would only find meaning in their sufferings. No matter how small a material gift is, it can represent an enormous sacrifice. Soon the poor realize that the visible gift given represents an unseen reality.

Gratitude teaches us to be thankful and helps us focus on what we have, and not on what we lack. The poor learn that God is a God of abundance and cannot be outdone in generosity. Suffering is an opportunity to see the good that it can cause instead of focusing on the burden it is. Those who identify with the poor through a spirit of poverty are evangelized to look past materialism. They too see our God who gives all and sustains all. They are as much the Church of the Poor as anyone else. The gift of offering one's suffering is a way to commend one's spirit to God. We learn that people are more important than things. God is the ultimate person we come to love and appreciate. He sets the example of giving meaning to suffering when Jesus says: "Father, into your hands I commend my spirit" (Lk 23:46).

Stewardship of Faith

In stewardship of faith we're working on the assumption that we have identity, trust, gratitude, and love. We look at faith as a treasure that God has given to us. Faith is then a gift. When I talk about gratitude, I talk about gifts given and gifts received. We thank God for gifts received. Everything is a gift. That's what gratitude is all about.

In gratitude, we see faith as the gift that it is. God gives us faith. So we thank God for the gift of faith. The way we thank God is to give a gift back. If you want to keep your faith, you have to give it away. How?

In stewardship spirituality, the way we appreciate the gift of faith is by receiving it as a gift that God has given to us and then giving the gift back to God in thanksgiving for what He has given us. Well, you can't give away something you don't have. So receiving the gift of faith means you have to develop the faith that God has given to you. This is what stewardship of faith is all about.

At St. Thomas More we encourage our parishioners to develop the faith and get it accurately and completely. A lot of people have an incomplete faith. Their faith has not been developed very much. In stewardship spirituality, we ask our people to make a commitment to expand their faith and to grow in their faith. So we ask our people to read the pastor's message, to attend lectures on faith, or to read the Bible. Our "Stewardship of Faith" commitment form (see pages 111-112) offers many ways for us to grow in faith in order to give it back in thanksgiving for what God has given us.

Of course we receive faith at different times of our life. Some receive it at birth or at baptism. Others receive at midlife or even at the point of death. And as the gift that it is, it is proof that there's God. It is reasonable and it is rational. But it is proof, because that's what faith is. You have to believe. It's a leap of faith to believe that there really is a God and that this generous, loving Creator has offered all this to us. And the only way we can keep this faith is if we give it away. You have to receive it well enough so that you are able to share it and give it away, hence, "go and make disciples." It is faith that gets us to practice the gifts of hope and love.

Stewardship of the Earth

THE *CATECHISM OF THE CATHOLIC CHURCH* uses the word stewardship in terms of the earth. ("In the beginning God entrusted the earth and its resources to the common stewardship of mankind to take care of them, master them by labor, and enjoy their fruits" (CCC 2402).) The Bible tells us that God gave us the earth to use wisely for our generation and the next. We need to use the resources to support human life. If we overuse the resources, we're stealing from the next generation.

And so we need to be good stewards of what God has given to us. We don't own them. We share them with the next generation. This means it is our responsibility to steward them, to use and to create resources that are renewable. That would be the best stewardship. Instead of using up resources that cannot be replaced, we have an obligation in stewardship of the earth to find resources that are renewable so that the next generation isn't stuck with a lack of the resources that God has given to them. And it's our responsibility to make sure that those resources are available to them. We need to do what we can to renew resources rather than waste them.

Also, while we may not be the ones who caused the problems, we have a responsibility to help fix them. Like it or not, we are in it together when it comes to stewardship issues. If we inherit problems caused by other people, our job is to be responsible in lessening the harm that any problem has caused in the world – including pollution or the misuse of resources and environmental damage. We need to take care of the world that God has given to us not just for ourselves but for future generations.

At St. Thomas More we encourage our people to thank God for the resources that they have received from God and to remember the three R's: reduce, reuse, and recycle. For instance, we ask our people to wash their clothes in cold water and to air dry them, if possible. We ask them to purchase products made from recycled products and to recycle engine oil.

Much of the secular view of "going green" is actually compatible with our spirituality of stewardship of the earth. The problem is some of the secular movements see humanity as the disease on the earth. We don't agree with that. We believe God has given us dominion over the earth, but we have to be responsible. Nor do we believe that animals have "rights." God did not give rights to animals. It's hard for people to understand that. We're not just an animal among animals. We're humans and we have rights that have been given to us by God. Humans have primacy over animals. And animals were not given these rights by God. Some people want to give rights to animals and that's an offense to God. They are acting like God. On the other hand, when we're good stewards of animals, we accept our responsibility toward them. We have to be good stewards as to how animals are used for food and leather goods. We have to do that in such a way that is responsible, not cruel, and allows for future generations to continue using these animals for the benefit of humanity.

We are not only *responsible* for the earth but also *accountable* for it.

Vocations

[As you will read in Section II, promoting and helping sustain vocations to the priesthood and religious life is also a key to the spirituality of stewardship.]

Vocation promotion has become everyone's job with the person in the pew at our parish nominating individuals through our "Called by Name" program. Our religious education programs and our school routinely teach about vocations. We regularly pray for vocations at Mass. We particularly pray that good and holy young men answer the call to the religious life. (We pray for our bishops, too!) And we mark "Religious and Clergy Appreciation Day."

I want to talk a little about that.

There's the story of a wife who always had to remind her husband of their wedding anniversary. Since this year was their twenty-fifth anniversary, she said nothing hoping that he would remember. The big day came and went. A while later the husband came home with flowers, tickets to a show, and a box of candy. The wife asked in surprise, "What's all this for?" The husband said, "Well, we've been married twenty-five years, two weeks, and three days!"

Husbands, wives, and children are expected to remember the important dates of the immediate family. Anniversaries, birthdays and holidays are times that don't pass by without notice. Among the holidays, there are Mother's Day, Father's Day, and even Grandparent's Day. Families become stronger and bonds grow deeper as a result of remembering.

Those of us who are ordained or in religious life come from families, but our vow of celibacy keeps us from starting our own families. Archbishop Charles Chaput reminds priests to see the Church as their spouse. When pastoral assignments are made, priests sometimes are placed far from siblings or parents. Having relatives nearby is a luxury for most clergy. "Holiday" often also means "holy day" and holy days are when priests are called to work. Many come to accept the fact of being away from families during the holidays. Having parish families remember priests during these days gives them consolation in their vocations and so the parish families in some aspect become a part of a priest's vocation. The bonds that result from being remembered make priests stronger in their resolve to be of service to the Church.

Many sacrifices are made within families. Spouses sacrifice for each other and parents make sacrifices on behalf of their children. Grown children eventually make sacrifices for their elderly parents. These sacrifices are not meaningless because they result in the expression of love for one another within the family. Those ordained to the priesthood or those in religious life have this same potential for expressed love when our sacrifices do not go unnoticed. This happens when the parish supplies the same kind of support a family would offer.

When my anniversary of priestly ordination is recognized, I imagine that it feels similar to the way spouses feel when they are remembered on their special day. This is probably the same for birthdays. Bonds grow deeper and memories result from the remembering. When the laity take their part in our celibate vocations, it is a reassuring sign to the young men and women considering a vocation. They will be bolstered by the fact that their sacrifices will not go unnoticed. They will not be alone, for the Church will supply the support needed to sustain their vocations. *Promoting vocations goes hand in hand with sustaining vocations.* Praying for new vocations means praying for those who have already answered the call.

St. Thomas More Parish celebrates a "Religious and Clergy Appreciation Day" to be on a par with, let's say, Mother's Day or Grandparent's Day. St. Thomas More Parish recognizes those who are in religious vows and who are currently in service to our parish. This includes sisters and brothers. In addition, we recognize those who are ordained to the priesthood and the diaconate. This includes active priests, retired priests, and deacons.

The hope is that the "Religious and Clergy Appreciation Day" will allow the families of the parish to realize their part in having a relationship to religious vocations. Perhaps those in religious life and the clergy are then better able to understand what it means that the Church is our spouse. Perhaps the laity will be enriched by the titles by which we are called: Brother, Sister, and Father. There is the potential that those who are considering a vocation would see the hope to which they are called.

Just as husbands, wives and children are expected to remember anniversaries, birthdays, and holidays within a family, please make those of us in vows or who are ordained feel like part of the family.

A Deeply Spiritual Meaning

A LITTLE BOY ASKED HIS MOTHER where he came from and where she came from when she was a baby. The mother told him a fantastic story about being brought by a stork. The boy ran into the next room and asked his grandmother and received a variation on the bird story. He then went outside to his playmates with the comment, "There hasn't been a normal birth in our family for three generations!"

Priestly and religious vocations are not delivered by the stork but are given to the Church by families. Since they are called "Father," "Brother," or "Sister," they are adopted as being part of the family by those they serve. That means that the laity has a role to play in their vocations. Treating priests like family means that we all see a deeply spiritual meaning to the vow of celibacy. Religious can recognize the Church as their spouse when they see a loving response of the Church to their vocations. This can happen when families remember their birthdays and important anniversaries. Therefore, when clergy are remembered on special days, they feel a part of a larger Church family.

At St. Thomas More Parish the weekend before Ash Wednesday has been set aside as the day we recognize and appreciate our clergy and religious. The laity is invited to participate in the important role that they have in vocations. That means that the clergy and religious, as part of parish families, are to be remembered in their sentiments.

Since vocations come from families, clergy and religious appreciation has an important influence upon families that produce vocations. Children see parents who appreciate the sacrifices that the priests, religious and deacons are making. They observe the interest that is shown in their well-being. Children hear the message that being a consecrated person is a worthy and noble position towards which to aspire. It shows everyone that the religious and clergy are not lonely people. They have good friends and have been adopted by a greater parish family. They feel good about their vocation when they are appreciated.

Thanks go out to those who have set a good example by showing gratitude and love to religious and clergy. Everyone has a role to play in vocations. As a family stays strong because of mutual love and respect, our parish family will become stronger when religious and clergy feel a part of that family. Let us not forget to thank God for the vocations that grace our parishes.

I Am Called "Father"

An observant young boy was trying to explain what Father's Day was all about. He said, "Father's Day is just like Mother's Day except you don't spend so much money."

When I first became a priest I was surprised that people came up to me and wished me a "Happy Father's Day." I thought about it briefly, and realized that I am called "Father." My role as a priest is to live up to that title in the way that I minister to the people of God. At first being called "Father" by people who were quite a bit older than I was felt a little odd, but as time went on, I realized the public role I play in everybody's life. My priesthood is not a personal accomplishment but is a grace that God shares with me and the community.

The priesthood of Jesus Christ is shared with all of us by virtue of our baptism. Old Testament practices required an ordinary person to go to a priest to offer his sacrifice to God. They could not do it themselves. Only the Levite priest was charged with making the offering and no one else. By being baptized into Jesus Christ we are baptized into his spiritual priesthood. We can offer our personal sacrifices directly to God. We do that by the common priesthood of believers. As an ordained priest, I share not only in the common priesthood of all believers, but I am called to function in the ministerial priesthood. That means that we priests are important to the sacramental life of the Church. The holy sacrifice of the Mass needs a priest to stand in the person of Christ. We priests are called to be holy. That is why one of the titles ascribed to us is "Reverend." We use it regularly in signing our names.

"Father" is a title that brings to mind a family relationship. Just as a father is called to provide, protect, and defend the family, so too does the priest provide, protect, and defend the parishioners in his care. Leadership and fatherhood go hand in hand. The pastor is the father and leader of the parish community. The very name "pastor" calls to mind the nurturing role of a father just as a shepherd tends his sheep.

Modern psychology tells us that our concept of God comes from our fathers. Mothers have special roles, but fathers in their leadership roles imprint a sense of authority in a child's mind. Obedience to a higher authority begins in the family; grows with teachers, coaches and civic authorities; and is ultimately realized in our obedience to God. People who have problems with authority usually have problems with their fathers and ultimately with God. Sometimes these people project those problems on priests whose authority represents both concepts. I suspect that anti-religious sentiments have a lot to do with a person's unresolved, immature feelings. Reconciliation is best achieved when those in a father's role follow the example of the parable of the forgiving father and his prodigal son. Mercy certainly triumphs over justice in these kinds of matters.

It is important to reflect upon the role that the priesthood plays in the context of the titles that are ascribed to us as priests. Being holy and called "Reverend" will only be meaningful if our title of "Father" is seen as an extension of God's love and mercy. All dads are setting an example of how authority is to be respected. Authority can be seen as being hard or soft and that will depend upon the care that fathers take in fulfilling their special roles. When we priests are called "Father" we carry the collective efforts of the men that have gone before us. Our legacy will be in providing for future men an example of how fathers make known the very presence of God.

NOTES, REFLECTIONS, & POINTS TO REMEMBER

For Part I: The Spirituality of Stewardship

NOTES, REFLECTIONS, & POINTS TO REMEMBER

For Part I: The Spirituality of Stewardship

NOTES, REFLECTIONS, & POINTS TO REMEMBER

For Part I: The Spirituality of Stewardship

PART II

Stewardship at St. Thomas More Parish

By Mila Glodava

I have to admit that everything I know about stewardship came from the school of hard knocks. In fact, I learned almost everything from scratch, from the spirituality and theology of stewardship to implementing the program through trials and errors. I believe this is the reason the St. Thomas More stewardship model has become one of the best and why it's one many parishes are emulating right now.

As Director of Communications and Stewardship at St. Thomas More Parish since 1989, I have served two pastors and a number of parochial vicars. I also have seen the parish staff grow from a handful to more than fifty, and that's not counting school staff! It has been a privilege for me to work with countless devoted volunteers. Learning from all of them about serving the Lord, I experienced my own transformation. In fact, my personal conversion has given me the passion to share with others what I have learned about stewardship as a way of life.

ST. THOMAS MORE, THE PARISH

As our pastor, Father Andrew Kemberling, accurately describes it: "St. Thomas More Parish, which was created in 1971 with fewer than six hundred families, is like no other." The parish, blessed with the stunning views of the foothills and the Colorado Front Range, is now home to approximately six thousand two hundred families or about twenty-one thousand individuals. Faith-filled and spiritually-alive, the parish has two spiritual hallmarks: stewardship and evangelization. As the St. Thomas More (STM) welcome packet describes, "Our parishioners' gifts of time, talent, and treasure make our multifaceted evangelization emphasis possible. And our evangelization bolsters our practice of stewardship. Both have contributed to the vibrancy of our faith community."

Indeed, the pages of the *More Informed*, the STM's bimonthly newsletter, are filled with a multitude of articles regarding the many happenings in the parish and the people behind those happenings.

I'll go through a — rather long — "litany" of parish programs and services, not to brag but to point out the "fruits" of the spirituality of stewardship and how a parish that focuses on giving to others can receive so very much itself.

In keeping with the goal to encourage prayer and making time for God, St. Thomas More offers many prayer and worship opportunities: perpetual adoration, pilgrim statue, prayer line, holy hour, ministry of praise (for the homebound), prayer groups, novenas, and living rosary crusade. The parish also offers numerous events for faith nourishment: adult education series; retreats and missions; and invitations to renowned speakers, biblical scholars, and theologians to speak here.

The weekend Masses are usually packed, bringing in for worship nearly seven thousand individuals, while weekday Masses attract about three hundred people daily. The Life Teen Masses are also usually packed with the youth and their families. These liturgies do not happen by chance. They are planned, implemented, and participated in by hundreds of volunteers — extraordinary ministers of the Eucharist, musicians, singers, ushers, lectors, greeters — as well as staff.

St. Thomas More Parish also can boast of outstanding religious education, youth and young adults ministry, and a parish school. Every year more than one thousand children enroll in religious education, preparing to receive the sacraments. At least three hundred receive their First Holy Communion every year and another three hundred receive the sacrament of confirmation.

The youth and young adult ministry's outstanding program has resulted in many of our young parishioners serving in the missions and other ministries in the church, including the priesthood. "I'm grateful for all the teachers at STM Parish School and for the mentors in STM's youth ministry who've pushed me to develop my gifts and talents throughout the years," said Patrick Reidy, who is currently pursuing a vocation to the priesthood as a member of the Congregation of the Holy Cross.

Not only does the parish help promote vocations to the priesthood (Patrick Reidy is the fourth parish-school graduate to enter the seminary) and women religious, it also has proven its merits when it comes to academic standards. The parish school, which first opened in 1994, received the prestigious Blue Ribbon award in 2006, and that speaks volumes about the quality of education that St. Thomas More offers.

The Rite of Christian Initiation of Adults (RCIA) program continues to bring to the fold an average of fifty new Catholics per year.

More than one thousand three hundred parishioners attend the many adult education programs offered in the parish, strengthening their faith commitment. One of the most successful programs for men, "That Man Is You," attracts more than three hundred men on Fridays (at 6:20 in the morning!) to strengthen their faith journey through guided studies and in-depth discussions. The women, on the other hand, have many options to choose from in their journey of faith, including ENDOW (Educating on the Nature and Dignity of Women), Women of Grace, FaithSisters, Moms and Tots, and others.

The parish also has many opportunities to promote the family, singles and seniors. Several marriage ministries — Marriage Encounter, Couple to Couple League, Covenant of Love, and Retrouvaille — provide assistance to couples who want to enhance their marriage or to save a marriage. The singles groups — New Life and STM Singles — offer more than dances and social events. They provide many activities for the spiritual growth and development of their members. The parish also encourages the senior members to participate in the many activities offered by the Forever Mores and the American Association of Retired Persons (AARP).

The Knights of Columbus and the Ladies Auxiliary are very busy administering the corporal works of mercy in the parish. The Knights also sponsor many family-oriented events such as the St. Patrick's Dinner Dance, Oktober Fest, and fish or steak fries. In addition, the parish offers activities for fun — golf, couple's bridge, scrapbooking, and physical fitness activities — as well as many family-friendly celebrations.

What about concerns for the poor, the sick, and those grieving? Extraordinary ministers of the Eucharist and members of the Legion of Mary visit those who are ill and the homebound. And the parish reaches out to those in need in many ways through the St. Vincent de Paul Society, Habitat for Humanity, and food banks. The Helping Hands and bereavement series reach out to those who are grieving. The Stephen Ministries serves those who need someone to walk with them on their spiritual journey. The Ambassadors of Hope serve the inner-city school children.

In the year 2000 we had one hundred ministries and programs. Today there are some three hundred involving nearly three thousand individual volunteers (or seven thousand volunteer positions being filled — some parishioners serve in a number of ways). We estimated the volunteers' service to the parish is worth at least $4 million.

Richly blessed, St. Thomas More has distributed, since fiscal year 2000-2001, nearly half a million dollars per year to various causes: the poor, the sick, children, youth, elderly, inner-city parishes, the religious, and the missions. While most of the grants are distributed locally, the parish also donates to various causes nationally and internationally. St. Thomas More has funded hospitals, schools, churches, special projects, and responses to emergencies around the globe. The parish also has sent youth and other lay missionaries to missions in the United States and around the world.

We have shared our stewardship program with many parishes not only in dioceses in Colorado, but also across the United States and other countries: Australia, Canada, Jamaica, England, Guam, and the Philippines. (In fact, it has almost single-handedly promoted stewardship as a way of life in the Philippines!)

Furthermore, St. Thomas More is fortunate to have been shepherded by pastors — Father Frederick McCallin (founding pastor); Father Michael A. Walsh; and, current pastor Father Andrew Kemberling — who believe in promoting vocations to the priesthood and religious life. Since 1984, St. Thomas More has seen ten young men ordained to the priesthood and ten men ordained as permanent deacons, six of whom serve at St. Thomas More. The other recently ordained clergy are serving in other parishes, even as far away as Kazakhstan. In addition, St. Thomas More has fostered the vocations of two sisters, a brother, six seminarians, and several lay missionaries serving in various parts of the world. One, who was very active in the youth ministry before going to college, is currently helping build water tanks in Nicaragua. Another has used YouTube to raise funds for a boarding school for boys in Africa. These are but a few vocations fostered at St. Thomas More.

ST. THOMAS MORE, A STEWARDSHIP MODEL

Over the years, following Father Joseph Champlin's sacrificial giving and other models, we have developed our very own St. Thomas More stewardship model. It has been recognized by the International Catholic Stewardship Council (ICSC) with numerous honors, including the Archbishop Thomas J. Murphy Memorial Award in 2007.

While the STM model was started to increase the offertory collection, in due time it has become a way of life in the parish.

As I will get into great detail later, the STM model has evolved into a six-phase program focusing on stewardship as spirituality and a life of thanksgiving for God's blessings:

1. Prayer (Time)
2. Ministry (Talent)
3. Faith
4. Treasure
5. Vocations
6. Earth

This model promotes making time for God in prayer, sharing our gifts and talents, nourishing our faith, giving of our treasure, promoting vocations, and caring for the earth.

Stewardship is an excellent response to the late Pope John Paul II's call for a "new evangelization." In his 1999 apostolic exhortation *Ecclesia in America*, the pope urged the bishops, priests, religious and people to make a commitment not to a re-evangelization but to a new evangelization — "new in ardor, methods and expression."

While the message of salvation through Jesus Christ is the same, evangelization should be carried out in new ways. Indeed, the fruits of stewardship enable the parish to carry out its mission to "go and make disciples." With the advent of high technology, St. Thomas More has taken advantage of the new and various methods of communication now available to bring the Good News of Jesus Christ to all nations.

Not only has St. Thomas More employed various methods of expression, it also has many faith-filled parishioners ready to serve as witnesses to the faith. In fact, as mentioned earlier, evangelization *is* the parish mission and so stewardship and evangelization have become the spiritual hallmarks of the parish.

MY "CONVERSION" STORY

It was not until 1991 that I experienced my own personal conversion to stewardship as a way of life. At that time STM parishioner Jean Harper wrote her story of conversion for our parish newsletter. (You can read it in Appendix 1). Jean's story personifies for me what Pope Paul VI observed in his 1975 apostolic exhortation *Evangelii Nuntiandi*: "Modern man listens more willingly to witnesses than to teachers, and if he does listen to teachers, it is because they are witnesses" (#41).

Jean's conversion story made me realize that although I had been a cradle Catholic, I had not made God a priority in my life. I also realized that, for me, giving was out of pride that I had something to give rather than in thanksgiving for all that God has given me. Also, at the time, it seemed that money was always tight for my family. Although my husband, Mark, and I were both working, it seemed that money just came in one hand and went out the other.

What made us rethink our way of life, however, was God's dare in Malachi 3:10: "Bring the whole tithe into the storehouse, That there may be food in my house, and try me in this, says the LORD of hosts, Shall I not open for you the floodgates of heaven, to pour down blessing upon you without measure?" I understand this is the only dare that God gave us in the Bible.

Mark and I took the dare and started giving God the tithe — the first and the best — and our lives were never the same after that.

Truly, when you make God your partner, he will take care of your needs.

Does this mean that we never had to experience any difficulties in life since we started embracing stewardship? On the contrary! Mark and I have been married since 1972 and during that period Mark has been laid off at least four times. Honestly, it was tough living on a church worker's salary. (I'm sure my colleagues can attest to this). The 1991 recession in the United States, however, was a real test for us, because we had just started practicing stewardship. When Mark lost his job, we were faced with a dilemma. Should we or should we not continue giving what we knew was a significant amount to the Church and to a few chosen charitable causes?

We decided to continue, knowing that we had to review our priorities in life and trust that God would provide for all our needs. And guess what? He did! God provided for all our needs during the five years that Mark, an electrical engineer, could not find a steady job. We had food on the table, our mortgage was paid, and the children had clothes on their backs. They also completed high school during that time. God provided for us in ways I never could have imagined.

I truly believe that my own personal conversion has changed *me*. Stewardship has changed my life. It has made me realize that I must make God the priority in my life and give him the first and the best, not out of fear, but out of love and thanksgiving. It also has given me the courage to speak about my faith to others and to speak out against injustice without fear of retribution.

I also realized that God had given me gifts to use for his glory, not mine, and that I have a responsibility to use my gifts for the benefit of others. I learned that I, alone, am accountable to him for my gifts. It was then I began to find ways to contribute to the building up of the Kingdom of God. It shows that it is never too late to embrace stewardship as a way of life.

Indeed, as the United States Conference of Catholic Bishops said in its 1992 pastoral letter titled *Stewardship: A Disciple's Response*: "To be a Christian disciple is a rewarding way of life, a way of companionship with Jesus, and the practice of stewardship is itself a source of deep joy. Those who live this way are happy people who have found the meaning and purpose of living."

Today, I feel that my own personal conversion has given me the grace to do my work at St. Thomas More with great conviction. My personal conversion also has given me the passion to share with others the message of stewardship. And that is one of the many lessons I have learned in embracing stewardship: "You cannot keep it to yourself." That is why Father Andrew and I have been promoting stewardship as a way of life beyond St. Thomas More. I can only say that the Holy Spirit must be at work here because it seems our work is just beginning.

This is also the reason Father Andrew and I decided to write this book on stewardship. With numerous requests coming our way from all corners of the United States and abroad, there is no way we could possibly accommodate all of them. While our priority will always be our work at St. Thomas More, we feel we also have a responsibility to share the STM stewardship model with others. We hope that this book will assist us in reaching more than we can possibly reach in person.

Further, although we are fully conscious that "Jesus is the supreme teacher of Christian stewardship" (*Stewardship: A Disciple's Response*), we also hope that the book will inspire others to make stewardship a way of life in their own lives as well as their own parishes or dioceses. My hope is that the gift of Christian stewardship will bless your life as it has blessed mine, and that it will bless your parish as it has blessed St. Thomas More.

NOTES, REFLECTIONS, & POINTS TO REMEMBER

For Part II: Stewardship at St. Thomas More Parish

NOTES, REFLECTIONS, & POINTS TO REMEMBER

For Part II: Stewardship at St. Thomas More Parish

PART III

Stewardship Methods

By Mila Glodava

"Therefore, from the day we heard this, we do not cease praying for you and asking that you may be filled with the knowledge of his will through all spiritual wisdom and understanding to live in a manner worthy of the Lord, so as to be fully pleasing, in every good work bearing fruit and growing in the knowledge of God, strengthened with every power, in accord with his glorious might, for all endurance and patience, with joy giving thanks to the Father, who has made you fit to share in the inheritance of the holy ones in light" (Col 1:9-12).

Stewardship at St. Thomas More is continuing to evolve as a total way of life with its current six-phase program consisting of the following:

Stewardship of Prayer (Time)
Stewardship of Ministry (Talent)
Stewardship of Faith
Stewardship of Treasure
Stewardship of Vocations
Stewardship of the Earth

Please remember, however, that this model did not happen overnight. There has been much trial and error since 1989 and what we have now are some tried and true ways of implementing stewardship in a parish. At our workshops and presentations Father Andrew often says that parishes should look for what they can use from the STM model, rather than simply comparing other parishes with St. Thomas More. Identifying ideas that can work in your parish is positive, comparing is negative.

Any parish — even poor parishes — can adopt the STM model to reflect their own parish personality. In fact, this model has been implemented in the poorest of the poor parishes in the Philippines with equal success. The Philippine Church has realized, and is now seemingly convinced, that stewardship as a way of life is a key to the sustainability of the Church of the Poor.

First World countries can just as easily use the STM model. The good news is it will probably not take your parish as long as it took us to achieve this model. With this book you will find not only the "how-to's" to make it happen, but also the basic "why": a compelling reason — the spirituality of stewardship — to embrace stewardship as a way of life. Father Andrew and I believe that to make stewardship a way of life in the parish, there must be a balance of both — the reason and the methodology.

Father Andrew is often invited to preach at Masses on the spirituality of stewardship. His talks on stewardship have made personal conversions. In fact, he converted me even more to this way of life. However, after giving talks at several parishes that did not make an effort to learn the "how-to's" of stewardship, he realized that his talks did not seem as effective as they could be. At the same time, learning only the methodology of stewardship without the spirituality is equally as ineffective.

Some people think that they are doing just fine without stewardship, and that they have enough money to take care of their needs. This reveals their misconception that stewardship is only about money. That is not true. While stewardship involves money and does provide the resources critical to promoting the mission of the Church to evangelize, stewardship is not just about money.

Stewardship practitioners, however, would readily agree that stewardship involves money. In fact, many parishes, including St. Thomas More, actually started to implement stewardship as a program because of money (or lack of it!) with impressive results. Eventually, however, the experts realized that to sustain stewardship in the parish, it must be more than just money.

Studies have shown that stewardship parishes have a healthier financial picture than those that do not practice stewardship. In fact, studies also show that if Catholic parishes become stewardship parishes it could mean billions of dollars in the coffers for them. Can you imagine what we can do collectively, if we have all the financial resources to do God's work?

Still, stewardship is much more than just money. At one of the workshops Father Andrew and I gave, a priest asked, "Why should I get into this stewardship kick?" My response was, "Stewardship is about conversion or transformation which leads to a deeper relationship with God. My own personal conversion or transformation has led me to a way of life that I would recommend to others. Why deprive parishioners the opportunity for conversion or transformation in a concrete way?" And transformed parishioners mean a transformed parish and community as well.

Stewardship Teaching

AGAIN, MAKING STEWARDSHIP A WAY of life at St. Thomas More did not happen overnight. In fact, it took years before it became the STM model we now share with others. Let me be frank. The STM model started with a real need to increase the offertory collection so we could pay the bills. That's why I can understand the need for many parishes to start with the treasure phase. If I were to start fresh, however, I would begin with the model in this book because it starts with developing or enhancing a relationship with God by making time with him.

Because Father Andrew has given an in-depth teaching on the spirituality of stewardship in Part I of this book, this will just be a brief overview. Stewardship teaching at St. Thomas More includes the following principles:

1. Stewardship is a way of life and a spirituality.
2. It promotes tithing and the need to give rather than giving to a need.
3. It has biblical foundation and is supported by the Catholic Church, including the United States Conference of Catholic Bishops.
4. Stewardship is a means to an end, and that end is evangelization.

Stewardship Is a Way of Life

AT ST. THOMAS MORE WE promote stewardship as a way of life. This means we emphasize the need for a life of thanksgiving for all of God's blessings by:

1. Making time for God in prayer and worship
2. Sharing time and talent for the common good
3. Nurturing faith in order to share it with others
4. Giving of treasure cheerfully
5. Promoting vocations for the abundant harvest
6. Preserving the earth for our generation and the next

Living this way of life is very much in keeping with the exhortations of the United States Conference of Catholic Bishops (USCCB), who, in their pastoral letter *Stewardship: A Disciple's Response* described the Christian steward as a Christ follower who:

1. Receives God's gifts gratefully
2. Cherishes and tends them in a responsible manner
3. Shares them in justice and love with all
4. Returns them with increase to the Lord

First, we welcome and accept the fact that God is the source of all things. We know how to receive gifts by being grateful for his blessings. Often we hear the adage that it is better to give than to receive but giving is not complete unless we know how to receive.

(Just a side story: When my husband was unable to find a steady job during a span of five years, my friends and relatives were very conscious of our needs and wanted to give us whatever they could to help us out. My ego, my pride, wanted to say no, until I realized, that if my giving must have meaning, I also must learn to receive not only gratefully, but also gracefully.)

Second, we are responsible and accountable for all of his gifts. (Our time, talent, and treasure; and our faith, vocation, and earth.) God trusted us with our gifts and to take care of them in a trustworthy manner. Romans 14:11-12 says, "For it is written, 'As I live, says the Lord, every knee shall bow to me, and every tongue shall give praise to God.' So [then] each of us shall give an accounting of himself [to God]." The bishops reiterated this in their pastoral letter on stewardship: "One day God will require an accounting of the use each person has made of the particular portion of these goods entrusted to him or her."

Third, we are to be generous. For the benefit of others, we are to give back a portion of the gifts that he has given us. We are to share our blessings with others, for the common good. In fact, this is not optional. The Scriptures say in 2 Corinthians 9:7-8, "Each must do as already determined, without sadness or compulsion, for God loves a cheerful giver. Moreover, God is able to make every grace abundant for you, so that in all things, always having all you need, you may have an abundance for every good work."

Fourth, we are to use — not bury — our gifts. That's how we honor the giver of the gifts. "Know thyself," Socrates said. I'll go a step further: "Know your gifts." In knowing and using our gifts we give glory to the Giver of the gift and "the Giver is more precious than the gift" (CCC 2604). There's a saying "if you don't use it, you lose it" but before we can use our gifts we need to become aware of those God-given gifts and talents.

Remember the Parable of the Talents? The master commended the first two who invested what they had been given: "Well done, my good and faithful servant. Since you were faithful in small matters, I will give you great responsibilities. Come, share your master's joy" (Mt 25:21).

Stewardship Is a Spirituality

As Father Andrew wrote in Section I, the four core values of stewardship spirituality are identity, trust, gratitude and love.

1. *Identity*: We need to know who and what we are. In Genesis 1:27 we find: "God created man in his image; in the divine image he created him; male and female he created them." God made us for him. We belong to God. We are his children. People usually want to be identified with a famous person, such as the president, a bishop, or a movie star. Our young people might say, "How cool is that!" Yet, how much cooler it is to identify ourselves as the "child of God," as "children of God."

2. *Trust.* We trust that God will provide for us. He will give us everything we need. This was very well expressed in 2 Corinthians 9:8, "Moreover, God is able to make every grace abundant for you, so that in all things, always having all you need, you may have an abundance for every good work." By the same token, we need to be trustworthy and honest in everything we do. In 1 Corinthians 4:1-2, St. Paul says, "Think of us in this way, as servants of Christ and stewards of God's mysteries. Moreover, it is required of stewards that they should be found trustworthy."

3. *Gratitude.* Jesus is our model of gratitude. He gave thanks to the Father always. We saw this especially when he shared food with others, as in the last supper and in the feeding of the multitude with five loaves and two fish. We know that God is the source of all. He has given us everything — our very life, our faith, our relationships, our intellect and will, our material possessions, the beauty of nature, and more.

Father Andrew suggests making a "Thank-God" list daily so we don't take things for granted. In doing this we truly live a life of thanksgiving for God's many blessings. Our gratitude is expressed by giving our time, talent, and treasure in thanksgiving for all he has given us.

4. *Love.* God loved us first. He created us in his image, then redeemed us with his only Son and sent us his Holy Spirit to sanctify us. In response to God's love, we give him our love, and we give thanks as in 1 Chronicles 16:34: "Give thanks to the Lord, for he is good, for his kindness endures forever." In 1 Corinthians 13:13, St. Paul said, "So faith, hope, love remain, these three; but the greatest of these is love." Love and charity are synonymous. The act of love requires that we give — our time, talent, and treasure — out of love. In giving, our first priority is God.

Stewardship Promotes Tithing: The First and the Best

"All the best of the new oil and of the new wine and grain that they give to the LORD as their first fruits; and likewise, of whatever grows on their land, the first products that they bring in to the LORD shall be yours" (Nm 18:12-13a).

"You shall take some first fruits of the various products of the soil which you harvest from the land which the LORD, your God, gives you, and putting them in a basket, you shall go to the place which the LORD, your God, chooses for the dwelling place of his name" (Dt 26:2).

SCRIPTURE MENTIONS THE WORD "TITHE" more than forty times so there is a solid biblical foundation to tithing. Even so, just the word itself seems to have a negative connotation among Catholics.

The same was true for many of St. Thomas More's parishioners. I did not understand why people reacted negatively to stewardship when we first started the program. It was because people immediately equated stewardship with tithing.

Actually, we did not use the word tithing much, mainly because it was just not part of my vocabulary at the time. Over time, however, I realized that the word scares a lot of people, or at least they frown upon the use of the word. Some say it's Protestant. Father Andrew disagrees. "It certainly is Catholic," he points out. "We just forgot its use until recently." When he first came to St. Thomas More, he gave due attention to tithing in his homilies and his teachings, not only in terms of money, but also in making time for God and in using our talents for God's glory.

Stewardship Promotes the Need to Give vs. Giving to a Need

Reminding people that we have a need to give makes a big difference in teaching people to give. The need to give comes from a meaningful relationship with God. In fact, the need to give is a very human experience.

Let's take the example of a child who depends a great deal on his or her parents — for food, shelter, and most of all, love. In turn, the child shows his or her love through simple expressions of affection — blowing a kiss, bringing in a flower from the back yard, or a simple hug. In adulthood, however, we express our love of God by giving of our time, talent, and treasure.

I still remember one afternoon waiting for my son, Kevin, to come home from school. Stepping out of the school bus, Kevin noticed a bright yellow dandelion, and without hesitation, he picked it and ran toward me with it. Then, stretching out his arms to offer his gift to me and giving me a hug, he said, "I love you, Mommy."

Do I have a need for the dandelion? Of course not... although I have heard some people actually put them in salads! My son's gesture is a prime example of the need to give. Kevin wanted to express his love for me by giving me a dandelion.

This is also true with God. If we have a deep relationship with him we will want to express our love for him by giving our time, our talent, and our treasure. That's why, in the spirituality of stewardship, the need to give is stressed instead of giving to a need. The latter emphasizes the needs of the parish — the boiler has to be repaired, the church roof is leaking, the parking lot has potholes, and more. We realize that when the gift is based on need, it stops after the need is addressed. However, when the gift is based on the "need to give" it does not stop. It is ongoing and there are no strings attached to the gifts. (The nameplate above the door or on the plaque, for example.) In other words, keep the parish budget needs separate from "stewardship of treasure weekends" when we ask parishoners to make a commitment of treasure.

Stewardship Has Biblical Foundation and Is Supported by the *Catechism of the Catholic Church* and the United States Conference of Catholic Bishops

In Appendix 4 you will find a list of biblical passages supporting stewardship and tithing. Throughout the book, there are citations from the *Catechism of the Catholic Church*. In 1992 the United States Conference of Catholic Bishops released its pastoral letter, *Stewardship: A Disciple's Response*. If you have not read or studied it, I hope you will soon. It is a valuable tool and reference material to inspire you to make stewardship a way of life in your parish.

In Scripture

These are just some examples of stewardship-related verses in Scripture. We first encountered the word "tithe" in Leviticus 27:30-32: "All tithes of the land, whether in grain from the fields or in fruit from the trees, belong to the Lord, as sacred to him. . . . The tithes of the herd and the flock shall be determined by ceding to the Lord as sacred every tenth animal as they are counted by the herdsman's rod."

Proverbs 3:9-10 reads: "Honor the Lord with your wealth, with first fruits of all your produce; Then will your barns be filled with grain, with new wine your vats will overflow."

Acts 2:44-45 says of the early Church: "All who believed were together and had all things in common; they would sell their property and possessions and divide them among all according to each one's need."

One of my favorite passages is Malachi 3:10: "Bring the whole tithe into the storehouse, That there may be food in my house, and try me in this, says the LORD of hosts: Shall I not open for you the floodgates of heaven, to pour down blessing upon you without measure?"

Indeed, God is daring us to tithe. To me, God's dare carries a lot of weight, and there's no way he will not fulfill his promise. As he said in Isaiah 42:16: "I will lead the blind on their journey; by paths unknown I will guide them. I will turn darkness into light before them, and make crooked ways straight. These things I do for them, and I will not forsake them."

Some people say that Jesus did not teach tithing. In fact, he required even more than tithing, said Bishop Broderick Pabillo, auxiliary bishop of Manila, at a stewardship conference in the Philippines. Remember the widow's mite? Jesus praised her for putting in "all she had, her whole livelihood" (Mk 12:44). Are you willing to give everything you have? If this is too much, how about Zacchaeus who, after welcoming Jesus to his home said, "Behold, half of my possessions, Lord, I shall give to the poor, and if I have extorted anything from anyone I shall repay it four times over"(Lk 19:8)?

These two examples make tithing easier to handle in comparison.

Jesus also warned us that to tithe is not enough, and that in practicing tithing, we cannot forget to love and to be just. "Woe to you Pharisees! You pay tithes of mint and of rue and of every garden herb, but you pay no attention to judgment and to love for God. These you should have done, without overlooking the others" (Lk 11:42).

Tithing means to give God the first and the best. In tithing we recognize that:

1. God is the owner, and we are only the managers of his treasure.
2. We give back ten percent — a tithe — the first and the best of what we have including our time, talent, and treasure.
3. A tithe is not a leftover or table droppings.
4. It is the best portion, the first portion.
5. It is a sign of our love to give the first and the best to God.

In the Catechism of the Catholic Church

As mentioned earlier, the *Catechism of the Catholic Church* supports stewardship as a way of life. In explaining the petition "give us this day our daily bread" from the Lord's Prayer, paragraphs 2828-2237 teach:

> 2828 *"Give us"*: The trust of children who look to their Father for everything is beautiful. "He makes his sun rise on the evil and on the good, and sends rain on the just and on the unjust." He gives to all the living "their food in due season." Jesus teaches us this petition, because it glorifies our Father by acknowledging how good he is, beyond all goodness.
>
> 2829 "Give us" also expresses the covenant. We are his and he is ours, for our sake. But this "us" also recognizes him as the Father of all men and we pray to him for them all, in solidarity with their needs and sufferings.
>
> 2830 *"Our bread"*: The Father who gives us life cannot but give us the nourishment life requires — appropriate goods and blessings, both material and spiritual. In the Sermon on the Mount, Jesus insists on the filial trust that cooperates with our Father's providence. He is not inviting us to idleness, but wants to relieve us from nagging worry and preoccupation. Such is the filial surrender of the children of God:
>
>> To those who seek the kingdom of God and his righteousness, he has promised to give all else besides. Since everything indeed belongs to God, he who possesses God wants for nothing, if he himself is not found wanting before God.
>
> 2831 But the presence of those who hunger because they lack bread opens up another profound meaning of this petition. The drama of hunger in the world calls Christians

who pray sincerely to exercise responsibility toward their brethren, both in their personal behavior and in their solidarity with the human family. This petition of the Lord's Prayer cannot be isolated from the parables of the poor man Lazarus and of the Last Judgment.

2832 As leaven in the dough, the newness of the kingdom should make the earth "rise" by the Spirit of Christ. This must be shown by the establishment of justice in personal and social economic and international relations, without ever forgetting that there are no just structures without people who want to be just.

2833 "Our" bread is the "one" loaf for the "many." In the Beatitudes "poverty" is the virtue of sharing: it calls us to communicate and share both material and spiritual goods, not by coercion but out of love, so that the abundance of some may remedy the needs of others.

2834 "Pray and work." "Pray as if everything depended on God and work as if everything depended on you." Even when we have done our work, the food we receive is still a gift from our Father; it is good to ask him for it and to thank him, as Christian families do when saying grace at meals.

2835 This petition, with the responsibility it involves, also applies to another hunger from which men are perishing: "Man does not live by bread alone, but… by every word that proceeds from the mouth of God," that is, by the Word he speaks and the Spirit he breathes forth. Christians must make every effort "to proclaim the good news to the poor." There is a famine on earth "not a famine of bread, nor a thirst for water, but of hearing the words of the Lord." For this reason the specifically Christian sense of this fourth petition concerns the Bread of Life: The Word of God accepted in faith, the Body of Christ received in the Eucharist.

> 2836 *"This day"* is also an expression of trust taught us by the Lord, which we would never have presumed to invent. Since it refers above all to his Word and to the Body of his Son, this "today" is not only that of our mortal time, but also the "today" of God....
>
> 2837 *"Daily"* (*epiousios*) occurs nowhere else in the New Testament. Taken in a temporal sense, this word is a pedagogical repetition of "this day," to confirm us in trust "without reservation." Taken in the qualitative sense, it signifies what is necessary for life, and more broadly every good thing sufficient for subsistence. Taken literally (*epiousios:* "super-essential"), it refers directly to the Bread of Life, the Body of Christ, the "medicine of immortality," without which we have no life within us. Finally in this connection, its heavenly meaning is evident: "this day" is the Day of the Lord, the day of the feast of the kingdom, anticipated in the Eucharist that is already the foretaste of the kingdom to come. For this reason it is fitting for the Eucharistic liturgy to be celebrated each day....

Stewardship: A Disciple's Response

In its 1992 pastoral letter *Stewardship: A Disciple's Response,* the United States Conference of Catholic Bishops wrote:

> All temporal and spiritual goods are created by and come from God. That is true of everything human beings have: spiritual gifts like faith, hope, and love; talents of body and brain; cherished relationships with family and friends; material goods; the achievements of human genius and skill; the world itself. One day God will require an accounting of the use each person has made of the particular portion of these goods entrusted to him or her.
>
> An oikonomos or steward is one to whom the owner of a household turns over responsibility for caring for the

property, managing affairs, managing resources to yield as much as possible, and sharing the resources with others. The position involves trust and accountability.

Stewardship Is a Means to an End: Evangelization

STEWARDSHIP, WHICH IS A CALL TO DISCIPLESHIP of Jesus Christ, is not the end. It is only a means to an end, and that end is evangelization. Again quoting the bishops' letter: "The authentic practice of stewardship inevitably leads to evangelization."

Thus as a community of disciples of Jesus Christ, our duty to evangelize is an obligation of love, for the "love of Christ impels us" (2 Cor 5:14).

In his apostolic exhortation, *Evangelii Nuntiandi*, Pope Paul VI noted:

> The presentation of the Gospel message is not an optional contribution for the Church. It is the duty incumbent on her by the command of the Lord Jesus, so that people can believe and be saved....
>
> Evangelizing is in fact the grace and vocation proper to the Church, her deepest identity. She exists in order to evangelize, that is to say, in order to preach and teach, to be the channel of grace, to reconcile sinners with God, and to perpetuate Christ's sacrifice in the Mass, which is the memorial of His death and glorious resurrection....
>
> The Church is an evangelizer, but she begins by being evangelized herself. She is the community of believers, the community of hope lived and communicated, the community of brotherly love; and she needs to listen unceasingly to what she must believe, to her reasons for hoping, to the new commandment of love. She is the People of God immersed in the world, and often tempted by idols, and she always needs to hear the proclamation of the "mighty works of God" which converted her to the Lord; she always needs to be called together afresh by Him and reunited. In brief this

> means that she has a constant need of being evangelized, if she wishes to retain freshness, vigor and strength in order to proclaim the Gospel.

At St. Thomas More we take our duty to evangelize very seriously, first at home and then to all nations. Using the USCCB's *Go and Make Disciples* (a national plan and strategy for Catholic evangelization in the United States), St. Thomas More's parish leaders developed a unique set of goals and objectives to carry out the parish mission to evangelize. The leaders chose three goals: share our faith, invite all people, and foster Gospel values. Under each goal are a number of objectives culturally sensitive to the faithful of St. Thomas More.

Every year each commission (groups, committees, and ministries with related interests and activities) chooses a specific objective and develops plans to carry out that objective with the ultimate goal of taking the Good News of salvation and the Kingdom of God to all peoples near and far. In the end, the entire parish carries out its mission to "go and make disciples."

As a stewardship parish, St. Thomas More is blessed with sufficient resources to evangelize. Additionally, as a stewardship and an evangelizing parish, St. Thomas More reaches out not only within the parish boundaries, but to those outside the parish boundaries as well. Indeed, evangelization activities cannot remain in the parish, but must be extended beyond its walls. Why? Because Jesus commanded his disciples to proclaim the Kingdom of God to all nations: "Go, therefore, and make disciples of all nations, baptizing them in the name of the Father, and of the Son, and of the holy Spirit, teaching them to observe all that I have commanded you. And behold, I am with you always, until the end of the age" (Mt 28:19-20).

If evangelization is the parish mission, then it makes sense for St. Thomas More to share its blessings with, and to be witness to, others at home and abroad. In the words of St. Paul: "If I preach the gospel, this is no reason for me to boast, for an obligation has been imposed on me, and woe to me if I do not preach it!" (1 Cor 9:16).

And so parishioners take the Good News of Jesus Christ outside the parish — to the inner-city schools, to food banks, and to parishes within and outside Colorado. The parish reaches out to the poor through the St. Vincent de Paul Society, the Knights of Columbus, the Angel Tree, and other ministries. St. Thomas More also funds numerous missionary activities in the United States and in developing countries such as Mexico, Nicaragua, the Philippines, and Peru; and in Africa. The Neo-Catechumenal Way, Legion of Mary, and the pilgrim statue visit families in their homes to bring Christ to them. We mail to all our registered members *More Informed*, our bimonthly newsletter, to take the good news of Jesus Christ to both active and inactive parish members.

Qualities of a Stewardship Parish Showcased at St. Thomas More

WHEN STEWARDSHIP BECOMES A WAY of life and evangelization truly becomes its mission, the parish with practicing Christian stewards becomes a praying, welcoming, serving, giving, and celebrating community.

1. Praying Community

A stewardship and evangelizing parish is a praying community. A praying and worshiping community makes time for God in prayer and it is rooted in the Eucharist. This means the parish gives special attention to all liturgical celebrations so that they are reverent yet joyful public worship.

Father Andrew has challenged parishioners to tithe a day a week or two hours and twenty-four minutes in prayer and time for God, whether in private and in public.

Indeed, prayer is a very important part of all activities, meetings, and events at St. Thomas More. For instance, Father Andrew usually assigns a person to prepare and lead the prayer before the staff or pastoral council meeting. It is not unusual for the prayer portion of the meeting to last twenty minutes.

The parish offers many opportunities to encourage prayer, whether private or public. At St. Thomas More perpetual adoration has grown and is still growing strong, with nearly five hundred adorers since its inception in the early 1990s. Daily communicants also pray the Liturgy of the Hours before Mass, while others pray the rosary after Mass.

A number of prayer groups — Centering Prayer, Intercessors of the Lamb, Men's Prayer Group, St. Peregrine Novena, Living Rosary Crusade, and others — offer various types of prayer to parishioners. The Ministry of Praise consists of members who are homebound praying daily for intentions of the parish, while the Prayer Line and the Book of Prayer and Healing pray for the intentions of individuals.

To help parishioners in their prayer life and in making time for God, the parish distributes many tools, such as rosaries and prayer booklets. A very active rosary makers group provides the parish with rosaries for distribution not only in the parish but also for the missions. Many of its members are those who live in assisted living communities, and they feel not only connected with the parish but enjoy a sense of belonging to it.

2. Welcoming Community

A stewardship and evangelizing parish is also a welcoming community. People who are grateful receivers and givers are usually cheerful and welcoming people. Thus, a parish full of cheerful and welcoming people also becomes a hospitable community. A smile usually draws another smile. A simple hello to another person across the hall makes him or her feel at home. "I just love the spirit here at St. Thomas More," said one visitor to me as he came down the stairs after Mass. "I cannot help but smile."

A welcoming and hospitable place gives parishioners a sense of belonging — even if they are homebound. Would you want to become involved in a parish that makes you feel like a stranger? People feel more comfortable coming to or getting involved in the parish if they feel they belong. This is possible even in a parish as large as St. Thomas More, where there are nearly three thousand individuals involved in approximately three hundred ministries and committees.

First-time visitors to St. Thomas More find it overwhelming because of its size. In order to alleviate this problem, volunteers serve as greeters before the liturgies. Some parishioners also serve at the information desk before and after the Masses to answer questions or to give directions to various venues. When the parish office is closed or no one is available to personally greet visitors, a computerized kiosk, computer, or marquee provides the necessary information listing the day's events and giving directions to safe, well-maintained, and handicap-friendly facilities. Indeed, these ministries are important in making guests or those new to the parish feel welcome.

Signs are very important to guests. When St. Thomas More was rebuilding, a sign committee made sure that there were many very visible signs around campus, so that parishioners and their guests could get through the maze of the construction. But signs should be visible not only for periods of construction, but also as an ordinary part of a welcoming community.

To be welcoming is actually more than all of the above. It is everybody's business to be welcoming and not the responsibility of only the welcome and donut Sunday committees. Let me give you an example which Notre Dame Sister Phyllis Heble related at a recent staff meeting. Sister Phyllis, who ministers before and after funerals, assisted at a Mass for the deceased on All Souls Day. At the reception later, she met a man who seemed to be in distress. Sister Phyllis started a conversation with him and later found out that the man's father died that very morning. He did not have any family around and somehow ended up at St. Thomas More at the Mass for the deceased. There he felt the comfort of family that he needed. Sister Phyllis' encounter with this man is the true meaning of what a welcoming community is.

3. Serving Community

A stewardship and evangelizing parish is a serving community. With nearly six thousand two hundred families, St. Thomas More Parish is, indeed, bursting at the seams. Yet people are still drawn to the parish. Why?

Many choose St. Thomas More Parish because they find that the parish addresses their needs, whether it is spiritual, physical, mental, social, or emotional. Like it or not, potential members check out churches to see if there's a fit with their needs. What are the services or programs the parish provides? At St. Thomas More, parishioners have ample opportunities to choose from the more than three hundred ministries, committees, and programs:

Spiritual: We emphasize the Eucharist as the center of all liturgical services. In addition, we offer outstanding faith formation in the parish.

Physical: We offer activities for health and well-being, exercise classes, weight programs, and recreational sports such as golf and bridge for adults and all sorts of sports activities for children and youth.

Mental: We have opportunities to stimulate the mind such as: writing for the parish newsletter; helping with the Web site; or taking leadership roles to plan, execute, review, or evaluate programs.

Social: We have many occasions to celebrate: appreciation parties, feast days, anniversaries, and others.

Emotional: We offer various support groups such as: AA, Al-Anon, AARP, Forever Mores Seniors, Stephen Ministries, and many more.

There's something for those who want to serve the poor, those particularly interested in worship, those seeking ways to evangelize, and more.

Many of our parishioners go outside of the parish to bring the Good News of Jesus Christ to others. We have Ambassadors of Hope whose members serve inner-city Catholic schools. We also have hundreds of volunteers for Habitat for Humanity and for many food banks in the metro Denver area.

In fact, there is something for those who want to serve the poor, those interested in worship, those who want to evangelize, and many other areas of ministry. This did not happen by chance. When parishioners suggest doing or starting a particular ministry, we let them as long as they are willing to keep it going and as long as the ministry falls under any of the commissions that carry out the parish mission to "go and make disciples."

I remember getting a visit from a parishioner, recently retired, who wanted to start the Living Rosary Crusade. She was so passionate about it that in no time she had more than one hundred members praying a decade of the rosary daily.

On the other hand, if a ministry no longer serves the parish and parishioners then there's no reason why the ministry should stay on the books. We let it go. The parish's "Leadership Days" in June are our opportunity to evaluate all our programs to see if they carry out our mission to "go and make disciples." That gathering is also a time for parish leaders to plan for the following year.

4. Giving Community

A stewardship and evangelizing parish is a giving parish. Just as we ask parishioners to give a tithe of their time, talent, and treasure, we also require the same for the parish.

At St. Thomas More, ten percent of the offertory collection goes to a charity account to be distributed to various charities locally, nationally, and internationally. Since 2000, the parish has distributed an average of $425,000 in grants annually. In addition to the charity grants, a significant budget is allocated for ongoing social concerns outreach such as Habitat for Humanity, Respect Life, Gabriel Project (for unwed mothers), Angel Tree (for children of prisoners), Project 600 (for inner-city school children), and others.

Parishioners also give through the St. Vincent de Paul Society, which provides financial assistance to the poor. The members of Knights of Columbus donate thousands of hours serving the parish and the community through their Easter Food Boxes, the Tootsie Rolls Drive (outside the parish), and many other outreach programs. Even the children in the religious education program and the parish school reach out to the poor and marginalized. The youth make sandwiches regularly for the Sandwich Line for the poor in Denver. They also collect food for the poor during the Thanksgiving and Christmas seasons. The children's entire offertory collection goes to the charity account which they distribute to many charitable organizations worldwide.

Of course, the parish has taken seriously its role as a mentor in the spreading of stewardship as a way of life. To Father Andrew's credit, he has made it his and the parish's mission to assist other pastors in making stewardship a way of life in their respective parishes. He feels that because St. Thomas More has been blessed the parish has an obligation to give back to God in many ways, including efforts to spread the message of stewardship beyond St. Thomas More. As

Luke 12:48 says: "Much will be required of the person entrusted with much, and still more will be demanded of the person entrusted with more."

5. Celebrating Community

A stewardship and evangelizing parish is a celebrating community. St. Thomas More is a celebrating parish. It is a spirit-filled and joyful parish. The parish celebrates the faith, the clergy, the volunteers, and the staff. The parish also celebrates the families, those who are single or married as well as seniors and the homebound. St. Thomas More celebrates all walks of life and ethnicities, making them feel important and making them feel they belong to this parish.

Parishioners have a choice of all kinds of celebrations: Volunteer Appreciation Party, Clergy and Religious Appreciation Day, STM Day, St. Patrick's Dance, Oktober Fest, Epiphany Celebration, Halloween, and Guppy Fest. Anniversaries of ordination and profession of vows, as well as wedding anniversaries, are regularly celebrated at St. Thomas More. (To mark wedding anniversaries, the parish encourages a public exchange of vows at Mass as a living witness to the sanctity of marriage.)

In addition, the youth ministry has traditionally celebrated with the poor through its Project 600, in which more than six hundred inner-city school children are entertained and presented with nicely wrapped Christmas gifts. For some youngsters, those gifts could very well be the only Christmas presents they receive that year.

Why Embrace Stewardship?

To be a Christian disciple is a rewarding way of life, a way of companionship with Jesus, and the practice of stewardship is itself a source of deep joy. Those who live this way are happy people who have found the meaning and purpose of living.

— *Stewardship: A Disciple's Response*
United States Conference of Catholic Bishops, 1992

In embracing stewardship as a way of life, practitioners find many rewards. Here are a few:

God cannot be outdone in generosity. Although we do not teach a *quid pro quo* approach, or see stewardship as a bargaining tool to get something, many give testimony to the fact that when they give they receive more than they have given.

Peace of mind. Trusting that God will provide for our needs keeps us from worrying about the future, and that gives us peace of mind. I experienced this peace of mind personally when my husband could not find a steady job for five years during the recession of the 1990s. It was not easy, but knowing and trusting God would take care of us, we did not have to worry about filling the needs of our family from my church salary.

Less attachment to money. We know everything we have is God's and that we are only his managers. That makes it easier to give back to him what does not belong to us anyway. As someone said, "It's easier to give somebody else's money."

Joy of giving. There's the expression "give until it hurts" but I would rather say, "Give until it becomes a joy to give." As Scripture says: "Each must do as already determined, without sadness or compulsion, for God loves a cheerful giver" (2 Cor 9:7). And in Acts 20:35 we read: "In every way I have shown you that by hard work of that sort we must help the weak, and keep in mind the words of the Lord Jesus who himself said, 'It is more blessed to give than to receive.'"

Resources are available to do God's work. When we give back to God, we give opportunities where none exist otherwise. Every time I think of the resources available at St. Thomas More and all the outreach opportunities made possible by our practice of stewardship, I cannot help but be in awe of what we all could do collectively to make the world a better place if all parishes were to practice stewardship as a way of life. While we probably cannot wipe out poverty and all the ills of society completely, we certainly could make a dent.

Again, quoting *Stewardship: A Disciples' Response*: "The life of a Christian steward models the life of Jesus. It is challenging and even difficult, in many respects. Yet intense joy comes to those who take the risk to live as Christian stewards. Women and men who seek to live as stewards learn that "all things work for good for those who love God" (Rom 8:28).

What Keeps Parishes from Embracing Stewardship as a Way of Life?

A NUMBER OF CONCERNS AND ISSUES have kept parishes or pastors from embracing stewardship as a way of life. Below are a few:

Stewardship is all about money. This is a common misunderstanding regarding stewardship. This is especially so with self-sufficient parishes. They don't feel the need to introduce stewardship because they have the funds to operate the parish. Just mention the word "stewardship" and people think that it's all about money and that someone is ready to pick their wallet.

It is easy to associate stewardship with money, because the early practitioners, and even those in recent times, used the word only when they wanted to increase the offertory collection. In fact, we started stewardship at St. Thomas More precisely because our offertory collection was dropping. However, money is only one-sixth of our stewardship program. With our emphasis on conversion and transformation, we hope that stewardship is becoming a way of life in the parish and for our parishioners.

Even the word "money" is dirty. This comes from the misunderstanding of the Scripture passage "For the love of money is the root of all evils" (1 Tm. 6:10). Often people forget the first four words of this verse and just believe the last six. Thus, they think, "Money is the root of all evil." Jesus did not see it that way, however. In fact, his parables contained references to money more than half the time. He must have thought it was an important topic for him to discuss it that many times. Does stewardship involve money? Sure it does. We need it to carry out Jesus' command to "go and make disciples."

Lack of training of priests in the spirituality of stewardship. While seminaries offer a multitude of classes on theology, dogma, philosophy, and other intellectual pursuits, the spirituality of stewardship is nowhere to be found in almost all the seminaries. When asked about this, one rector said, "We don't have the time to add another class." The problem is that priests should have some training in the spirituality of stewardship and as managers of time, talent, and treasure for parishes.

Concept of giving to a need vs. need to give. Many parishes have resorted to all sorts of fundraising (raffles, bingo, and bazaars, for example) but they are still kept wanting for more. They never seem to have enough when paying the bills becomes the goal rather than conversion or transformation and a meaningful relationship with God. When the motivation is giving to a need, it stops the moment the need has been addressed. On the other hand, we continue to give when we recognize we have a need to give. Then, too, there are no strings attached to the gifts when they are based on a need to give.

Stewardship will continue to work on its own after starting the program. If this were the case, there would be more stewardship parishes. One of the reasons stewardship does not work in the parish is a failure to make it an annual parish program. Sometimes a parish declares itself a "stewardship parish" and thinks, just by doing that, it is. What helps make stewardship a way of life in the parish and for individuals are the annual renewals. Remember those New Year's resolutions? We make them year after year because we slack off, simply forget, or need to update them.

The same is true with making stewardship a way of life. The annual renewals are a big part of the success of the stewardship program. People have a tendency to let things slide and to focus on other pursuits. That's why they need to be reminded to recommit to making time for God, to sharing their gifts and talents, to nourishing their faith, to giving of their treasure, to promoting vocations, and to caring for the earth — all in thanksgiving for God's blessings. It's in the annual renewals that we ask people to make a recommitment of their time, talent, and treasure.

One parish talked about prayer for an entire month with beautiful homilies, but did not ask people to make a commitment to pray. What a missed opportunity! In marketing, we know that we need to educate, inform, and then invite to act. The third one, the action, is the reason for the annual renewal.

Great homilies, beautiful choirs, outstanding religious education and youth programs will compel people to give without stewardship. Not necessarily. Otherwise, many parishes would not be hurting for resources. In reality, a stewardship parish tends to have the above and much more. Many cathedral parishes and other faith communities have the most beautiful and awe-inspiring buildings as well as the best choirs and great homilies (usually from the bishops themselves), but are known to be struggling for funds and for human resources.

That's why Charles Zech — a professor of economics at Villanova University and the author of numerous books on Catholic giving — recommends in his *Why Catholics Don't Give and What Can Be Done About It* (Our Sunday Visitor, 2000) that a parish "instill among its members a sense of stewardship." I could not agree more. Asking parishioners to make a commitment to give back to God in thanksgiving for all his blessings is the best way to compel people to give. Just waiting for people to be generous because the parish offers some great qualities is not necessarily the best approach to giving. Asking is the best way to receive. As Jesus said, "Ask and it will be given to you" (Mt 7:7).

Stewardship Is an Ongoing Process!

STEWARDSHIP IS, INDEED, A WAY of life. It is a process and, therefore, it is ongoing. Stewardship takes time to evolve and so it requires patience. Remember, it took many years for the St. Thomas More model to become what it is today.

Some priests or lay leaders who ask us to help them make stewardship a way of life in their parish want to see immediate results and then they're easily disappointed when they don't see that. The parish doesn't succeed because leaders think this would all just happen without any planning, or that it would go on "autopilot" after starting the program. On the contrary! It takes time to plan and to make stewardship happen in the parish.

When we started implementing stewardship in 1989, we decided early on that we would need to educate the parish throughout the year. In addition to the homilies, we used — and continue to use — the Sunday bulletin and the newsletter for this purpose. With the advent of high technology, we have added the Web site, e-mails, a computer kiosk, and digital videos to teach stewardship. More importantly we use these communication tools to show how the parish has embraced stewardship and how our parishioners are living the life of a good steward, the life of Jesus' disciple.

Stewardship is a way of life and must be *lived*. It's a lifetime process that involves conversion and transformation. Yes, it is also a "program," which means there is a time when the parish is engaged in the active phase of the process. There is a beginning and an end in the parish stewardship program.

The next section, Part IV, of this book will explain more about the program, but please note, it describes our experiences at St. Thomas More, which has gone through more than a few trials and errors. We feel that we can speak with authority on what we know well — the St. Thomas More model — rather than other parish models.

Certainly, there are many more models, which we might mention from time to time, but they are not the subject of this book. We encourage you, however, to learn more about other models and see what will best fit your parish. Two ways of doing this are by attending conferences offered in your diocese; or by going to those presented by the International Catholic Stewardship Council (ICSC) on an international level, by Our Sunday Visitor on a regional level, or by your diocese on a local level.

The choice is yours!

NOTES, REFLECTIONS, & POINTS TO REMEMBER

For Part III: Stewardship Methods

NOTES, REFLECTIONS, & POINTS TO REMEMBER

For Part III: Stewardship Methods

NOTES, REFLECTIONS, & POINTS TO REMEMBER

For Part III: Stewardship Methods

PART IV

The "How-to" of Stewardship

By Mila Glodava

Now we will look at the "nuts and bolts" of the St. Thomas More Parish Program. In television, we hear of "must-see TV." In stewardship, we recommend a number of "must-do" and "must-have" items.

At a recent meeting, someone said, "All we need is to know the theology of stewardship or that if there's good liturgy, great homilies, or outstanding choirs in the parish, parishioners would feel compelled to give of their time, talent, and treasure."

Well, that's not exactly true. If that were the case, many parishes would never have to want for anything, whether it's for volunteers or for the financial resources to run the parish. There are a few "must-do" and "must-have" items for parishes to make significant progress towards embracing stewardship as a way of life in the parish. There may be others that have worked successfully in other parishes, but the ones we talk about here are the ones that have worked at St. Thomas More.

Let's look at STM's "must-do" and "must-have" items we recommend parishes to consider implementing in their parishes:

1. Organizational requirements
2. Liturgical components
3. Educational plans

These requirements actually resemble the three roles of the pastor as priest (liturgical), prophet (educational), and king (organizational).

Organizational Requirements

Making stewardship a way of life in the parish is no easy task. In fact, it involves a lot of work. That is why it is necessary that there is maximum support from the pastor, the parish staff, and parish leaders.

Pastor: The role of the pastor is essential if the parish is to embrace stewardship as a way of life. As the principal leader of his parish, his support or lack of support can mean the success or failure of this way of life. When I first started stewardship at St. Thomas More, my pastor was definitely the initiator of the program. Father Walsh encouraged me to develop, coordinate, and monitor the progress of our stewardship program. His main role was to give a homily on stewardship and to give the spiritual side of stewardship during commitment Sundays. The pastor must not only believe in giving it a try but also in supporting the process. If he does not have time to oversee its implementation, he must allow others to carry out its implementation. That's why if people request us at St. Thomas More to help them introduce stewardship in their parish, we require that the pastor be involved in the process.

Parish staff: It is ideal to have a communications and stewardship staff to develop, coordinate, and monitor the stewardship program. The parish staff may be privy to data that may not be readily available to a volunteer committee. As mentioned before, I have coordinated all aspects of stewardship from the early years of stewardship at St. Thomas More. Over time, my office has grown into a six-member department helping me with all six phases of our stewardship program.

At a meeting of several stewardship parishes, one of the pastors said that the reason St. Thomas More has developed stewardship into what it is today is because one person acts as an "engine" to make the program run over an extended period of time. He also noted that the success of St. Francis of Assisi Parish in Wichita, Kansas, was because Monsignor Thomas McGread was its "engine" for more than three decades.

After nearly two decades coordinating the stewardship program at St. Thomas More, I tend to agree that it's important to have at least one person monitoring the stewardship activities of the parish.

Parish leaders: Many parishes don't have the funds to hire a staff person. It is advisable to form a stewardship commission or committee to assist the pastor in implementing stewardship in the parish. An important aspect of a successful stewardship parish, the stewardship committee oversees how stewardship is carried out in the parish, and distributes the charity account.

Please note that while we did not initially have a stewardship commission to run the program, we did rely on various stewardship committees (ministry fair, vocations and others) to assist us in implementing the program.

Stewardship commission/committee: At St. Thomas More a stewardship commission or committee oversees all aspects of stewardship in the parish. The stewardship commission meets at least six times a year. Members are past lay witness speakers who have expressed their embracing of stewardship as a way of life. In addition, the finance and pastoral councils send liaisons to the stewardship commission. The commission determines the allocation of the parish tithe and reviews the implementation of parish goals and objectives. They also help formulate plans to implement the focus objective for the coming year for the commission.

In cooperation with the pastor and/or staff, the stewardship committee determines how stewardship will become a way of life in the parish. It involves making a commitment to do annual renewals for parishioners to make a commitment of time, talent, and treasure, whether for the first time or simply to recommit for another year. The committee plans when and how stewardship will be implemented during the calendar or liturgical year. The stewardship committee also assists the pastor with the tithe of the tithe — giving to charity ten percent of the parish offertory (see page 91) — and its distribution as well as how to ensure transparency and accountability.

Stewardship Calendar

Stewardship at St. Thomas More is year-round. As mentioned earlier, we find it helpful to keep the six active phases of the program scheduled for the same time each year. The stewardship office coordinates the parish's "master calendar" and this includes a "stewardship calendar" which helps in implementation. This is important for the staff and commission so that they will be able to plan and incorporate stewardship in their respective programs and activities.

For instance, during the stewardship of vocations weekends and special dates associated with it, the parish school, religious education, and youth ministries can talk about vocations to the priesthood and religious life. They may also want to invite a priest, brother or sister to a class to talk about his or her own vocation.

SAMPLE STEWARDSHIP CALENDAR

JANUARY

- ❍ year-end statements are sent

FEBRUARY

- ❍ clergy and religious appreciation (the last weekend before Ash Wednesday)
- ❍ send second letter to nominees of "Called by Name"

MARCH

- ❍ volunteer database is updated
- ❍ Easter letter with offering envelope sent to all parishioners

APRIL

- ❍ Archbishop's Catholic Appeal (ACA)
- ❍ Earth Day
- ❍ Stewardship of the Earth
- ❍ World Day of Prayer for Vocations
- ❍ volunteer appreciation (second Friday after Easter)

MAY

- ❍ new pastoral council members selected on Pentecost Sunday

JUNE

- ❍ Leadership Days
- ❍ St. Thomas More Day
- ❍ Pastor's Annual Award
- ❍ Alumni Day
- ❍ mission appeal

JULY

- ❍ start meetings for ministry fair
- ❍ contact lay witness speakers

AUGUST

- ❍ Stewardship of Prayer: prayer rally and mini-ministry fair on prayer groups
- ❍ Stewardship of Time and Talent: ministry fair
- ❍ work on renewal letters

SEPTEMBER:

- ❍ Stewardship of Faith (on Catechetical Sunday)

OCTOBER

- ❍ Stewardship of Treasure
- ❍ send out three Stewardship of Treasure letters: thank you, commitment forms, and acknowledgement of commitments

NOVEMBER

- ❍ Stewardship of Vocations
- ❍ send follow-up letter for Stewardship of Treasure
- ❍ send first letter to nominees of "Called by Name"

DECEMBER

- ❍ year-end giving
- ❍ Christmas letter with offering envelope sent
- ❍ financial statement from an audited report published in the parish newsletter
- ❍ year-end brochures to encourage other forms of giving

YEAR-ROUND

- ❍ ongoing stewardship education through faith formation and homilies and through special events, office requirements, and various communications tools
- ❍ newcomer's welcome packet
- ❍ stewardship articles published in Sunday bulletin and parish newsletter
- ❍ monthly statements sent along with parishioners' offertory envelopes
- ❍ parish tithe distributed and published in the bulletin
- ❍ clergy and religious remembered on special days
- ❍ mini-ministry Fair on the fourth Sunday of each month (except June and August)

Annual Renewals

IF THERE IS ONE CONSTANT since we started stewardship at St. Thomas More in 1989, it is the annual renewals. We have made a conscious decision to encourage parishioners to make an annual commitment to all phases of stewardship: time, talent, faith, treasure, vocations, and earth.

The result of the commitments is unmistakable. Although the initial response was nothing to brag about, we are pleased at how we continue to show an increase in volunteers and treasure year after year, and in growing as a spirit-filled parish.

Parishes that do not consistently schedule annual renewals usually see a different picture. They cannot get enough volunteers for their ministries. Their offertory collection stays stagnant or attendance at Mass or other liturgical services may dwindle.

It's important to have an annual renewal of commitments to allow families to review past giving of time, talent, and treasure; and to adjust accordingly for the coming year. The annual renewal is a good time to educate the parish on the spirituality and the practice of stewardship as a way of life. It also helps newcomers who may be learning about stewardship for the first time.

Commitment Cards

COMMITMENT CARDS MAY BE CALLED pledges, covenants, or faith promises. We have a commitment card for all phases of stewardship — for adults and for children and youth. As Father Andrew often says, stewardship is a spirituality and that means doing rather than thinking. A former Benedictine monk, he describes his life in the monastery as doing vs. thinking. "*Ora et labora*" — prayer and work — is the motto of the Benedictine. They pray and work at certain hours, until it becomes a way of life for them. Stewardship spirituality means making a commitment to become a good steward and commitment cards are important in the process of making stewardship a way of life.

SAMPLE COMMITMENT CARDS

Stewardship of Faith Commitment

Keep this copy for your records.

(Please indicate what you will do to strengthen and renew your faith.)

- ☐ Participate in one or more of the following:
  - ☐ Advent / Lenten series
  - ☐ Catholic Biblical School
  - ☐ Catechism Class
  - ☐ Family Program
  - ☐ Parish Mission
  - ☐ Stations of the Cross (Lent)
  - ☐ Sponsor RCIA
- ☐ Attend a Catechetical Conference.
- ☐ Attend Mass weekly, daily. (Circle one or both.)
- ☐ Attend a retreat.
- ☐ Help those in need: family/friends/neighbors.
- ☐ Join a Small Christian community.
- ☐ Join a Bible Study.
- ☐ Listen attentively to the homily on Sundays and discuss with family after Mass.
- ☐ Make a 15 minute visit per week to the Adoration Chapel.
- ☐ Pray each day—at least 15 minutes.
- ☐ Pray Grace before/after meals.
- ☐ Pray the Rosary daily/weekly.
- ☐ Read Spiritual books.
- ☐ Receive the Sacrament of Reconciliation 3 times per year or more often
- ☐ Read the following on a regular basis: STM bulletin, Denver Catholic Register, papal documents, *Grace in Action.*
- ☐ Share your faith story with a friend/ family member.
- ☐ Spend one hour per week in the Adoration Chapel.
- ☐ Read Scripture each day—15 minutes or more.

Stewardship of Faith Commitment

Please return this copy to the parish.

(Please indicate what you will do to strengthen and renew your faith.)

- ☐ Participate in one or more of the following:
  - ☐ Advent / Lenten series
  - ☐ Catholic Biblical School
  - ☐ Catechism Class
  - ☐ Family Program
  - ☐ Parish Mission
  - ☐ Stations of the Cross (Lent)
  - ☐ Sponsor RCIA
- ☐ Attend a Catechetical Conference.
- ☐ Attend Mass weekly, daily. (Circle one or both.)
- ☐ Attend a retreat.
- ☐ Help those in need: family/friends/neighbors.
- ☐ Join a Small Christian community.
- ☐ Join a Bible Study.
- ☐ Listen attentively to the homily on Sundays and discuss with family after Mass.
- ☐ Make a 15 minute visit per week to the Adoration Chapel.
- ☐ Pray each day—at least 15 minutes.
- ☐ Pray Grace before/after meals.
- ☐ Pray the Rosary daily/weekly.
- ☐ Read Spiritual books.
- ☐ Receive the Sacrament of Reconciliation 3 times per year or more often
- ☐ Read the following on a regular basis: STM bulletin, Denver Catholic Register, papal documents, *Grace in Action.*
- ☐ Share your faith story with a friend/ family member.
- ☐ Spend one hour per week in the Adoration Chapel.
- ☐ Read Scripture each day—15 minutes or more.

Stewardship of Faith

Keep this copy for your records.

Please check the things you will do to strengthen and renew your faith.

Faith is a spiritual gift that helps us believe in God and trust that the Lord loves us. Like other gifts, faith requires care.

HOW WILL YOU STEWARD YOUR FAITH?

- ☐ Dress modestly.
- ☐ Learn your Catholic prayers. *(Ask your parents to help you.)*
- ☐ Go to Mass each week on Sunday and on Holy Days. *(Parents will take you.)*
- ☐ Say a decade of the Rosary each day. *(Great to do in the car!)*
- ☐ Read your Bible—a passage each day or every other day.
- ☐ Study the life of your patron saint. How can you follow your patron saint's example?
- ☐ Celebrate the true spirit of holidays, especially Christmas and Easter.
- ☐ Keep the Fourth Commandment: Honor thy father and mother.
- ☐ Play a Bible game or Catechism game. (*Check them out from our parish library!*)
- ☐ Watch a video about the Bible or a saint.
- ☐ Pray for your family and friends each day.
- ☐ Go to Religion class/youth group each week.
- ☐ Go to the Sacrament of Reconciliation at least 3 times a year. *(More often is better!)*
- ☐ Pray to your Guardian Angel. *(Your parents can teach you the prayer.)*
- ☐ Help with chores around the house.
- ☐ Do your homework.
- ☐ Respect your parish priests, your teachers, your neighbors and friends.
- ☐ Say Grace before and after meals, thanking God for your food.
- ☐ Wear a crucifix, scapular medal or other jewelry that symbolizes your Catholic faith.
- ☐ Live the Beatitudes.
- ☐ When cruising the Internet, visit our website or another Catholic page.

Stewardship of Faith

Return this copy to the parish.

Please check the things you will do to strengthen and renew your faith.

Faith is a spiritual gift that helps us believe in God and trust that the Lord loves us. Like other gifts, faith requires care.

HOW WILL YOU STEWARD YOUR FAITH?

- ☐ Dress modestly.
- ☐ Learn your Catholic prayers. *(Ask your parents to help you.)*
- ☐ Go to Mass each week on Sunday and on Holy Days. *(Parents will take you.)*
- ☐ Say a decade of the Rosary each day. *(Great to do in the car!)*
- ☐ Read your Bible—a passage each day or every other day.
- ☐ Study the life of your patron saint. How can you follow your patron saint's example?
- ☐ Celebrate the true spirit of holidays, especially Christmas and Easter.
- ☐ Keep the Fourth Commandment: Honor thy father and mother.
- ☐ Play a Bible game or Catechism game. (*Check them out from our parish library!*)
- ☐ Watch a video about the Bible or a saint.
- ☐ Pray for your family and friends each day.
- ☐ Go to Religion class/youth group each week.
- ☐ Go to the Sacrament of Reconciliation at least 3 times a year. *(More often is better!)*
- ☐ Pray to your Guardian Angel. *(Your parents can teach you the prayer.)*
- ☐ Help with chores around the house.
- ☐ Do your homework.
- ☐ Respect your parish priests, your teachers, your neighbors and friends.
- ☐ Say Grace before and after meals, thanking God for your food.
- ☐ Wear a crucifix, scapular medal or other jewelry that symbolizes your Catholic faith.
- ☐ Live the Beatitudes.
- ☐ When cruising the Internet, visit our website or another Catholic page.

Stewardship of Prayer

Keep this copy for your records.

Please check Prayer and Intentions to which you plan to commit.

PRIVATE PRAYER

- ☐ Church Visits
- ☐ Daytime Prayer
- ☐ Litany
- ☐ Liturgy of the Hours
- ☐ Morning Offering
- ☐ Morning Prayer
- ☐ Night Prayer
- ☐ Novenas/Devotions
- ☐ Perpetual Adoration
- ☐ Prayer Line
- ☐ Quiet Time
- ☐ Reading the Sunday Reading Prior to Mass
- ☐ Rosary
- ☐ Scripture Reading
- ☐ Spiritual Reading
- ☐ Other__________

PUBLIC PRAYER

- ☐ Centering Prayer
- ☐ Daily Mass
- ☐ Family Prayer
- ☐ Grace before Meals
- ☐ Holy Hour
- ☐ Men's Saturday Group
- ☐ Parish Mission
- ☐ Pilgrimages
- ☐ Prayer Groups
- ☐ Prayer Line
- ☐ Retreat
- ☐ Weekly Mass
- ☐ Other__________

CHECK INTENTIONS for which you will pray:

- ☐ Abuse: Substance, Physical, Emotional
- ☐ Addictions
- ☐ Children
- ☐ Church
- ☐ Clergy
- ☐ Crisis of Faith
- ☐ Divorced
- ☐ Engaged
- ☐ Family Life
- ☐ Homebound
- ☐ Increase in Knowledge of Faith
- ☐ Increase in Parish Involvement
- ☐ Married Couples
- ☐ Nation
- ☐ Non-Practicing Catholics
- ☐ Sick
- ☐ Singles
- ☐ Vocations
- ☐ World
- ☐ Youth
- ☐ Those who have no one to pray for them
- ☐ End of Abortion
- ☐ Other__________

Would you like to invite a person who is homebound to join our Ministers of Praise Group? This person will be asked to uphold the parish in prayers every month.

☐ Yes! I recommend____________________

Name of homebound person

____

Phone number

____

Parishioner submitting name

Stewardship of Prayer

Return this copy to the parish.

Please check the types of Prayer and Intentions. (Please indicate the hours per week).

PRIVATE PRAYER

- ☐ Church Visits
- ☐ Daytime Prayer
- ☐ Litany
- ☐ Liturgy of the Hours
- ☐ Morning Offering
- ☐ Morning Prayer
- ☐ Night Prayer
- ☐ Novenas/Devotions
- ☐ Perpetual Adoration
- ☐ Prayer Line
- ☐ Quiet Time
- ☐ Reading the Sunday Reading Prior to Mass
- ☐ Rosary
- ☐ Scripture Reading
- ☐ Spiritual Reading
- ☐ Other__________

PUBLIC PRAYER

- ☐ Centering Prayer
- ☐ Daily Mass
- ☐ Family Prayer
- ☐ Grace before Meals
- ☐ Holy Hour
- ☐ Men's Saturday Group
- ☐ Parish Mission
- ☐ Pilgrimages
- ☐ Prayer Groups
- ☐ Prayer Line
- ☐ Retreat
- ☐ Weekly Mass
- ☐ Other__________

CHECK INTENTIONS for which you will pray:

- ☐ Abuse: Substance, Physical, Emotional
- ☐ Addictions
- ☐ Children
- ☐ Church
- ☐ Clergy
- ☐ Crisis of Faith
- ☐ Divorced
- ☐ Engaged
- ☐ Family Life
- ☐ Homebound
- ☐ Increase in Knowledge of Faith
- ☐ Increase in Parish Involvement
- ☐ Married Couples
- ☐ Nation
- ☐ Non-Practicing Catholics
- ☐ Sick
- ☐ Singles
- ☐ Vocations
- ☐ World
- ☐ Youth
- ☐ Those who have no one to pray for them
- ☐ End of Abortion
- ☐ Other__________

Would you like to invite a person who is homebound to join our Ministers of Praise Group? This person will be asked to uphold the parish in prayers every month.

☐ Yes! I recommend____________________

Name of homebound person

____

Phone number

____

Parishioner submitting name

Commitment Form

Envelope Number: ______ Date: ______

Name: ______

Address: ______

City: ______ State: ______ Zip: ______

Phone (Home) ______ (Work) ______

E-mail address: ______

Please complete one form per individual in the family.

If you need additional forms you may make copies of this original or contact the parish office at 303-770-1155.

Stewardship of Time & Talent for Adult Stewards

St. Thomas More Catholic Church

Please check the box for each ministry that you are interested in, as well as those you are already doing. If you check "interested in" you will be notified by the leader of the ministry. Please complete one form per individual in the family.

1 Communications & Stewardship Commission

	Please check box	Interested in:	Already doing:
1a	**Communications:**		
1a3	General Office Volunteers	☐	☐
1a4	Information Desk	☐	☐
1a5.1	More Informed Writers	☐	☐
1b	**Stewardship:**		
1b8	Ambassadors of Hope (Volunteers for Inner City Schools)	☐	☐
1b1	Cloister Cove Volunteers	☐	☐
1b2	Ministry Fair/Time & Talent	☐	☐
1b3	Newcomers' Welcome	☐	☐
1b5.1	Rosary Makers	☐	☐

2 Facilities Support Commission

	Please check box	Interested in:	Already doing:
2b	Handy Man Maintenance	☐	☐
2d	Landscaping/Flowers	☐	☐

3 Faith & Academic Formation Commission

	Please check box	Interested in:	Already doing:
3a1	**Faith Formation & Catechists:**		
	Adult Faith Formation/Adult Volunteers		
3a1.2	Bible Studies	☐	☐
3a1.1	Catechism Class	☐	☐
3a1.3	ChristLife	☐	☐
3a1.18	Confirmation Class	☐	☐
3a1.26	ENDOW	☐	☐
3a1.20	FAMILIA	☐	☐
3a1.4	Family Program Catechists	☐	☐
3a1.24	Grades 1-5 Catechists	☐	☐
3a1.5	Legion of Mary	☐	☐
3a1.21	Men Among Men	☐	☐
3a1.22	Ministry of Mothers Sharing (MOMS)	☐	☐
3a1.7	Mom & Tots	☐	☐
3a1.8	Neo-Catechumenal Way	☐	☐
3a1.25	Office Helpers	☐	☐
3a1.9	Parish Library Volunteer	☐	☐

3c3	**Young Adults (Ages 18-39)**		
3c3.5	College Life Leader	☐	☐
3c3.1	Oasis	☐	☐
3c3.2	Retreat Leaders	☐	☐
3c3.3	Service Coordinator	☐	☐
3c3.4	Special Events	☐	☐

4 Family Life Commission/ Adult Volunteers

	Please check box	Interested in:	Already doing:
4a	Bridge Club	☐	☐
4b	Forever Mores STM Senior Ministry	☐	☐
4c	Foster Parenting	☐	☐
4e	Knights of Columbus (K of C)	☐	☐
4e.1	K of C Ladies Auxiliary	☐	☐
4d.1	Ladies' Golf League	☐	☐
4d.2	Men's Golf League	☐	☐
4g	New Life Singles Ministry	☐	☐
4h	Parish Special Events	☐	☐
4i	STM Singles Ministry	☐	☐
4j	STM Stitchers	☐	☐
4k	Scrapbooking	☐	☐

5 Liturgy Commission/ Adult Volunteers

	Please check box	Interested in:	Already doing:
5g1	Accompanist	☐	☐
5b	Art & Environment	☐	☐
5f1	Caritas (10:30 a.m.)	☐	☐
5f2	C.H.AL.I.C.E. (4:00 p.m. Sat.)	☐	☐
5m	Funeral Choir	☐	☐
5c	Extraordinary Ministers of Holy Communion	☐	☐
5c1	Ministry to the Sick / Dying	☐	☐
5c1.1	Homebound	☐	☐
5c2	Nursing Homes	☐	☐
5c3	Swedish Hospital	☐	☐
5c4	Porter Hospital	☐	☐
5d	Greeters	☐	☐
5f10	Knights of Columbus Men's Choir	☐	☐
5f11	Magnificat Woman's Choir(8:30)	☐	☐
5g	Musicians	☐	☐
5h	Perpetual Eucharistic Adoration	☐	☐
5l	Pew Brigade	☐	☐
5b1	Sewing Group	☐	☐
5k	Ushers	☐	☐
5f17	Young Adult Choir	☐	☐

6 Parish Life Commission

	Please check box	Interested in:	Already doing:
6i	Ambassadors of Mary, Pilgrim Statue (Men)	☐	☐
6a	Baptism Preparation Couples	☐	☐
6b	Couple to Couple League	☐	☐
6g	Couples Retreat (Fall)	☐	☐
6j	Covenant of Love (Marriage Enrichment)	☐	☐
6d	Eucharistic Apostles of Divine Mercy	☐	☐
6c	Marriage Encounter	☐	☐
6k	Marriage Works N-HIM (Married Couples Ministry)	☐	☐
6e1	Ministry of Praise	☐	☐
6e2	Prayer Line	☐	☐
6e3	Centering Prayer	☐	☐
6e4	Men's Saturday Group	☐	☐
6e6	Daily Mass Prayer Companion (after 6:30 Mass)	☐	☐
6h	Novena to St. Peregrine and St. Jude (Cancer Patients)	☐	☐
6f	Retrouvaille (For Troubled Marriage)	☐	☐

7 Social Concerns Commission

	Please check box	Interested in:	Already doing:
7a	Angel Tree	☐	☐
7b	Blood Drive Volunteer	☐	☐
7b.1	Blood Drive Donor	☐	☐
7c	Discovery: Job Network (D:JN)	☐	☐
7k	Gabriel Project	☐	☐
7d	Habitat for Humanity	☐	☐

Stewardship of Time & Talent for Young Stewards

Commitment Form

Envelope Number: ______ Date: ______

Name: ______

Address: ______

City: ______ State: ______ Zip: ______

Phone (Home) ______ (Cell) ______

E-mail address: ______

Please complete one form per child in the family. *(Parents please help your child as needed). If you need additional forms you may make copies of this original or contact the parish office at 303-770-1155.*

Stewardship of Time & Talent for Young Stewards

St. Thomas More Catholic Church

Please sign up for each ministry that you are interested in, as well as those you are already doing.
If you check "interested in" you will be notified by the leader of the ministry.

What will you do for God?

	Please check box	Interested in:	Already doing:
	Faith Formation & Catechists: Children's Faith Formation/ Children Volunteers		
3a2.6	Catechist Helpers	□	□
3a2.7	Child Care Aides	□	□
3a2.1	Junior Legion of Mary	□	□
3a2.4	Office Helpers	□	□
3a2.5	Summer Bible School Helpers	□	□
	Parish School: Youth Volunteers		
3b.1a	Campbell Soup Labels	□	□
3b.1b	Lenten Family Liturgy	□	□
3b.1c	Yearbook	□	□
	Youth & Young Adult Ministries High School Youth Ministry/ Youth Volunteer Opportunities		
3c1.b8	Mentors	□	□
3c1.b16	Servant Leadership Team	□	□
	Middle School Youth Ministry/ Youth Volunteers		
3c2.a8	8th Grade Leadership Team	□	□
3c2.a1	Boy Scouts	□	□
3c2.a2	Girl Scouts	□	□
3c2.a4	Mentor for Crossfire (Sophomore & Above)	□	□
3c2.a3	Office Help	□	□
3c2.a9	Service Club	□	□
3c2.a5	Spark Writers & Photographers	□	□

	Please check box	Interested in:	Already doing:
	LIFE TEEN/ Liturgy & Music Ministry Youth Volunteers		
3c2.c3	Advanced Guitar Class	□	□
3c2.c2	Beginning Guitar Class	□	□
3c1.a5	Breakaway LIFE TEEN Core Team (Juniors and Seniors)	□	□
3c2.c8	LIFE TEEN Lectors	□	□
3c2.c5	LIFE TEEN Mass Setup/Cleanup	□	□
3c2.c7	LIFE TEEN Ushers	□	□
5.1e	LIFE TEEN Youth Choir	□	□
3c2.c9	Praise, Worship & Adoration	□	□
3c1.a3	Project 600	□	□
3c2.c10	Sound & Media Ministry	□	□
3c1.a9	Venture Club Leader	□	□
3c2.c4	Voice Class	□	□
3c2.c11	Worship Team for Breakaway	□	□
3c2.c12	Worship Team for Crossfire	□	□
	Liturgy Commission/Youth Volunteers		
5.1a	Altar Servers	□	□
5.1b	Children's Choir	□	□
5.1d	Church Ushers (Sat. eve., Sun. morn.)	□	□
5.1c	Instrumental Musicians (e.g. Guitar, Flute, Violin, etc.)	□	□
5.1f	Pew Brigade	□	□

IMPORTANT NOTICE!

To ensure the safety and well being of all parishioners and participants in our ministries and programs, St. Thomas More Catholic Church complies with the following Archdiocese of Denver requirements for all volunteers:

- All volunteers will be required to attend a safe environment workshop.
- All volunteers must sign a waiver stating that they have received and read the archdiocesan policy manual addressing sexual misconduct.
- All volunteers working with children will be required to sign a form agreeing to a criminal background check.

For more information, please contact the parish.

STM Stewardship Prayer

O God, our loving creator and giver of all good gifts,
bless our parish and our archdiocese,
strengthen our faith and grant us the spirit
of Christian stewardship
so that we may give generously of our
time, talent and treasure to the spreading of Your kingdom
here at St. Thomas More and throughout the world.
We ask this through our Lord Jesus,
your Son, who lives and reigns with You and
the Holy Spirit, one God forever and ever.
Amen.

Stewardship: For a Better Life. ✦ For a Better World.

ADULT COMMITMENT CARDS

(Bangtail envelopes are practical because the form is attached — see page 201.)

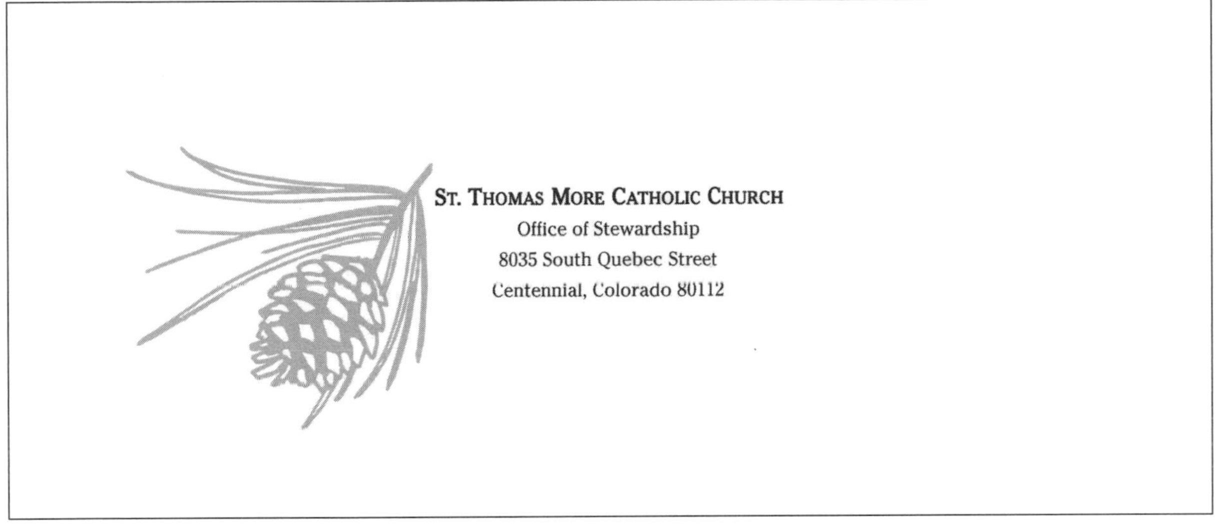

St. Thomas More Catholic Church
Stewardship of Treasure Commitment

Envelope Number

Name

Address

City Zip Code

E-mail Address

Parishioner's Signature

In thanksgiving for God's blessings and in support of my parish

Please choose one:

I will give $ ______________ Weekly

I will give $ ______________ Monthly

I will give $ ______________ Yearly

☐ Please take me off your mailing list for envelopes.

☐ Please delete me from your parish.

Reason

To register, please stop by the Parish Office.

CHILDREN'S COMMITMENT ENVELOPES

STM Stewardship Prayer

O God, our loving creator and giver of all good gifts, bless our parish and the archdiocese, strengthen our faith and grant us the spirit of Christian stewardship so that we may give generously of our time, talent and treasure to the spreading of Your kingdom here at St. Thomas More and throughout the world. We ask this through our Lord Jesus, Your Son, who lives and reigns with You and the Holy Spirit, one God forever and ever. Amen.

✻ Giving Guideline ✻

Time: Time given to Church other than attending Mass

____

Talent: How you help at home, Church or school

____

Treasure: Weekly gift of your own money

5% of your weekly allowance __________

10% of your weekly allowance __________

____

"God loves a cheerful giver."

2 Corinthians 9:7

St. Thomas More Catholic Church
Office of Stewardship
8035 South Quebec Street
Centennial, Colorado 80112

Young Steward's Commitment

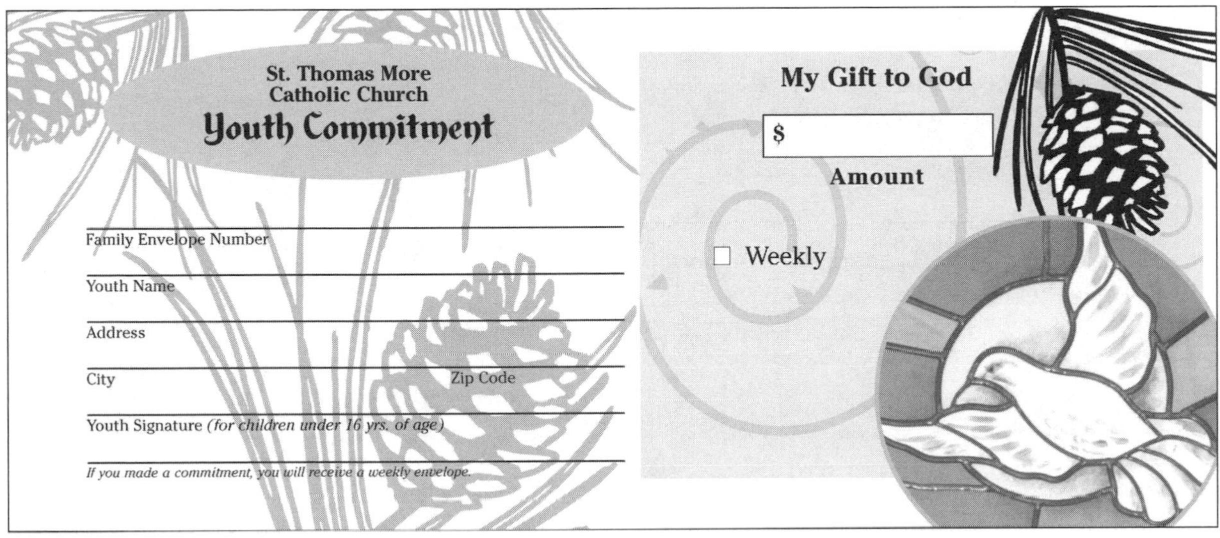
St. Thomas More
Catholic Church
Youth Commitment

Family Envelope Number

Youth Name

Address

City Zip Code

Youth Signature *(for children under 16 yrs. of age)*

If you made a commitment, you will receive a weekly envelope.

My Gift to God

$

Amount

☐ Weekly

"STEWARDSHIP OF EARTH AND VOCATIONS" CARDS

Adult Stewardship of Earth Commitment

Please return this copy to the parish.

(Please indicate what you will do to care for God's creation.)

- □ Recycle newspaper, paper, cardboard,glass, tin and aluminum.
- □ Wash clothes in cold water and air dry when possible.
- □ Use old clothes and cloth for cleaning, instead of paper towels.
- □ Reduce use of disposable products, or, if you must buy disposable, buy paper or glass products instead of plastic.
- □ Recycle engine oil.
- □ Invest your money in environmentally and socially conscious businesses.
- □ When purchasing a car, select an energy-efficient model.
- □ Avoid buying aerosol cans and Styrofoam products.
- □ Purchase products made from recycled materials.
- □ Ask candidates for office what they are prepared to do to pursue environmental justice.
- □ Go to the Catholic Relief Services website at www.catholicrelief.org and get involved in an international relief campaign.
- □ Go to the Bread for the World website at www.breadfortheworld.org and help fight world hunger.
- □ Consider purchasing fair-trade coffee. Go to www.cafecampesino.com and learn more about fairly traded, shade grown coffee.

Adult Stewardship of Earth Commitment

Keep this copy for your records.

(Please indicate what you will do to care for God's creation.)

- □ Recycle newspaper, paper, cardboard,glass, tin and aluminum.
- □ Wash clothes in cold water and air dry when possible.
- □ Use old clothes and cloth for cleaning, instead of paper towels.
- □ Reduce use of disposable products, or, if you must buy disposable, buy paper or glass products instead of plastic.
- □ Recycle engine oil.
- □ Invest your money in environmentally and socially conscious businesses.
- □ When purchasing a car, select an energy-efficient model.
- □ Avoid buying aerosol cans and Styrofoam products.
- □ Purchase products made from recycled materials.
- □ Ask candidates for office what they are prepared to do to pursue environmental justice.
- □ Go to the Catholic Relief Services website at www.catholicrelief.org and get involved in an international relief campaign.
- □ Go to the Bread for the World website at www.breadfortheworld.org and help fight world hunger.
- □ Consider purchasing fair-trade coffee. Go to www.cafecampesino.com and learn more about fairly traded, shade grown coffee.

Children's Stewardship of Earth Commitment

Please return this copy to the parish.

(Please indicate what you will do to care for God's creation.)

- □ Recycle newspaper, paper, cardboard, glass, tin and aluminum.
- □ Use reusable containers for sandwiches instead of baggies.
- □ Do not leave the water running when brushing your teeth or doing the dishes.
- □ Turn off lights and appliances (TV, video game player, etc.) when you leave the room.
- □ Donate unwanted clothing and other items to charity or a thrift shop.
- □ Enjoy recreational activities that use your energy instead of electricity: for example, go hiking instead of watching TV.
- □ Don't use aerosol spray can products, look for pump sprays instead.
- □ Avoid buying Styrofoam.
- □ Reuse paper grocery bags.
- □ Buy and use rechargeable batteries.
- □ Do not litter.
- □ Bike or walk for short trips.
- □ Go to www.catholic relief.org (Catholic Relief Services website) and click on "get involved then go to the Kid's page.

Children's Stewardship of Earth Commitment

Keep this copy for your records.

(Please indicate what you will do to care for God's creation.)

- □ Recycle newspaper, paper, cardboard, glass, tin and aluminum.
- □ Use reusable containers for sandwiches instead of baggies.
- □ Do not leave the water running when brushing your teeth or doing the dishes.
- □ Turn off lights and appliances (TV, video game player, etc.) when you leave the room.
- □ Donate unwanted clothing and other items to charity or a thrift shop.
- □ Enjoy recreational activities that use your energy instead of electricity: for example, go hiking instead of watching TV.
- □ Don't use aerosol spray can products, look for pump sprays instead.
- □ Avoid buying Styrofoam.
- □ Reuse paper grocery bags.
- □ Buy and use rechargeable batteries.
- □ Do not litter.
- □ Bike or walk for short trips.
- □ Go to www.catholic relief.org (Catholic Relief Services website) and click on "get involved then go to the Kid's page.

Stewardship of Vocations Commitment

"Called by Name"

Prayer for Vocations

*Heavenly Father,
bless your Church,
with an abundance of holy
and zealous priests, deacons,
brothers and sisters.*

*Form us all in the likeness
of your Son so that through Him,
with Him, in Him we may love you
more deeply and serve you
more faithfully,
always and everywhere.*

*We ask this through
Christ our Lord.*

Amen

The CALLED BY NAME program reflects the Second Vatican Council's vision that all God's faithful people share responsibility for calling forth and fostering vocations to the priesthood, permanent diaconate and Religious life.

Office Use Only

Stewardship of Vocations Commitment

Please return this copy to the parish.

The CALLED BY NAME program reflects the Second Vatican Council's vision that all God's faithful people share responsibility for calling forth and fostering vocations to the priesthood, permanent diaconate and Religious life.

Stewardship of Vocations "Called by Name"

I nominate the following person as an individual who may be called to a vocation as a priest or deacon or religious man or woman.

Nominee (*last name, first name*)

☐ Male ☐ Female Age (if known)

Phone (*if known*)

Mailing Address (*if known*)

City State Zip Code

Name of Parishioner submitting nomination (*optional*)

( )
Phone

One of the mistakes I made when I started stewardship at St. Thomas More was asking for time, talent, and treasure all at the same time! I had decided to copy a form from another parish, and did not consider the size of our parish. It was a disaster for us in terms of data entry! There was too much information to be entered into our database. Since then, we have simplified data entry by keeping a separate commitment card for each phase of stewardship.

Giving the children and youth their own version of commitment cards has worked very well for data entry, too. It also has made the children and youth feel that we value them as individuals. Moreover, we are able to identify their gifts easily.

Our commitment cards include a prayer. In Mass during commitment weekends, after the homily, Father Andrew or the presiding cleric asks each person to pick up a commitment card from the pew. Everyone is asked to say the prayer on the back side of the card. Here is a sample:

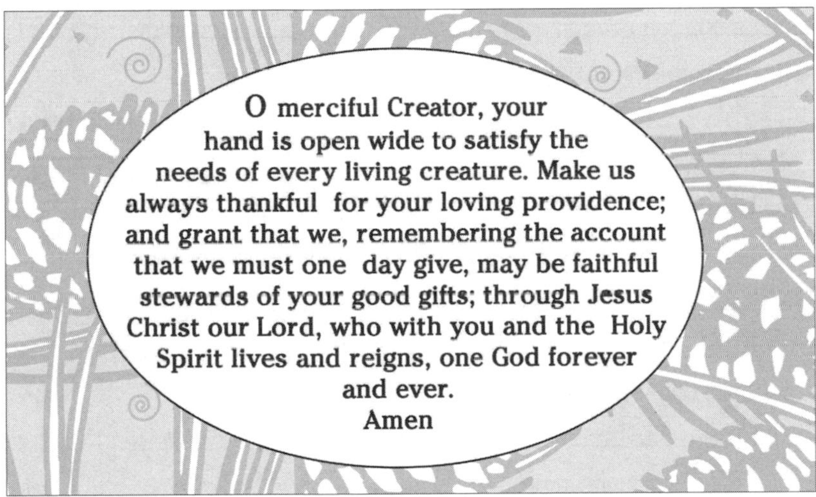

O merciful Creator, your
hand is open wide to satisfy the
needs of every living creature. Make us
always thankful for your loving providence;
and grant that we, remembering the account
that we must one day give, may be faithful
stewards of your good gifts; through Jesus
Christ our Lord, who with you and the Holy
Spirit lives and reigns, one God forever
and ever.
Amen

Praying the prayer on the commitment cards is a great way to get the cards into the hands of the parishioners. Remember that some parishioners are suspicious of commitment cards. Some would not want to touch the card, for fear of making a commitment. Father Andrew often would say to them, "You're all here to pray, aren't you?" and so they pick up the card. We ask them to pray a stewardship prayer together. After the prayer, the pastor, presiding cleric, or lay person asks them to turn the card over and encourages them to fill it out and then come forward to the altar to hand their commitment card to the presiding cleric or altar servers. This ritual is not mandatory and so only those who feel comfortable with this "altar call" come forward. (The children love this opportunity to move out of the pews and head up to the altar!)

The only time we mail the commitment cards is for stewardship of treasure. Because of the size of our parish, we outsource our mailings during this renewal process. (We pay a fundraising and public relations company, but volunteers can manage this in smaller parishes.)

At all other commitment weekends, we distribute the cards in the pews. Although some families mail their commitment cards, we recommend that parishioners offer their cards as part of the liturgy. That's why an altar call has become a part of our commitment weekends. Please be aware: Parishes interested in adopting this ritual might expect only a handful of parishioners to participate the first few times. As the program continues, the altar call becomes a natural part of commitment weekends.

Why do we use commitment cards or pledges? Because they work! (*See Part II.*)

For those still not convinced, consider our offertory collection. When we started stewardship at St. Thomas More Parish in 1989, our offertory was $1.2 million. We collected only 421 pledges, even though the parish had 4,573 registered families. Still, there was an eighteen percent increase (more than $220,000).

Today, our annual renewal is generating new pledges, and commitments have grown to more than 2,700. With registered families at 6,200, we still have a long way to go to make it 100 percent. Now the offertory collection is close to $4.5 million.

We have tracked our growth more closely since Father Andrew came to St. Thomas More in June 2000. The following report and charts show how stewardship makes a difference in increasing the offertory collection, even after factoring the rate of inflation.

DATA ANALYSIS: WHY PLEDGES ARE IMPORTANT

By Michael P. Angell

About the author: Prior to joining the St. Thomas More parish staff in 2008, Michael Angell served the local community as a licensed financial advisor. He holds a Bachelor of Science degree in mathematics from Creighton University. He and his wife, Leanell, reside in Castle Rock, Colorado.

We're going to take a moment to talk about financial data. We won't explore formulas in depth because that is beyond the scope of the text. You don't have to be a financial planner to be a good steward. That is why you have a parish finance council. That said, it is important to understand the basics.

The Time Value of Money

Suppose a man visits his local bank. The bank president greets him and proudly announces "Sir, we can guarantee you a one hundred percent increase in your savings if you simply follow our advice!"

"Great!" said the man eagerly as he stumbled to pull out his checkbook. "By the way, how long will all this take?"

"Only one hundred years, sir! We'll pay you one percent interest a year."

If you were that customer, you might march out immediately, right? Most people would. This lighthearted story demonstrates the time value of money. When looking at increases of 25%, 50% or even 100% in the offertory, it is important to ask, "How much time passed?" Stewardship takes time. For example if a parish increases its offertory by 10% in ten years, that isn't necessarily very impressive. However if a parish increases its offertory by 10% in one year... well, that is another story.

The Effects of Inflation

A good financial planner will tell you there are three natural enemies to your money: debt, inflation, and taxes. Fortunately as nonprofit organizations, churches do not have to worry about taxes much, but they still have to worry about debt and inflation.

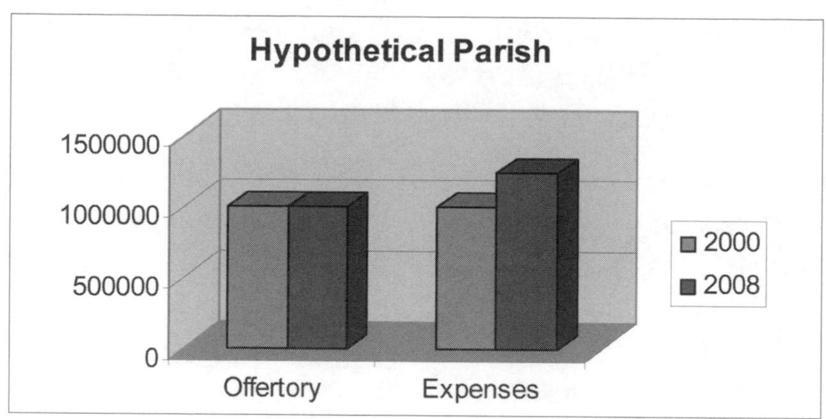

Here we see a hypothetical parish. In 2000 it is living within its means. Both offertory and expenses equal $1 million. Eight years later, the same parish still has an offertory of $1 million, but expenses have increased to $1.2 million. It hss serious cash-flow problems and may not understand why.

Our case studies in this book are based on real parishes. We have changed the names and numbers to protect privacy. We measured offertory growth from 2000 to 2008. Inflation during that period averaged 2.8%. (Source: Bureau of Labor Statistics) Why is that important? Because inflation plays a huge role in our society and therefore our parish expenses!

Consider this example. Suppose a couple buys a home in 1970 for $70,000. They live in it for 30 years. They raise their children and send them to good, Catholic schools. One becomes a priest. Another marries and becomes a lay missionary. One day the nest is empty and Mom and Dad decide they need a smaller place. It's just too much work to keep the yard in shape and the house clean! So they decide to buy a condo. They sell their home for $250,000, even after 30 years of depreciation. That is inflation at work!

Does that happen a lot? Sure! It happens every day. Why? Because inflation changes the value of dollars! It is important to understand that the exact same goods and services often cost *more* today than they did yesterday.

The math behind calculating inflation is very complex, but you can use this rule of thumb:

Growth Rate - Inflation ≈ Real Return

In other words, if the offertory grew by 5% in a given year, and inflation was 3%, the Real Return is approximately 2% (the national inflation rate is released by the U.S. Bureau of Labor and Statistics). For a complete explanation of the Data Analysis formula, please see Appendix 6.

Pledges . . . and Cell Phones

The fundamental concept driving stewardship of treasure is to obtain pledges. You may recall from Sunday school that King Solomon built the first temple in Jerusalem. He used the abundant wealth and natural resources he inherited from his father, David. Where did King Solomon get the workers? Scripture tells us he largely used the forced labor of the peoples the Israelites conquered. Breaking News: That approach won't work in your parish. We're pretty sure on that point! Nor are we the tax collector. We can't simply raise taxes every time we have a great idea that just needs funding. If you want to fund your parish expenditures, you need to do as Our Lord Jesus, and later the apostles, did. You need to rely on the goodwill of your followers. You need to humbly and respectfully ask for alms.

We live in a capitalistic society. To quote Will Rogers, "The Lord must love the common folk. He sure made a lot of 'em." Most pews are filled with working class people. That is just the way it is. Occasionally a large donor will step forward, but we all know those people are few and far between. The bread and butter of any offertory is composed of small monthly donations. People buy their cars, homes, and other items these days on monthly installments. Why should we expect to be any different?

Consider this example. Most Americans own cell phones these days but few realize it costs more than $400 in most cases to manufacture a cell phone. How, then, are retailers able to sell them at a mere $50? Because they ask for a contract! In the first year, those retailers are in the red. It is only because of a customer's steady monthly payments that manufacturers are able to recover their costs. Without a commitment, they would be sunk.

The point is this: Relying simply on the spontaneous goodwill of parishioners is a dangerous proposition at best. When times are hard, discretionary spending and giving dry up. Therefore you need to ask people to *plan* their giving. Ask people to treat their donations as a small, predictable, and manageable household expense. When you do this through a pledge, the likelihood of success greatly increases!

Measuring the Unknown: Donors without Pledges

WHEN ASKING FOR PLEDGES, it is natural to wonder, "How many *unregistered* families are currently giving?" This can be a difficult proposition because, by definition, this is an unknown variable.

In the Bible, there are many numerical references to the size of groups. For example, Jesus fed the crowd with loaves and fishes and "Those who ate were about five thousand men, not counting women and children" (Mt 14:21). Did Matthew know exactly how many people were there? By his own testimony, the answer is no. However he made an educated guess. We're forced to make the same kinds of estimates even today.

We know pews at St. Thomas More seat a maximum of about 1,000. On a typical weekend with seven Masses, we serve 7,000 people. Also we know approximately 3,500 families give annually. Therefore we can conclude most of the crowd is already accounted for. Gifts of unknown origin comprise less than 5% of the total offertory.

The Numbers: Increasing Donors and the Average Gift

THIS TEXT IS NOT A MATH BOOK. It is a stewardship book. Still we need to prove to you how stewardship works *on the budget sheet.* At the end of the day, there are only two ways to increase your offertory. Either: a) increase the number of donors; or b) increase the average gift. For the mathematically inclined:

Total offertory = number of donors x average gift

and

Total offertory increase ≈ gift size increase + donor increase

For example, if a parish has 2,000 donors and the average annual gift is $1,000, the offertory will be $2,000,000. If the number of donors increases 10% to 2,200 and the annual gift increases 10% to $1,100, the total offertory will increase to $2,420,000 or an increase of approximately 20%. (For a complete formula explanation please see the Data Analysis Appendix at the end of this section.)

This formula *proves* mathematically what good stewards already know. *An increase in either gift size or the number of families making a pledge has a substantial impact on your total offertory.*

Stewardship parishes often face "chicken and the egg" skepticism. Do parishes enjoy success because they are wealthy, or do parishes become wealthy because they are successful? In other words, which came first, the stewardship program or the money? To the casual observer, good fortune may appear to be a matter of circumstance or luck. Let us assure you, the stewardship program by necessity preceded the success.

Do you still think you need a lot of money for stewardship to work? By no means! For example, if Wall Street has taught us anything through the years, it is this: No matter how much money you have, it is still possible to make huge mistakes. The financial crisis that exploded in 2008 was basically fueled by irresponsible financial decisions. Hedge funds were in many cases poor stewards of their clients' money. We know there are plenty of good hedge funds out there, too, but many are not. Consider also the sad and tragic story of Bernie Maddoff. Yes, he was wealthy but was he a good steward? Certainly not! Despite all the billions under his management, he still failed. We call that a case of bad stewardship. Consider also the sad case of General Motors. As recently as 2005 the company was reaching record profits as the largest auto manufacturer in the world. Yet a few short years later it filed for bankruptcy!

You don't need a lot of money to be a good steward. In fact, having more money is sometimes more dangerous, because small mistakes are potentially magnified a hundred- or even a thousand-fold.

What is true in life is true in finance. The Lord will not give you more than you can handle if you obey him. Be content with your portion.

"Yes, but what if my parish is a 'poor' parish? Will stewardship still work for me?"

The answer is "Yes!" Consider this example. We have taken our stewardship program to the Church in the Philippines. There is little disagreement among us that the Philippines is an extremely poor nation. Our Catholic brothers and sisters there are considered among the poorest of the poor. Yet within a few years of beginning stewardship, they too have been able to see significant progress. Formerly these people relied almost entirely on donations from overseas. Today the Philippine Church is looking forward to becoming self-sufficient. The Lord uses the small and weak to humble the mighty, does he not? They have proven by their example that you don't need to live in an affluent neighborhood for stewardship to work.

Recall the Parable of the Talents (Mt 25:14-30). If it is important for the steward who was given five talents to practice good stewardship, how much more important is it for the steward who was only given two talents, or even one! Don't commit the same folly as the lazy steward. Whatever your means, be prepared to return them to the Lord with increase. For Our Lord says: "Bring the whole tithe into the storehouse that there may be food in my house. Try me in this, says the LORD of hosts: Shall I not open for you the floodgates and pour down blessings upon you without measure?" (Mal 3:10).

Sample Financial Reports

IN THIS SECTION WE PROVIDE financial charts for a hypothetical parish, St. Jerome Catholic Church in Whiterose, California. The purpose is to demonstrate how you can statistically measure the progress of your stewardship campaign over time. In the private sector, these are generally called metrics. We track the following variables:

	2000	2008
Total Offertory	$3,000,000	$4,100,000
Gifts with Pledges	$1,640,650	$3,585,419
Gifts without pledges	$1,099,895	$299,994
Donors	3,871	3,440
Registered Parish Families	5,102	5,896

Average gift	$775	$1,192
Loose cash	$223,047	$190,187
Loose checks	$36,408	$24,400

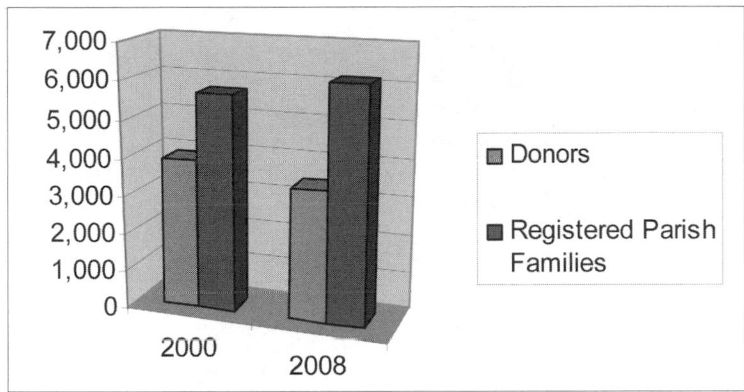

This chart demonstrates that between 2000 and 2008 the number of registered families and donors remained relatively constant. In other words, the offertory increase was not due to a dramatic increase in weekly attendance. Offertory growth was pledge driven. Also, in this example we show a slight decrease in the number of donors. Why? In 2004, St. Jerome simultaneously ran a separate $10 million dollar building campaign. The campaign was a huge success. However, a small percentage of parishioners simply diverted their offertory gift to the building fund. Please be cautious of this phenomenon when asking for building fund pledges!

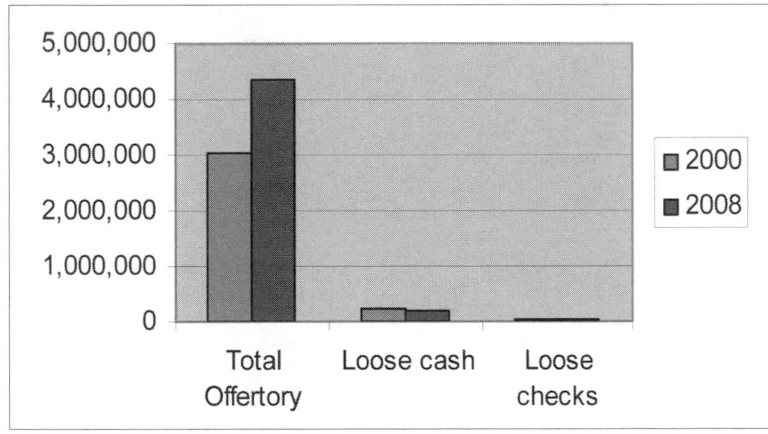

Know most of your donors by name by creating a database. This chart illustrates that loose cash and checks not associated with any known registered families compose a relatively small fraction of totals.

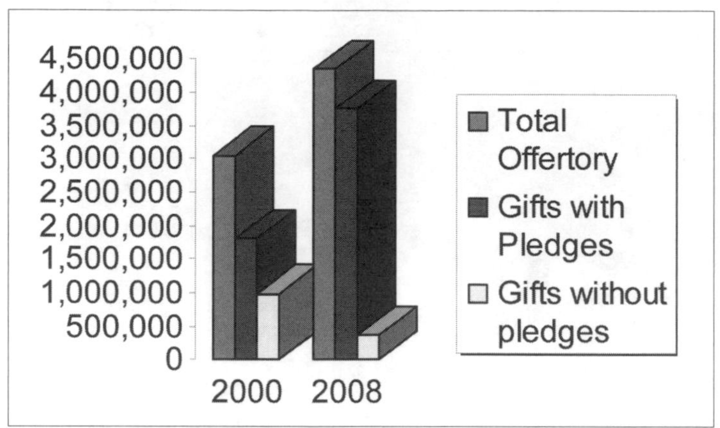

As one can see, the offertory is composed almost entirely of pledges.

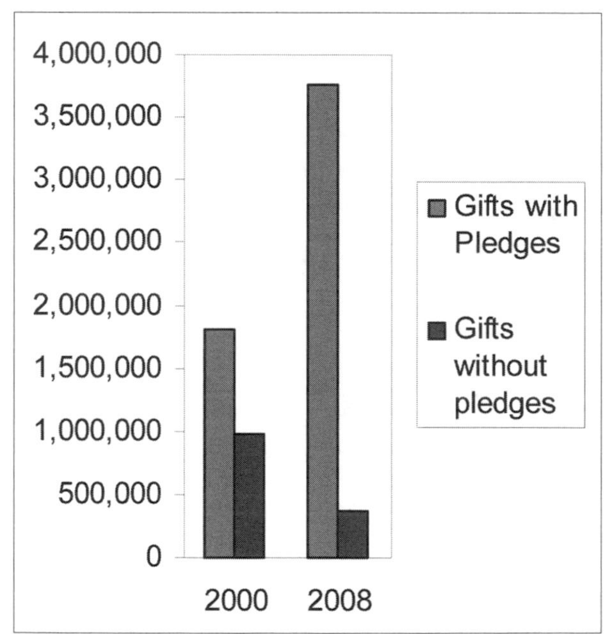

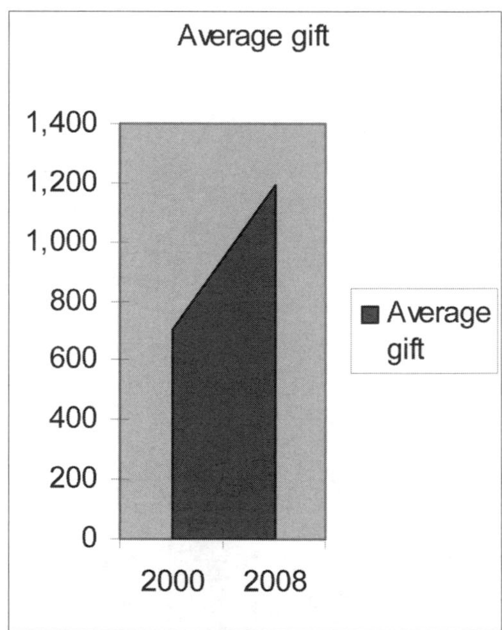

Here the average gift increased dramatically in our sample period.

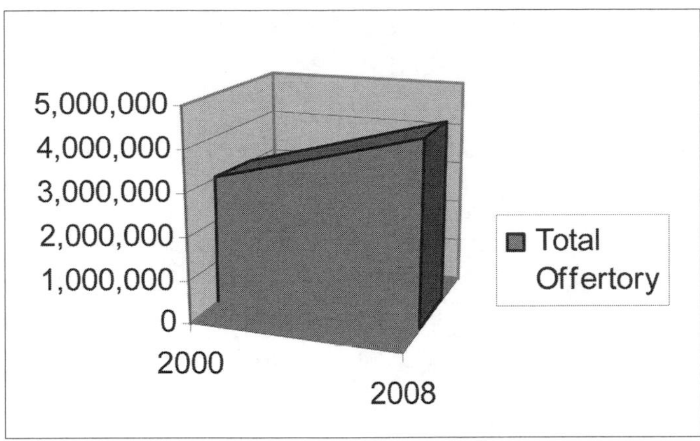

The offertory as a whole grew as a result.

Case Studies

In this section, we explore three case studies. Again, the names and numbers are hypothetical but are based on real parishes that we encountered in our ministry. All parishes have a natural life cycle: inception, peak, and decline. Each example represents a parish in a different phase of the cycle. Perhaps you will find your own situation mirrored here. The purpose of this section is to demonstrate how stewardship can benefit any parish in any situation. Our hypothetical parishes are:

1. St. Augustine
2. St. Benedict
3. St. Catherine

1. St. Augustine

Profile: St. Augustine is a new parish located in a posh suburb. Less than 15 years old, it is the only parish within a 20-mile radius. Enthusiasm is high and the parishioners are affluent. The offertory is growing by leaps and bounds with no end in sight. All Masses are standing-room only. Various ministries are competing for work space. The facilities are limited and inadequate. Although the offertory is growing at over 12% annually, it does not yet provide the millions needed to build additional facilities.

Main Objective: To expand and accommodate the needs of a growing flock.

	2000	2008
Total Offertory	$2,043,731	$6,352,872
Gifts with Pledges	$798,136	$4,752,868
Gifts without pledges	$1,004,463	$1,385,417
Donors	2,928	3,855
Registered Parish Families	4,696	5,155
Average gift	$698	$1,648
Loose cash	$133,724	$190,187
Loose checks	$107,408	$24,400

St. Augustine's decided to implement stewardship with the following programs:

1. *Prayer:* They started an adoration chapel to pray for God's guidance.
2. *Vocations:* The *Traveling Chalice* program was created for families to encourage vocations to the priestly life.
3. *Time and Talent:* They held a ministry fair and 400 new volunteers signed up. Their donated time and service would have normally cost millions in the private sector.
4. *Treasure:* They began a building campaign. They steadily raised $4 million in two years over and above the regular offertory.
5. *Earth:* As a new parish, the grounds were largely undeveloped. A parishioner with his own landscaping business donated his services and planted a beautiful lawn with shrubbery.

2. St. Benedict

Profile: St. Benedict was built more than 40 years ago in a middle-class neighborhood. The offertory is keeping pace with inflation. Funds are adequate, but there is nothing left over after expenses. The pastor has to watch every penny carefully to make sure the parish does not go over budget. He would like to remodel and start new programs, but the money just isn't there. Sunday attendance is at an all-time high but volunteers are scarce. Most work just doesn't get done. The parish feels more like a sacramental machine than a community filled with the Holy Spirit.

Main Objective: Reinvigorate a parish that is still in its prime.

	2000	2008
Total Offertory	$1,143,731	$1,387,800
Gifts with Pledges	$398,136	$677,763
Gifts without pledges	$602,463	$586,789
Donors	3,628	3,855
Registered Parish Families	8,096	7,806
Average gift	$315	$360
Loose cash	$115,724	$110,444
Loose checks	$27,408	$12,804

St. Benedict's decided to implement stewardship with the following programs:

1. *Prayer:* They started a Rosary Makers club. Volunteers gather once a week to pray the rosary, then spend the rest of the time socializing as they craft rosaries by hand to donate to the parish.
2. *Vocations:* They began a "Called by Name" program. People who are nominated for vocations by their friends and family are contacted. This has produced six seminarians.
3. *Time and Talent:* When it came time to update the parish database, they also asked people their profession. When needs arose, the pastor would approach parishioners to ask if they would be interested in donating their time and services.
4. *Treasure:* They asked people that were giving spontaneously to fill out a pledge card. Spontaneous giving became planned giving. The average gift size increased 14%. Registered donors increased by over 6%.
5. *Earth:* The school children planted trees to beautify the grounds.

3. St. Catherine

Profile: St. Catherine's is an inner-city parish in danger of closing. Built over 100 years ago, the original founders have long since passed away and their children have moved to distant suburbs. Many lower-income families have moved into the neighborhood. The offertory has been in decline for years. Facilities are in dire need of repair. The rectory has mice. In a difficult economy, the archdiocese can no longer subsidize the parish. Families are worried that if the parish and school close they will have no place to go.

Main Objective: To fulfill its mission to minister to the poor, the parish needs to stay open and become self-sufficient again.

	2000	2008
Total Offertory	$304,624	$435,310
Gifts with Pledges	$179,813	$375,268
Gifts without pledges	$95,356	$45,455
Donors	1,928	2,155
Registered Parish Families	2,396	2,205
Average gift	$158	$202
Loose cash	$23,047	$10,187
Loose checks	$6,408	$4,400

St. Catherine's decided to implement stewardship with the following programs:

1. *Prayer:* They renewed their use of extraordinary ministers of the Eucharist, including visiting and bringing Communion to the homebound.
2. *Vocations:* They have begun a weekly holy hour to pray for vocations. Since then three men have come forward and been ordained as permanent deacons.
3. *Time and Talent:* They held a volunteer appreciation party. People that had not volunteered in years turned out. Professional handymen donated their services at half price. A "Supper Club" ministry was started to provide meals for parish events, including funerals. With renewed warmth and enthusiasm, lay ministry flourished.

4. *Treasure:* They began a tithe of the tithe. In the spirit of the widow's mite, they donated 10% of their offertory to the local food bank. With a sudden confidence that they could help others, they realized they could also help themselves. They organized an annual silent auction. Businesses around the state donated goods and services that were in turn auctioned off at a charity dinner.
5. *Earth:* The Knights of Columbus were recruited to restore run-down flower beds and reseed the lawn. Broken fences were repaired. Used computers were donated to create a student computer lab.

Children's Offertory: Start Them Young

This is a true story. A six-year-old boy asked his father a question at the dinner table. "Dad, what would you do with a million dollars?"

Nonchalantly the father replied, "Give ten percent to the church and put the rest in the bank where it will earn interest." The father did not even bother to look up from his meal. Between two spoonfuls of soup he had communicated to his son his entire financial philosophy. He did not think his paternal advice was extraordinary and to him, it really wasn't. It was what he already did every paycheck. To him it was just business as usual. The son grew up to be an investment professional. The father, by the way, retired early.

How do children learn about giving? By example! As good stewards, we have a responsibility to train the next generation to be good stewards. We have to teach them to give. The amount is not important. Even a penny is enough. What *is* important is that children learn how to give at an early age. It is no secret that habits people form as children often last them their entire lives.

No Gift Is Too Small

There is another reason we have a children's offertory. Sometimes adults are too ashamed to give. They realize their means are limited. They see the wads in the basket as it passes by and say to themselves,

"My gift is just too small. They'll laugh at me and my worthless contribution. There is no way I can help." So they don't give at all.

By having a children's offertory, we communicate to the adults one simple truth: No gift is too small. When adults see the gifts of children graciously accepted, their hearts open up. It becomes easier to give.

More than one adult has said, "Well, heck, I can certainly give more than *that*," and a steward is born.

It Really Does Add Up

Children get statements every six months. It is a special treat for a youngster to get his or her very own mail. The administrative expense is negligible. A hypothetical children's offertory may look something like this.

	2000	2008
Children donors	57	573
average weekly gift	0.75	1
average annual gift	39	52
Total	$2,223	$29,796

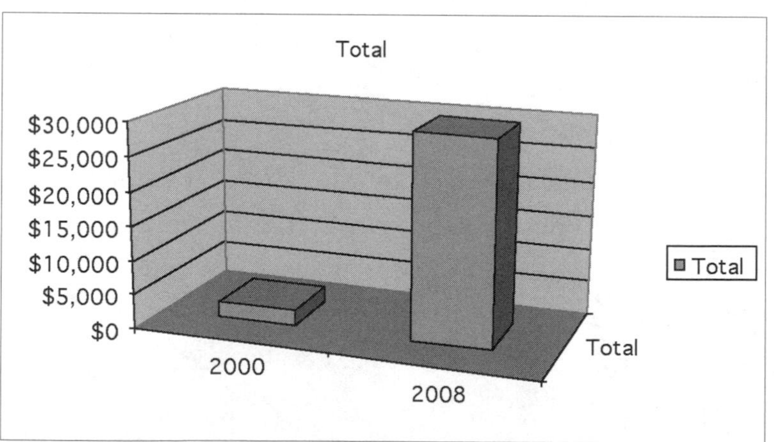

Impressive isn't it? Again we stress, 100% of the children's offertory is donated to charity. The objective of a children's offertory is not to raise money, even though it does. The objective is to educate children about the need to give and be productive members of society.

Tithe of the Tithe

"You are to make a contribution from them to the LORD, a tithe of the tithes" (Nm 18:26).

When Father Andrew came to St. Thomas More, one of the first things he did was to start a charity account from the offertory — the tithe of the tithe. Why would any parish, already serving the Lord in so many ways, give away one-tenth of its offertory collection? This is what Numbers 18:26-29 says:

> "Give the Levites these instructions: When you receive from the Israelites the tithes I have assigned you from them as your heritage, you are to make a contribution from them to the LORD, a tithe of the tithes; and your contribution will be credited to you as if it were grain from the threshing floor or new wine from the press. Thus you too shall make a contribution from all the tithes you receive from the Israelites, handing over to Aaron the priest the part to be contributed to the Lord. From all the gifts that you receive, and from the best parts, you are to consecrate to the LORD your own full contribution."

Some parishes give ten percent of their offertory collection from a particular week to charity. For example, when a missionary comes to a parish for a mission appeal, the parish gives him ten percent of the collection for that week. Doing it this way may not be as practical as you might think because not all charities have the same exact needs.

At St. Thomas More ten percent of the weekly collection is deposited immediately to an STM charity account. As Father Andrew often says, "This is God's money, not that of the parish." It is given to charity in the name of God. It is a restricted fund that can only be used for charitable causes *outside* of St. Thomas More. It cannot benefit St. Thomas More or its staff.

How is the charity account allocated? Who decides the allocation?

Since Fiscal Year 2000-2001, St. Thomas More has distributed more than $3 million to various charities, locally, nationally, and internationally. Each week we publish in the weekly bulletin the recipients of grants that provide much needed assistance to benefit various causes: education, the poor, children, youth, seniors, the sick, and those marginalized, as well as religious congregations, inner city parishes, and the missions.

The pastor works with the stewardship committee to determine the allocation of these funds by cause and by geographic area — local, national and international. At St. Thomas More, the current seventeen special collections mandated by the Archdiocese of Denver are taken from the charity account.

Rather than taking a second collection, we publish a notice in the Sunday bulletin that week reminding our parishioners that they were spared a second collection. A specific amount is then sent to "Such and Such" a cause on behalf of St. Thomas More parishioners.

Generally, the stewardship committee allocates more for the poor locally than to various causes nationwide. Money distributed from the St. Thomas More charity account may be allocated by the pastor and/or the stewardship committee. Both must follow guidelines which include the following:

1. The pastor may approve grant requests up to $2,500. The check request requires his signature as proof of approval.
2. The stewardship committee must approve grants above $2,500 prior to disbursement. The check request for grants approved for processing requires the signature of the pastor and the chair of the stewardship committee.
3. The vicar general must approve grants above $25,000. The check request for grants approved for processing requires the signature of the pastor, the chair of the stewardship committee, and the vicar general.

4. The vicar general also must be informed of multiple disbursements to a specific organization, if in the fiscal year these disbursements total more than $25,000.
5. A member of the finance council and pastoral council each will serve as a liaison to the stewardship committee.
6. On a monthly basis, the accounting department will provide to the stewardship committee and the finance council a listing of disbursements made out of the charity account.

In addition, the entire amount from envelopes in the children's offertory collection goes to the children's charity account. Then the children and youth in religious education, parish school, and youth ministry distribute to causes they choose. Please note that we encourage children to give to the offertory in their own envelopes. Every Sunday the children are invited to place their offertory in a special jar at the altar, so their offertory gift is kept separate from the adult offertory. All cash deposited in the children's jar does go to the regular offertory collection, in order to encourage the children to use envelopes. During renewal weekends children are advised that their envelope money will not be used to operate the parish. Their entire collection goes only to the poor and to causes the children themselves choose.

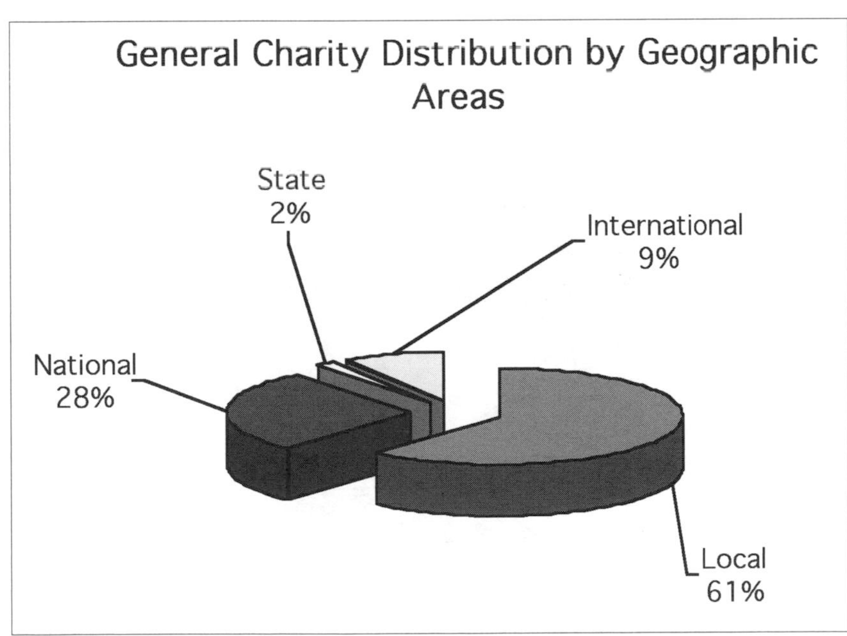

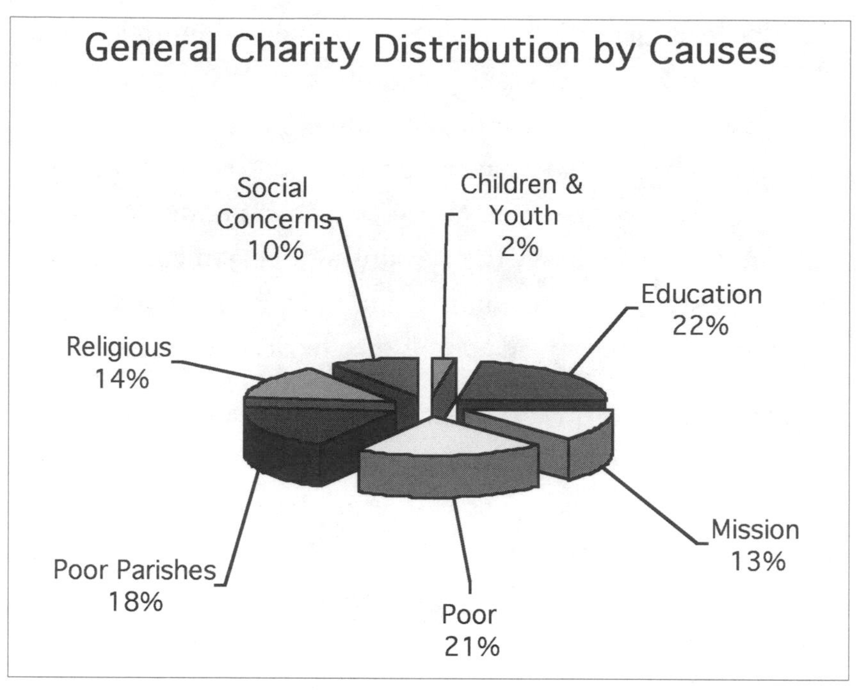
General Charity Distribution by Causes
Social Concerns 10%
Children & Youth 2%
Education 22%
Religious 14%
Mission 13%
Poor Parishes 18%
Poor 21%

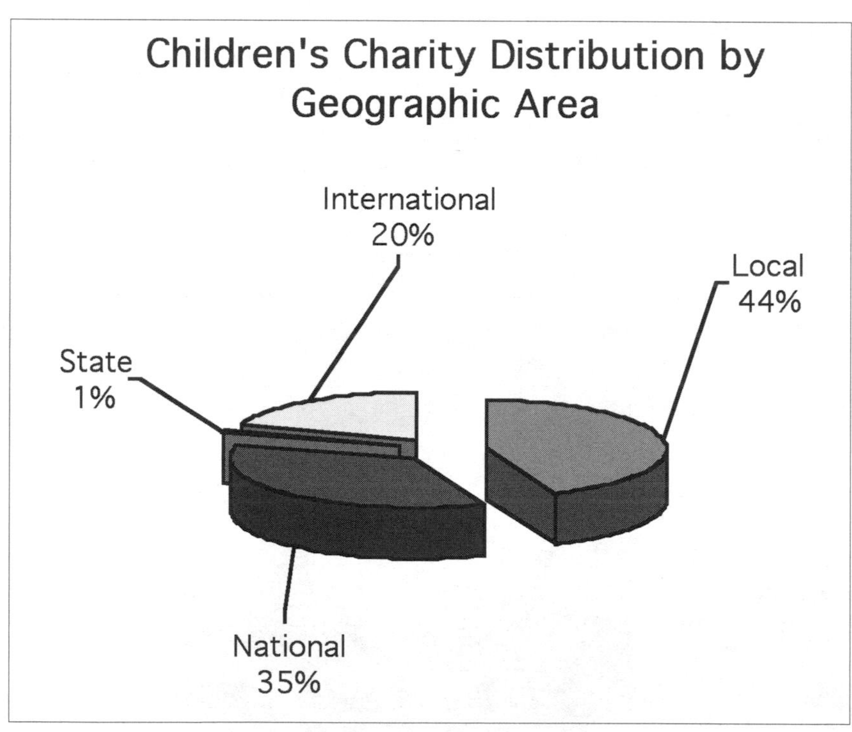
Children's Charity Distribution by Geographic Area
International 20%
Local 44%
State 1%
National 35%

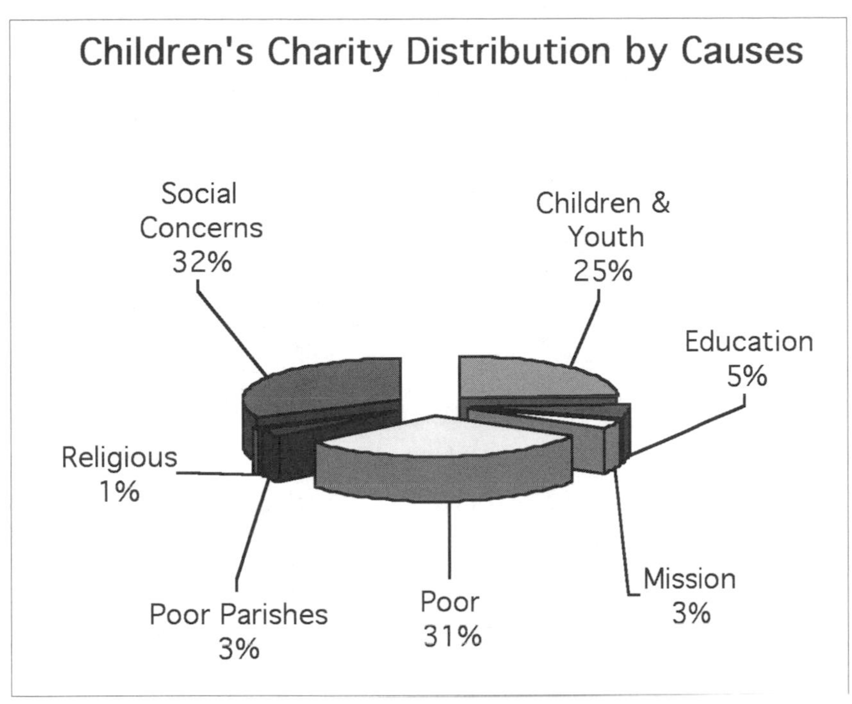

Children going to the altar to place their offering in a special glass jar

Monthly Statements; Offertory Envelopes

When Father Andrew first told me in 2000 that we would be sending out monthly statements, I balked immediately knowing how much time and effort would be needed to make this happen. I knew because in the past we have regularly sent statements twice a year — in August and January.

He also wanted to change the envelopes from the colorful Stewardship Series to a plainer but mail-able business-reply envelope, which is pre-stamped; or to a courtesy-reply envelope, which is not pre-stamped. Of course, you know who won this debate. I can truly say that this was one argument I needed to lose. Why? Because our offertory jumped by twelve percent following the first month we implemented this change in 2001. I never expected this increase because our offertory, by many standards, was already quite high. Yet the increase was real and the numbers continue to increase year after year.

Statements are mailed so they arrive before the beginning of the month. It is a first-class mailing and may include a parish calendar of events and/or other enclosures. There are computer systems that can do this, or a parish can use a company such as Our Sunday Visitor.

The statement presents the amount given each week for the previous month, and for the monthly givers what they gave the previous month. The statement also shows the information about how much they have pledged, if any, and a summary for the year to date. We recommend that a contact person's name appear somewhere on the statement. It is important to note that the contact person is someone who does not receive the funds nor record the gifts, so that there's no conflict of interest when questions regarding the offertory or other gifts are researched. At St. Thomas More I serve as the contact person for our parishioners when they have questions, complaints, or problems regarding their gift records or about their giving of time and talent.

Since we do not provide postage, what we use at St. Thomas More is a courtesy reply envelope. The back is preprinted with the envelope or member number, name, and address and a space for counters to record the amount of the gift. It also includes an appropriate scriptural message.

Sample Monthly Statement, Adults

"Try Me In This"

Envelope No. 00000

Mr. & Mrs. John Doe
123 Shepherd's Path
Centennial, CO 80112

Says the Lord of Hosts. Shall I not open the floodgates of heaven, to pour blessings upon you without measure?

- Malachi 3:10

0001708

May Statement | Total Gifts in 2009: $1,500.00

	Pledged Amount	Prior Years Gifts	Gifts YTD 2009	Pledge Balance
General Fund 2009	$2,400.00	N/A	$1,025.00	$1,375.00
	Detail for May: 05/03/2009		$200.00	
	Total for May:		$200.00	
Jubilee Vision Building Fund $1,375.00	$3,600.00	$2,700.00	$500.00	$400.00
	Detail for May: 05/04/2009		$100.00	
	Total for May:		$100.00	
Phase II Jubilee Building Fund	$3,600.00	$0.00	$0.00	$3,600.00

In thanksgiving for God's many blessings, and in fulfillment of my responsibilities as a Christian steward, I welcome the privilege of honoring the commitment made to St. Thomas More Parish. Please call 303-770-1155 with questions.

Children's Statement (sent in July and January)

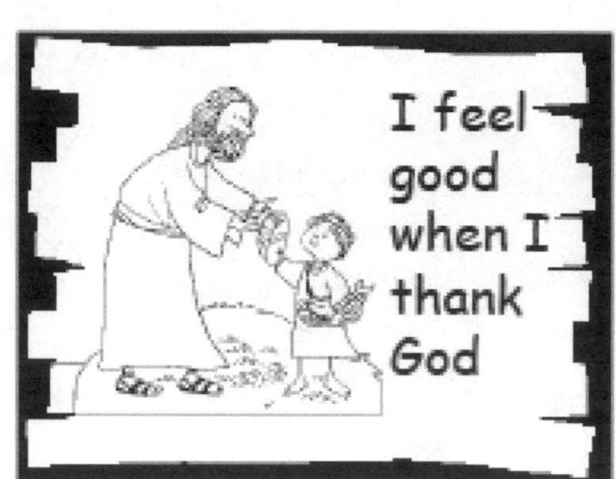

Envelope No. 00000

Johnny Doe
123 Shepherd's Path
Centennial, CO 80112

0001708

January - June 2009

You have thank God
with your gift of **$3.73**

For the year you plan
to give to God **$52.00**

All your gifts to God
go to the Children's Charity Fund!

"God loves a cheerful giver."
2 Corinthians 9:7

Courtesy-reply envelopes are effective because they can be mailed back to our parish when parishioners are out of town. If they dropped their stamped envelope at an out-of-town parish, there's a great likelihood that it would be mailed back to us. We hope that parishes will practice the honor system here. This way our parish does not lose the use of that particular offertory in a given week. At St. Thomas More we would lose at least $14,000 to $16,000 worth of offertory collection per week without the use of these envelopes.

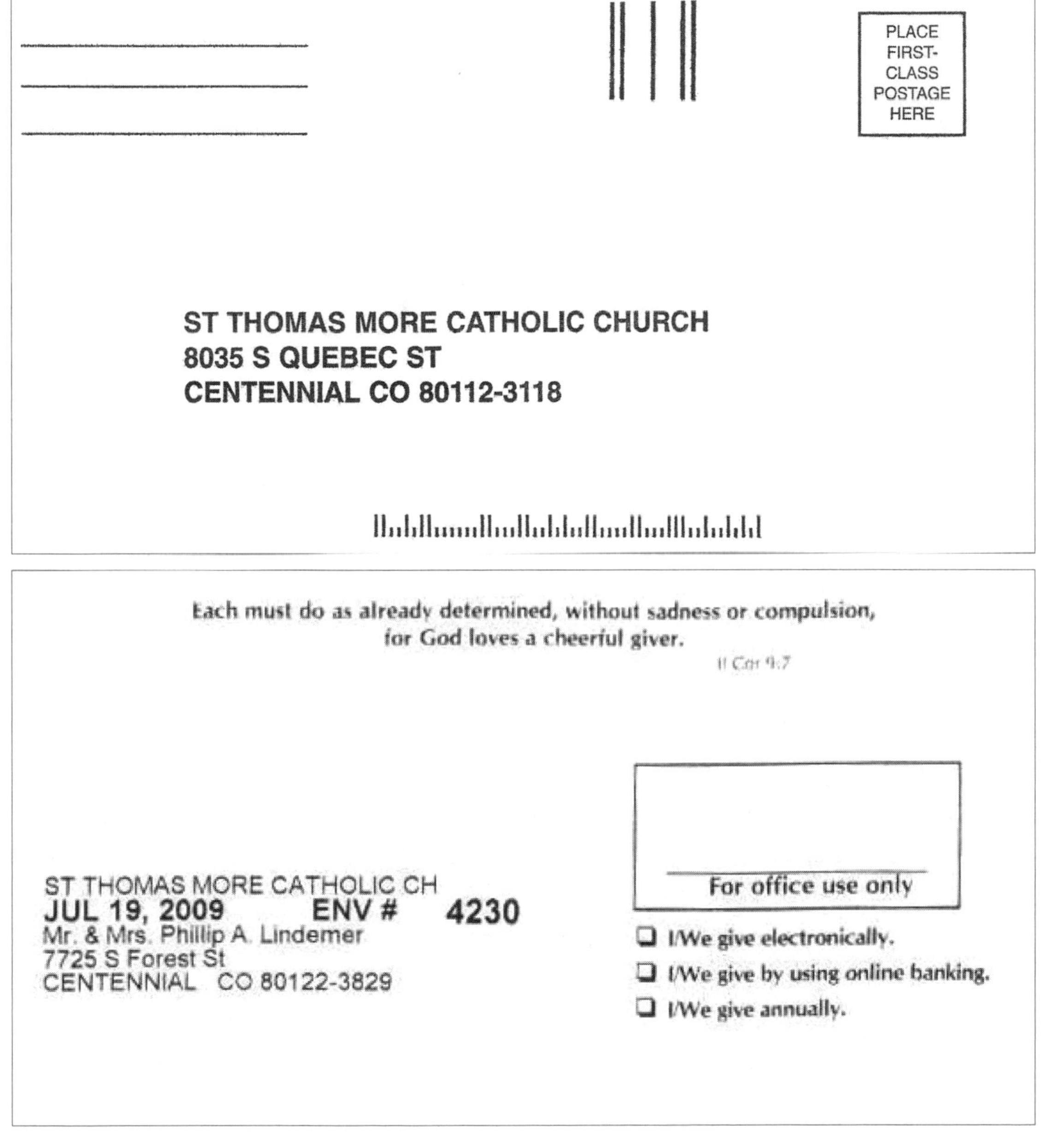

PLACE FIRST-CLASS POSTAGE HERE

ST THOMAS MORE CATHOLIC CHURCH
8035 S QUEBEC ST
CENTENNIAL CO 80112-3118

Each must do as already determined, without sadness or compulsion,
for God loves a cheerful giver.
II Cor 9:7

ST THOMAS MORE CATHOLIC CH
JUL 19, 2009 ENV # 4230
Mr. & Mrs. Phillip A. Lindemer
7725 S Forest St
CENTENNIAL CO 80122-3829

For office use only

- ❑ I/We give electronically.
- ❑ I/We give by using online banking.
- ❑ I/We give annually.

Children's Offertory Envelope

Charity Joy Peace Patience Kindness Goodness Generosity Gentleness Faithfulness Self-Control Modesty Chastity

The Fruits of the Holy Spirit

"Taste and See the Goodness of the Lord."

Psalm 34:8

ST. THOMAS MORE CATHOLIC CHURCH
8035 S. QUEBEC ST.
CENTENNIAL, CO 80112

DATE ________________

ENV. # ________________

NAME ________________

Joyfully Sharing the
Fruits of the Holy Spirit

Time ________________

Talent ________________

Treasure
$________________

Our Sunday Visitor, Inc.

In addition, we have also implemented the use of the electronic fund transfers (EFTs) called ACH (Account Clearing House) — an effective way of offertory collection. At St. Thomas More we add an average of about $20,000 via EFTs per month. Some frown upon this practice, however, because it loses the liturgical aspect of giving the offertory at Mass. One way to offset this is by using an offertory envelope that is marked "EFT." Many, however, feel that it's a waste of an envelope. So there are pros and cons to this practice.

Why are these tools effective? Father Andrew explains that the monthly statement serves as a reminder of what the family has pledged and the payment to date. When a statement arrives it usually is placed along with all the other bills so that when the time comes for the family-designated bill payer to work on the bills, the envelope is readily available. Father Andrew further recommends that the first bill they pay is to God, who deserves to receive the first and the best, not the leftover.

Father Andrew explains that sometimes when it comes to expenses spouses hide some from the other. So with the parish sending a statement there's a record of the family's giving to Church. It becomes an open book in the family.

To generate both tools effectively, an efficient tracking record of gifts and pledges must be in place, along with very important backup and recovery procedures for all critical information, which brings us to the next important element of stewardship: accountability and transparency.

Accountability and Transparency

If we manage our affairs well, then God will say, "Well done, my good and faithful servant.... Come, share your master's joy" (Mt 25:31).

It is imperative that the parish also practices good stewardship of all parish resources, including safeguarding the offertory gifts. Thus, accountability and transparency are a must in the parish. Internal controls have to be in place from the time the offertory is dropped in the collection basket until it is deposited and recorded in the database; and finally reviewed, audited and approved by the finance council and the finance office of the diocese.

The Archdiocese of Denver urges the pastors to understand the internal control structure in parishes, and to have knowledge about all parish financial operations. They need to familiarize themselves with all revenues (cash receipts), expenses (cash disbursements), assets, and liabilities. Are there adequate checks and balances over these activities to protect against theft, inappropriate uses of funds and other assets, inaccurate recording in the financial statements, and increased liability?

Procedures for offertory fund collection, counting, and deposit should be documented and communicated, and if possible performed by separate individuals.

At St. Thomas More we follow the guidelines of the Archdiocese of Denver regarding offertory collection, counting and deposits:

1. Rotate the teams of counters every month. There should be at least two teams.
2. Counters must sign the counter's collection form upon completion of counting the offertory.
3. No one person, including staff or family relations, is left alone with the offertory.
4. There is no handling of offertory funds after the end of counting.
5. Bags used are to be tamper resistant with pre-numbered and locking tabs. Ushers must record and sign the number. The counters verify.
6. Weekly deposits are reconciled with offertory records.
7. Each batch on the counter's form receives a deposit batch number. The amounts recorded in the deposit database must be the same as the amount on the counter's form.
8. The accounts payable office gives a weekly report to the pastor and the office of stewardship. It includes the weekend collection, the amount of tithe for the week, and the balance of the charity accounts.

In addition, the office of stewardship and the accounting department must reconcile the gifts records and deposits monthly. If there are discrepancies, efforts must be made to determine the differences before the statements go out. The reconciliation sheet for the month also compares the weekly totals from the previous year as shown in the following examples.

In the December issue of the parish newsletter we publish a financial report with charts showing revenues and expenses for the year. If parishioners need more details than the newsletter allows, we invite them to visit the parish office to look at the financial reports.

Sample: Counter's Collection Form

COUNTER'S COLLECTION FORM

Date: ______________________________

Env. Checks	Batch 1	Batch 2	Batch 3	Batch 4	Batch 5	Batch 6	Batch 7	TOTAL
	Batch 8	Batch 9	Batch 10	Batch 11	Batch 12	Batch 13	Batch 14	
	Batch 15	Batch 16	Batch 17	Batch 18	Batch 19	Batch 20	Batch 21	
Loose Checks	Batch 22	Batch 23	Batch 24	Batch 25	Batch 26	Batch 27	Batch 28	
Env. Cash	Batch 29	Batch 30	Batch 31	Batch 32	Batch 33	Batch 34	Batch 35	
Misc. Cash	Batch 36	Batch 37	Batch 38	Batch 39	Batch 40	Batch 41	Batch 42	
Children	Batch 43	Batch 44	Batch 45	ACH Weekly	ACH Weekly	ACH Monthly	ACH Monthly	
TOTAL								

DEPOSITS	AMOUNT	COUNTER'S NAME IN PRINT	COUNTER'S SIGNATURE
No. 1			
No. 2			
No. 3			
TOTAL			

Sample: Weekly Offertory Collection Report

Description	2006	2007	Difference
Week 19	30,655.92	39,951.59	9,295.67
Week 20	22,016.89	23,676.76	1,659.87
Week 21	23,457.48	25,749.94	2,292.46
Week 22	19,660.62	17,283.81	-2,376.81
TOTAL	95,790.91	106,662.10	10,871.19
Average	$23,947.73	$26,665.53	$2,717.80
% of Increase			11%

Sample: Weekly Offertory Comparison Report

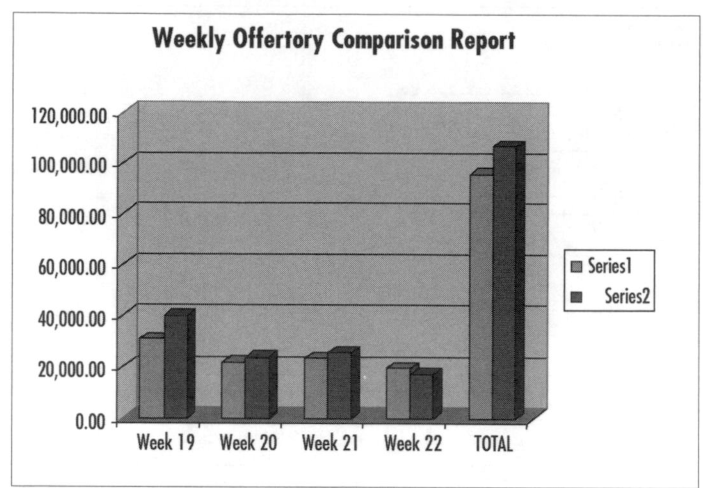

Sample Financial Report: Revenues

Revenue	Amount	% of Total
Offertory	$1,425,223	91.6%
Religious Education Programs	$59,193	3.8%
Interest	$1,170	0.1%
Gifts & Bequests	$18,412	1.2%
ACA Rebate	$2,258	0.1%
Youth Programs	$37,068	2.4%
Other Revenue	$12,061	0.8%
Total Revenue	**$1,555,385**	

Sample Financial Report: Expenses

Operating Expenses	Amount	% of Total
Personnel Costs	$597,835	45.6%
Utilities, Maintenance & Insurance	$196,591	15.0%
Charity*	$142,522	10.9%
Archdiocesan Assessments	$95,791	7.3%
Stewardship & Communications	$45,782	3.5%
Interest Expense	$4,806	0.4%

Religious Education Programs	$43,203	3.3%
Youth Programs	$29,227	2.2%
Social Concerns	$38,402	2.9%
Other Operating Expense	$93,666	7.2%
Capital Acquisitions	$21,796	1.7%
Total Expenditures & Loan Reduction	**$1,309,621**	

Liturgical Components

We recommend that commitment weekends are liturgical, which means that asking for parishioners to make a commitment must be part of the liturgy rather than just an afterthought. This also means that at the beginning of Mass, pulpit announcements, prayers of the faithful, liturgical music, and the environment with a stewardship message should be evident during commitment weekends.

Here are some examples from St. Thomas More:

At the beginning of Mass: "Today is the twentieth Sunday in Ordinary Time and the stewardship of prayer weekend at St. Thomas More."

Prayers of the faithful: "For all parish pastoral council members, that through their stewardship of time and talent, they will find greater personal and communal faith, we pray to the Lord."

Stewardship music: Sacred music that is consistent with the liturgy of the day or the weekend enhances the worship experience of the congregation. During the stewardship weekends, we recommend that liturgists or directors of music find appropriate music which conveys that sense of stewardship. For example:

> "Seek Ye First," by Karen Lafferty, is based on Matthew 6:33 and encourages us to make God the priority in our life and that God will provide. "Take My Hand," by Sebastian Temple, is appropriate for time and talent weekend. "Our

Blessing Cup," by Bob Hurd, talks about giving back for all of God's goodness.

The "Hymn of Thanksgiving," a stewardship song based on Psalm 24:1-6 and written anonymously for the International Catholic Stewardship Council (ICSC), speaks about time, talent, and treasure. We have obtained permission to give you a few lines of the hymn:

O Make us faithful stewards of your bounty,
Give us the grace to bring your love to birth.
We place our time, our talent and our treasure,
We place our work and worship without measure
All at your service, God of all the earth.

Altar call: Deuteronomy 26:2-4 says, "You shall take some fruits of the various products of the soil which you harvest... and putting them in a basket... you shall go to the priest... [who will] set it in front of the altar of the LORD, your God." I have always felt that the altar call which our Protestant brothers and sisters use in their ministry is very effective in drawing people to participate at liturgies. At STM, resistance was immediate when I first introduced the altar call to receive the commitment cards. It was not an easy sell, considering not only the size of the parish, but also the perceived sophistication of parishioners. "It will take more time." "People will never go for it." "It's so dumb!"

Undaunted, yet considering the strong opposition, I decided to purchase huge baskets (Father Walsh called them the "Moses baskets"), and I asked couples to hold the baskets at a particular station of the aisle to receive the commitment cards. It worked well but did not have the same effect as actually going toward the altar.

The following year, we decided to use only one basket and to place it at the foot of the altar. We asked people to come forward (soft music is nice at this time) to offer their gift to God. The response was incredible! Today, the altar call probably is one of the most touching parts of our commitment weekends, especially seeing children run up to the altar to give to the presiding priest or altar servers their own commitment cards. Moreover, it didn't, as some feared, take more time than the usual offering, so the Mass wasn't longer. Although we understand that this may not be for everyone, we recommend the altar call as one of the most important parts of commitment weekends.

Preaching on stewardship: In 1 Corinthians 9:16, we read: "If I preach the gospel, this is no reason for me to boast, for an obligation has been imposed on me, and woe to me if I do not preach it!"

Preaching on stewardship is a very important part of our program. The message must be incorporated in the homily and not just be an afterthought during stewardship weekends. Pastors could easily weave the stewardship message into the Gospel of the day. We recommend highly, though, to plan the commitment weekends with Sunday readings that may be "stewardship friendly."

We also recommend that during "stewardship of treasure" weekend the pastor preaches at all Masses and he, not an associate or a member of the finance council, talks about, or asks for, money. Father Andrew explains, "If I am God's representative in forgiving sins, why shouldn't I be his representative in talking about, or asking for, money to build his Kingdom on earth?"

(See Appendix 2 for samples of stewardship homilies.)

Lay witness speakers: To repeat Pope Paul VI's message in his apostolic exhortation *Evangelii Nuntiandi:* "Modern man listens more willingly to witnesses than to teachers, and if he does listen to teachers, it is because they are witnesses."

Lay witness speakers are a very important aspect of stewardship. They give testimonials of their personal story of conversion and can be very persuasive in the practice of stewardship. In fact, my own personal conversion to stewardship as a way of life happened because of a lay witness.

We ask parishioners but, if necessary, in the beginning a parish may need to ask people from other parishes to be lay witness speakers. They speak on or offer witness to their own embrace of stewardship during the stewardship of ministry (talent) and stewardship of treasure weekends. They speak after a very short homily. Parishes should keep in mind, however, the liturgical requirements in their dioceses regarding lay witness speakers.

How do I find the lay witness speakers? I rely on the inspiration of the Holy Spirit and actually praying about it to help me find the right person to serve as a lay witness speaker. Often I would see a person at church and somehow, I am compelled to ask if he or she would be interested in serving as a lay witness speaker. Most are usually very active in the Church and daily communicants, and I usually recognize them as regular givers or as having a record of giving financially. The amount of money the speakers give should not be an issue; only that they are faithful givers of time, talent, and treasure.

I try to have the lay witness speakers in place a year before the next commitment weekends. Although it is not always possible, we find it preferable to have one speaker for all Masses so we avoid comparisons between speakers. In the past twenty years we have had the blessing of lay witness speakers that included couples, singles, children, youths, and seniors. It is also important that lay witness speakers are inclusive of ethnic representation.

When the lay witness speakers agree, I give them some pointers on how long their talk should be (no more than seven minutes is the rule at St. Thomas More), and what their talk may or may not include. Scripture passages that support their life as stewards are powerful and convincing, while the *quid pro quo* or some kind of bargaining with God for things received must be avoided.

I also ask them for a copy of their talk two weeks before commitment weekend to double check for dos and don'ts, and to give the pastor a chance to review the talk and spot-check questions of dogma.

Here lay witnesses give a talk following a short homily at the weekend Masses. Items to be included are:

1. Thankfulness for all that God has given both materially and spiritually
2. The need to give vs. giving to a need
3. Trust that God will provide for their needs
4. God cannot be outdone in generosity
5. Scripture passages that support their talk

In other words, the lay speakers give witness to how they live their faith as good stewards. As St. Francis of Assisi said, "Christians should always preach the Gospel, sometimes using words."

(See Appendix 1 for samples of lay witness talks at St. Thomas More.)

Money Talks

"Each must do as already determined, without sadness or compulsion, for God loves a cheerful giver"(2 Cor 9:7).

THE ST. THOMAS MORE STEWARDSHIP model generally calls for talks about money on three different occasions annually: the Archbishop's Catholic Appeal (ACA) in April or May (depending on when Easter falls), the stewardship of treasure weekends in October, and the mission appeal in June. A capital fund campaign is in addition to these weekends.

Archbishop's Catholic Appeal

IN APRIL OR MAY, OR two weeks after Easter, we have two weekends of talks about the Archbishop's Catholic Appeal (ACA). Father Andrew recommends that rather than simply talking about the needs that the ACA addresses, the celebrant talks about stewardship — about thanking God for his blessings and our need to give because of our deep relationship with God. He also recommends that families allocate at least one or two percent of their tithe to the ACA. This approach has been very successful here, judging from the response of families to this annual appeal.

Sometimes, Father Andrew assigns a parochial vicar or a deacon to preach on stewardship and ACA at all Masses. Otherwise, the presiding cleric facilitates the two weekends, usually with a letter from the archbishop.

"For where your treasure is, there also will your heart be" (Lk 12:34).

Stewardship of Treasure Weekends

We have three active-phase weekends during which we talk about money. The first weekend, Father Andrew preaches at all the Masses on the spirituality of stewardship. He also asks parishioners to pray for guidance and inspiration on how they will respond to God's call to discipleship through their treasure. The second weekend lay witness speakers talk about their embrace of stewardship as a way of life. If necessary, the first two weekends may be combined. And the third weekend is commitment weekend when we ask parishioners to make a commitment to support the parish and its mission to "go and make disciples."

Mission Appeal

"Go, therefore, and make disciples of all nations" (Mt 28:19).

The Cooperative Mission Appeal generally requires not only talks about money, but — at most parishes — also a second collection. Not here. The missionary, who is informed ahead of time that the stewardship committee has allocated a significant contribution for them (currently $25,000), simply thanks parishioners for their practice of stewardship and the parish's contribution on their behalf. The missionary then describes how the parish contribution would help them in their missionary activities, and how parishioners become missionaries without leaving their homes.

The mission appeal is one of the current seventeen mandated special collections in the Archdiocese of Denver. Since Father Andrew came to St. Thomas More, all mandated collections' contributions come from the parish "tithe of the tithe" and are allocated by the stewardship committee. Thus, St. Thomas More has no second collections or holy day collections except on Christmas.

Capital Fund Campaign

"Thus says the Lord: The heavens are my throne, the earth is my footstool. What kind of house can you build for me; what is to be my resting place?" (Is 66:1-2).

It is inevitable that a parish will need an extraordinary campaign to raise funds for capital needs — build a new parish hall or a school, renovate the church, and more. When any of these needs arises, a capital fund campaign can be a necessity, without abandoning stewardship principles.

What does that mean? First, make sure that the fund-raising consultants practice stewardship in their approach to fund raising. This must be reflected in the language they use in the campaign.

Father Andrew also promotes the "jubilee gift" or a once-in-a-lifetime gift to God through the parish. He notes that Leviticus 25 says a jubilee year proclaims liberty in the land for all inhabitants, with slaves being set free, and debts forgiven or justly settled. He asks parishioners to stretch themselves in determining what gift they can give in thanksgiving for all that God has given them. Even when members feel that they have made their once-in-a-lifetime gift (donating toward the building of a church at another time and place, for example), they need to reflect on their current circumstances and stretch themselves to consider making another once-in-a-lifetime gift.

Here all three pastors have engaged in at least one capital campaign for building projects. Father McCallin built the church and the youth center, while Father Walsh built the parish school and evangelization center. I helped coordinate both of Father Walsh's capital campaigns as well as Father Andrew's building project which involved major facilities renovations as well as a new rectory and adoration chapel. These building projects cost at least $27 million.

Limited Collections or Fund Raisers

With a few exceptions, we have eliminated fund-raising events at St. Thomas More. The children and youth are *not* out selling tickets, entertainment books, or any kind of food products. Father Andrew often says this practice only makes our children "little salespeople."

One major fund raiser we allow is the school's dinner and auction event, which is an opportunity for many services and in-kind donations to be converted into cash. What about those Boy Scout spaghetti dinners or the Knights of Columbus fish fries? Because the cost of these events are usually minimal, we allow these but only if they are promoted as community builders rather than as fund raisers. We also allow in-kind donations — canned food, used clothing, or gifts to prisoners, the homeless, and food banks during special holidays like Christmas and Easter, because parishioners want to give tangible gifts to the poor and needy.

Meanwhile, we discourage our ministries from raising funds. Instead, we allocate a budget for valid parish ministries under a particular commission. This way, the ministries can concentrate on the reason they exist in the parish. For instance, the respect life committee is there to help educate the parish regarding respect life issues and not to have to worry about how they will cover expenses. When they give away roses on Mother's Day, the cost has already been budgeted for them.

NOTES, REFLECTIONS, & POINTS TO REMEMBER

For Part IV: The "How-to" of Stewardship

NOTES, REFLECTIONS, & POINTS TO REMEMBER

For Part IV: The "How-to" of Stewardship

NOTES, REFLECTIONS, & POINTS TO REMEMBER

For Part IV: The "How-to" of Stewardship

NOTES, REFLECTIONS, & POINTS TO REMEMBER

For Part IV: The "How-to" of Stewardship

PART V

Six-Phase Program of Stewardship

By Mila Glodava

At St. Thomas More, stewardship is a year-round, six-phase program consisting of:

1. Stewardship of Prayer (Time), second week of August
2. Stewardship of Ministry (Talent), fourth week of August
3. Stewardship of Faith, third week of September, usually on Catechetical Sunday
4. Stewardship of Treasure; second, third, and fourth week of October
5. Stewardship of Vocations, second week of November
6. Stewardship of the Earth, Friday around Earth Day which is April 22

We usually implement each of the six phases around the same time each year so the parish gets used to the program year after year. Of course, each parish will have to decide what time of year is most appropriate for itself. It goes without saying that the success of implementing stewardship in a parish will depend a great deal on how efficient the parish office and/or stewardship committee perform certain tasks before, during, and after commitment weekend. These are lists of what items need attention:

Before Commitment Weekend

1. Prepare all letters, brochures, prayer cards, commitment cards, name labels, postage, sharpened golf pencils, receptacles for the commitment cards and visual aids.
2. Work with the liturgy committee or office about procedures to follow regarding lay witness talks, altar call, prayers of the faithful, music, pulpit announcements, and others.
3. If there will be a telephone follow-up, prepare a script, and call-information sheets and other instructions on further steps after the telephone follow-ups.

4. If using visual aids, make sure that television monitors, tape players, and projectors and screens are in good working condition. Find someone who can operate the AV equipment without difficulty. A dry run usually will avoid embarrassing situations and loss of precious time during liturgy.

During Commitment Sunday

1. Have commitment cards available in pews even though you may have mailed them to parishioners. Some parishioners forget or lose their copy so will need replacements. There also may be people who are not on the parish roster yet. Also have sharpened golf pencils in the pews.
2. Have the AV operator ready to start the equipment on cue.
3. Have a basket or some kind of receptacle ready to receive the commitment cards.

After Commitment Sunday

1. Collect all leftover commitment cards/forms as well as golf pencils for future use.
2. Send thank-you letters/cards to respondents.
3. Monitor and evaluate the level of giving and number of participants. Some parishes do not monitor the pledges. Rather, they keep the commitment cards in a receptacle in full view of parishioners all year long, until their next annual renewal.
4. Publish results (the number of pledges and total amount of pledges). Thank all participants. Compare results from previous year.
5. Identify those who did not return their cards for follow-up letters, phone campaign, or home visitation.
6. Prepare list of parishioners who signed up for church ministry. Give the list to parish leaders for follow-up contact.

STEWARDSHIP OF PRAYER: TIME

"Every one of us needs at least half an hour each day, except when we're busy, then we need an hour" (St. Francis de Sales).

We kick off our stewardship renewal program with the stewardship of prayer weekend in August. The celebrant preaches at all the Masses about giving time to God in prayer and then invites parishioners to make a commitment of time in prayer. After the homily he asks each person to pick up a prayer commitment card in the pew to pray the prayer on the back side of the card. Because they are asked to pray the prayer together, they may pick up a card. After the prayer, he asks them to turn the card over and encourages them to fill it out.

Father Andrew usually says, "The two sides are not identical." One is to keep for their records and the other is to return to the parish. Parishioners tear the card in two and the half for the parish is collected as soft music is played. All the collected halves are then placed in the basket in front of the ambo.

The prayer commitment card is divided into public and private prayer, and also intentions for which to pray. We ask parishioners to make a commitment of two hours and twenty-four minutes per week (a tithe of ten percent of the one thousand four hundred forty minutes in one day). Some people tithe that amount daily. Parishioners are reminded they are giving their tithe of time in thanksgiving for all of God's blessings.

During the stewardship of prayer weekend, we give away "tools" for prayer: rosaries, prayer booklets, holy cards, and anything else that can act as a prayer aid. We continue to give away these items throughout the year. We encourage our rosary makers ministry to make rosaries year-round so we have a supply when there's a need in the parish and in the missions.

In the past we had a holy hour on Thursday following the stewardship of prayer weekend. However, with only a handful of people coming we decided to have a prayer rally instead on the Saturday of the weekend. We are very pleased with the response to the rally, which continues to grow in attendance.

The rally starts with Mass, followed by a light supper, a short Eucharistic service such as a Holy Hour with Benediction (featuring sacred music), a talk on prayer, a procession around campus featuring banners depicting the various ministries in the parish, and an outdoor benediction. During the rally, we pray for all of St. Thomas More's nearly three hundred ministries and committees as we kick off the school year. The rally is an example of how we stay responsive: we try something, and if it's not working, we change it and find something that works better. Thus, if the rally no longer works, we'll find other ways to promote prayer.

There are also various prayer opportunities throughout the year including perpetual adoration, rosary after Mass, novenas (Divine Mercy and St. Peregrine), and various prayer groups (prayer line, centering prayer, men's group, school parents, and others). We host a mini-ministry fair on the various prayer groups during the stewardship of prayer weekend.

Here's something we ask our parishioners to think about. There are 365 days or 8,760 hours in a year. Typically, an adult spends 2,080 hours at work and 4,185 eating and sleeping. That leaves 2,495 disposable hours. How much do we give to God? Father Andrew says: "If we spend 4,185 hours eating and sleeping, don't we need to allot time for God, also?" People will do this if they see time as a gift and they realize something needs to be returned to God from their time as well.

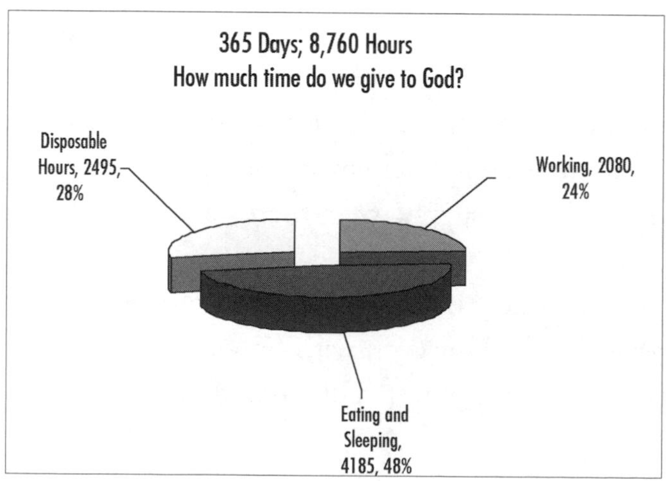

"Stewardship of Prayer" Commitment Card

Stewardship of Prayer

Keep this copy for your records.

Please check Prayer and Intentions to which you plan to commit.

PRIVATE PRAYER

- ☐ Church Visits
- ☐ Daytime Prayer
- ☐ Litany
- ☐ Liturgy of the Hours
- ☐ Morning Offering
- ☐ Morning Prayer
- ☐ Night Prayer
- ☐ Novenas/Devotions
- ☐ Perpetual Adoration
- ☐ Prayer Line
- ☐ Quiet Time
- ☐ Reading the Sunday Reading Prior to Mass
- ☐ Rosary
- ☐ Scripture Reading
- ☐ Spiritual Reading
- ☐ Other________________

PUBLIC PRAYER

- ☐ Centering Prayer
- ☐ Daily Mass
- ☐ Family Prayer
- ☐ Grace before Meals
- ☐ Holy Hour
- ☐ Men's Saturday Group
- ☐ Parish Mission
- ☐ Pilgrimages
- ☐ Prayer Groups
- ☐ Prayer Line
- ☐ Retreat
- ☐ Weekly Mass
- ☐ Other

CHECK INTENTIONS for which you will pray:

- ☐ Abuse: Substance, Physical, Emotional
- ☐ Addictions
- ☐ Children
- ☐ Church
- ☐ Clergy
- ☐ Crisis of Faith
- ☐ Divorced
- ☐ Engaged
- ☐ Family Life
- ☐ Homebound
- ☐ Increase in Knowledge of Faith
- ☐ Increase in Parish Involvement
- ☐ Married Couples
- ☐ Nation
- ☐ Non-Practicing Catholics
- ☐ Sick
- ☐ Singles
- ☐ Vocations
- ☐ World
- ☐ Youth
- ☐ Those who have no one to pray for them
- ☐ End of Abortion
- ☐ Other________________

Would you like to invite a person who is homebound to join our Ministers of Praise Group? This person will be asked to uphold the parish in prayers every month.

☐ Yes! I recommend ________________________
Name of homebound person

____
Phone number

____
Parishioner submitting name

Stewardship of Prayer

Return this copy to the parish.

Please check the types of Prayer and Intentions. (Please indicate the hours per week).

PRIVATE PRAYER

- ☐ Church Visits
- ☐ Daytime Prayer
- ☐ Litany
- ☐ Liturgy of the Hours
- ☐ Morning Offering
- ☐ Morning Prayer
- ☐ Night Prayer
- ☐ Novenas/Devotions
- ☐ Perpetual Adoration
- ☐ Prayer Line
- ☐ Quiet Time
- ☐ Reading the Sunday Reading Prior to Mass
- ☐ Rosary
- ☐ Scripture Reading
- ☐ Spiritual Reading
- ☐ Other________________

PUBLIC PRAYER

- ☐ Centering Prayer
- ☐ Daily Mass
- ☐ Family Prayer
- ☐ Grace before Meals
- ☐ Holy Hour
- ☐ Men's Saturday Group
- ☐ Parish Mission
- ☐ Pilgrimages
- ☐ Prayer Groups
- ☐ Prayer Line
- ☐ Retreat
- ☐ Weekly Mass
- ☐ Other

CHECK INTENTIONS for which you will pray:

- ☐ Abuse: Substance, Physical, Emotional
- ☐ Addictions
- ☐ Children
- ☐ Church
- ☐ Clergy
- ☐ Crisis of Faith
- ☐ Divorced
- ☐ Engaged
- ☐ Family Life
- ☐ Homebound
- ☐ Increase in Knowledge of Faith
- ☐ Increase in Parish Involvement
- ☐ Married Couples
- ☐ Nation
- ☐ Non-Practicing Catholics
- ☐ Sick
- ☐ Singles
- ☐ Vocations
- ☐ World
- ☐ Youth
- ☐ Those who have no one to pray for them
- ☐ End of Abortion
- ☐ Other________________

Would you like to invite a person who is homebound to join our Ministers of Praise Group? This person will be asked to uphold the parish in prayers every month.

☐ Yes! I recommend ________________________
Name of homebound person

____
Phone number

____
Parishioner submitting name

STEWARDSHIP OF MINISTRY: TIME AND TALENT

"As each one has received a gift, use it to serve one another as good stewards of God's varied grace" (1 Pt 4:10).

The stewardship of ministry/time and talent is usually scheduled on the fourth weekend in August. It includes a short homily on giving of time and talent as well as lay witness speakers who talk about why giving of their time and talent as a gift to God is important to them, and how stewardship has changed their lives. They also lead the volunteers' sign-up in church. (Again, see Appendix 1 for samples of lay witness talks.)

As part of the stewardship of time and talent we hold a ministry fair to educate, inform, and invite parishioners to participate in parish life. In the past we held it in the gymnasium, but not many people came. Several years ago, we began to hold it in the courtyard where people can't miss the booths when they come to and from Mass. It made a big difference in getting the interest of new volunteers. We also entice them with refreshments and games for children so they feel comfortable staying around.

The fair offers many areas of volunteering or serving in ministries in each of the seven commissions:

1. Communications and Stewardship
2. Facilities Support
3. Faith and Academic Formation (catechesis, parish school, youth)
4. Family Life
5. Liturgy
6. Parish Life
7. Social Concerns

We assign tables for ministries according to their respective commission. For instance, the altar servers, music, extraordinary ministers of the Eucharist, and more would fall under the liturgy commission. Each of the three branches of the faith and academic formation commission would get a section for their ministries.

During the ministry fair parish leaders make themselves available to promote their committees or ministries and to answer questions. The fair is a great community builder for the parish, and it is an opportunity for volunteers to see they are not alone in their service to God.

At Mass the celebrant gives a very short homily and then invites lay witnesses to share their story. Later, they ask the parishioners to pick up time and talent sheets in the pews, pray the stewardship prayer, and then check off the ministries that appeal to them. It is important that the lay ministers point out a few of the many and varied ministries available.

It is necessary that parishioners write in their name, address, and telephone number, not only for recording purposes but also for contact reasons. The lay witness speakers emphasize that every person signs up on a separate and individual time and talent sheet. This is helpful in keeping records straight. If everyone in a family signed up on one form it would be a nightmare for data entry.

SAMPLE LAY WITNESS TALK

"I Got Involved in Ministry When I Was Invited. Today I Invite You."

By John Longo

Hi! I am John Longo, and I've been asked by Father Walsh and the parish to speak to you about time and talent, but to answer your first question: "Yes, I am blind!"

I lost my sight in an automobile accident many years ago. I nearly lost my life. It was then that I had to make a considerable lifestyle adjustment; not out of choice but out of necessity.

After fearing that I had nothing left in life but poverty and despair, a friend of mine (later my wife) brought me out of my self-pity and invited me to get involved in the church and so she had me assist her in teaching Sunday school. After my health improved I started college; I made a career choice to serve God by serving others, through Scripture. I had desired to make a lifelong Christian commitment to serving others, and now it is a lifestyle.

When I finished my schooling in Sacred Scripture and moved back to Denver, I was asked by then Archbishop Stafford to teach for the Archdiocese of Denver and help prepare men for the diaconate.

Shortly after we had just joined the parish, a pair from the evangelization team invited us to participate in the church ministries, and so we began to help with confirmation, and later with the Small Wonders program. When our first child was baptized, we were invited to help prepare couples for that sacrament.

A year or so ago, I was invited to help with the respect life committee and, just recently, I was invited to add my thoughts to the parish newsletter.

> These invitations are graces from God, but I am a weak vessel of clay, who also depends on the help of others — those who read for me, assist me in my ministries — for we are all servants to one another, members of the Body of Christ.
>
> All of you have been given abilities by God, to serve the Body of Christ. Even if you think your talents are small, they can get mightily used by God. God wants a cheerful giver; not a tearful giver. I got involved in ministry when I was invited.
>
> Today, I invite *you!*
>
> Today, there are time and talent forms in the pews, that we ask you to fill out, especially those of you who have never participated in a ministry before, being generous with your time and talent. We need ushers, Eucharistic ministers, teachers and ministers of all kinds.

As you probably can imagine, John Longo was a very powerful lay witness speaker. Indeed, his invitation challenged many parishioners — whether they had a physical handicap or not — to become involved in the parish. To date, many of those who accepted the challenge in 1998 are still involved in parish ministries. No wonder the number of ministries at St. Thomas More grew from ninety-four that year to nearly three hundred by 2007, attracting more than eight thousand five hundred individuals in multiple ministries.

Sample Memo: Lay Witness Speaker

DATE: July 21, 2006
FROM: Mila Glodava
TO: John Doe
RE: Stewardship of Time and Talent: Aug. 26/27

Thank you for agreeing to give the lay witness talk for the Stewardship of Time and Talent weekend Aug. 26/27 at all the Masses.

On Sunday, Aug. 27, I have made arrangements for you to have breakfast, brunch, and/ or refreshments in the Padre Restaurant. All you need to do is tell the maitre'd you're there for stewardship.

Below are a few pointers for you.

1) Please prepare a 5-minute talk regarding your own stewardship of time and talent as your way of thanking God for His blessings upon you and your family (please see attached to assist you in preparing your talk). I would appreciate getting a copy of your talk by Aug. 8 (I'm leaving Aug. 13 for the Philippines, so I need a couple of days to review it and give to all the priests).

2) Please arrive at least 15 minutes before your scheduled talk to give you time to let the presiding cleric know that you are speaking and where you will be so he can introduce you after a very short homily. You might want to sit in the first pews right in front of the pulpit.

3) Please deliver your talk immediately after the presiding priest has introduced you. Speak slowly. You'll be tempted to read too fast. Speak slowly, pause... take deep breaths.

Tips on Giving the Time and Talent Talks

1. Call to holiness: Please remind parishioners that each one of us is called to holiness by virtue of our baptism. This call to holiness involves not only service at church but also people's everyday life at work, at home or on the job – a steward way of life.
2. Making time for God: This is important in building a relationship with God. Reading the Bible is a good way to learn about God. And that stewardship is deeply rooted in the Bible (See Appendix for Scripture passages on stewardship). Quote from the Bible regarding stewardship.
3. Receiving and giving: The cycle of receiving and giving are natural part of a serious relationship with God. Knowing everything we have and are belongs to God, we thank Him for all of His blessings.
4. Generosity: Reflect on all of God's blessings and what Psalmist says in 116:12, "What shall return to the Lord for all of His bounty to me?" God has been generous; we need to be generous as well.
5. The first and the best: We give God the first and the best, not the leftovers. We encourage giving the tithe.
6. Love: Invite them to give because they love God and would like to express that love by giving back a tithe of our time, talent and treasure.

Sample Talent Commitment Form

Commitment Form

Envelope Number: ______ Date: ______

Name: ______

Address: ______

City: ______ State: ______ Zip: ______

Phone (Home) ______ (Work) ______

E-mail address: ______

Please complete one form per individual in the family.

If you need additional forms you may make copies of this original or contact the parish office at 303-770-1155.

Stewardship of Time & Talent for Adult Stewards

St. Thomas More Catholic Church

Please check the box for each ministry that you are interested in, as well as those you are already doing. If you check "interested in" you will be notified by the leader of the ministry. Please complete one form per individual in the family.

1 Communications & Stewardship Commission

Please check box		Interested in:	Already doing:
1a	**Communications:**		
1a3	General Office Volunteers	☐	☐
1a4	Information Desk	☐	☐
1a5.1	More Informed Writers	☐	☐
1b	**Stewardship:**		
1b8	Ambassadors of Hope (Volunteers for Inner City Schools)	☐	☐
1b1	Cloister Cove Volunteers	☐	☐
1b2	Ministry Fair/Time & Talent	☐	☐
1b3	Newcomers' Welcome	☐	☐
1b5.1	Rosary Makers	☐	☐

2 Facilities Support Commission

Please check box		Interested in:	Already doing:
2b	Handy Man Maintenance	☐	☐
2d	Landscaping/Flowers	☐	☐

3 Faith & Academic Formation Commission

Please check box		Interested in:	Already doing:
3a1	**Faith Formation & Catechists:**		
	Adult Faith Formation/Adult Volunteers		
3a1.2	Bible Studies	☐	☐
3a1.1	Catechism Class	☐	☐
3a1.3	ChristLife	☐	☐
3a1.18	Confirmation Class	☐	☐
3a1.26	ENDOW	☐	☐
3a1.20	FAMILIA	☐	☐
3a1.4	Family Program Catechists	☐	☐
3a1.24	Grades 1-5 Catechists	☐	☐
3a1.5	Legion of Mary	☐	☐
3a1.21	Men Among Men	☐	☐
3a1.22	Ministry of Mothers Sharing (MOMS)	☐	☐
3a1.7	Mom & Tots	☐	☐
3a1.8	Neo-Catechumenal Way	☐	☐
3a1.25	Office Helpers	☐	☐
3a1.9	Parish Library Volunteer	☐	☐

3c3	**Young Adults (Ages 18-39)**		
3c3.5	College Life Leader	☐	☐
3c3.1	Oasis	☐	☐
3c3.2	Retreat Leaders	☐	☐
3c3.3	Service Coordinator	☐	☐
3c3.4	Special Events	☐	☐

4 Family Life Commission/ Adult Volunteers

	Please check box	Interested in:	Already doing:
4a	Bridge Club	☐	☐
4b	Forever Mores STM Senior Ministry	☐	☐
4c	Foster Parenting	☐	☐
4e	Knights of Columbus (K of C)	☐	☐
4e.1	K of C Ladies Auxiliary	☐	☐
4d.1	Ladies' Golf League	☐	☐
4d.2	Men's Golf League	☐	☐
4g	New Life Singles Ministry	☐	☐
4h	Parish Special Events	☐	☐
4i	STM Singles Ministry	☐	☐
4j	STM Stitchers	☐	☐
4k	Scrapbooking	☐	☐

5 Liturgy Commission/ Adult Volunteers

	Please check box	Interested in:	Already doing:
5g1	Accompanist	☐	☐
5b	Art & Environment	☐	☐
5f1	Caritas (10:30 a.m.)	☐	☐
5f2	C.H.AL.I.C.E. (4:00 p.m. Sat.)	☐	☐
5m	Funeral Choir	☐	☐
5c	Extraordinary Ministers of Holy Communion	☐	☐
5c1	Ministry to the Sick / Dying	☐	☐
5c1.1	Homebound	☐	☐
5c2	Nursing Homes	☐	☐
5c3	Swedish Hospital	☐	☐
5c4	Porter Hospital	☐	☐
5d	Greeters	☐	☐
5f10	Knights of Columbus Men's Choir	☐	☐
5f11	Magnificat Woman's Choir(8:30)	☐	☐
5g	Musicians	☐	☐
5h	Perpetual Eucharistic Adoration	☐	☐
5l	Pew Brigade	☐	☐
5b1	Sewing Group	☐	☐
5k	Ushers	☐	☐
5f17	Young Adult Choir	☐	☐

6 Parish Life Commission

	Please check box	Interested in:	Already doing:
6i	Ambassadors of Mary, Pilgrim Statue (Men)	☐	☐
6a	Baptism Preparation Couples	☐	☐
6b	Couple to Couple League	☐	☐
6g	Couples Retreat (Fall)	☐	☐
6j	Covenant of Love (Marriage Enrichment)	☐	☐
6d	Eucharistic Apostles of Divine Mercy	☐	☐
6c	Marriage Encounter	☐	☐
6k	Marriage Works N-HIM (Married Couples Ministry)	☐	☐
6e1	Ministry of Praise	☐	☐
6e2	Prayer Line	☐	☐
6e3	Centering Prayer	☐	☐
6e4	Men's Saturday Group	☐	☐
6e6	Daily Mass Prayer Companion (after 6:30 Mass)	☐	☐
6h	Novena to St. Peregrine and St. Jude (Cancer Patients)	☐	☐
6f	Retrouvaille (For Troubled Marriage)	☐	☐

7 Social Concerns Commission

	Please check box	Interested in:	Already doing:
7a	Angel Tree	☐	☐
7b	Blood Drive Volunteer	☐	☐
7b.1	Blood Drive Donor	☐	☐
7c	Discovery: Job Network (D:JN)	☐	☐
7k	Gabriel Project	☐	☐
7d	Habitat for Humanity	☐	☐

As we said earlier, all commitment weekends are liturgically based. We ask parishioners to make a commitment at Mass. During the time and talent weekend, however, we realize that some parishioners may need more information before they sign up. In this case we encourage them to visit the ministry fair to talk to someone in their ministry of interest. We also encourage volunteers to renew their commitments of time and talent every year. This offers an excellent opportunity for those experiencing burnout to change ministries.

Also, mindful of current concerns for safe environment for children, we include the following "Important Notice" in our time and talent commitment form:

Important Notice!

To ensure the safety and well-being of all parishioners and participants in our ministries and programs, St. Thomas More Catholic Church complies with the following Archdiocese of Denver requirements for all volunteers who work with children:

- All volunteers who work with children will be required to attend a safe environment workshop.
- All volunteers who work with children must sign a waiver stating that they have received and read the archdiocesan policy manual addressing sexual misconduct.
- All volunteers working with children will be required to sign a form agreeing to a criminal background check.

We prepare the time and talent commitment form many weeks before the commitment weekend. The form, which is grouped according to our commissions, changes from year to year. We include only the ministries that need volunteers because some ministries can accommodate only a specific number. For instance, we have more than four hundred volunteers who provide food for receptions after a funeral. If we add more, chances are they could not all be scheduled during the year. If we cannot schedule them, they feel undervalued.

It may be a little bit different in smaller parishes, as Father Andrew describes: "In my previous parish, which was considerably smaller in size than St. Thomas More, we did it differently. We had a write-up of all the activities on one sheet, like a want ad of a newspaper, and a volunteer sheet was attached. Parishioners would circle the want ad and then mark it down on the volunteer sheet. When they tore the two apart, they would keep the want-ad section and the other part went to the parish. This way they had a reminder of what they did, and the parish got a reminder of what they would do."

Because of the sheer number of ministries and committees at St. Thomas More, we cannot possibly list all the descriptions on the time and talent form. Instead, we publish a program directory which describes succinctly each ministry: its purpose, when and where meetings are held, and who the contact person is. The directory also contains our parish mission statement, our organizational chart, our parish staff roster, and our goals and objectives. The publication comes in handy for someone who wants to know more about the parish.

We do all this because we need to help people discover their talent and then make sure their talent and the ministry match. That is important. For example, if they don't have a good voice, they should not be in the choir. If they are good writers, they should find the ministries that can employ that talent.

On a personal note, when I started a ministry regarding the marginalization of women through the mail-order brides business, I began getting more public attention than I ever had before, causing my head to swell a little bit. Then I discovered stewardship. I realized that God has given me the ability to voice our protest of the marginalization of women. Because of my conversion to this new way of life, my attitude changed. I realized I have a responsibility to use my gifts and that I alone was accountable to God for all the gifts He has given me.

According to Father Andrew, this is the change that is most important. Knowing their gifts and talents and realizing that using them glorifies the Giver of the gifts, parishioners could become more inspired to get involved in parish ministries or in community service.

This is where their conversion comes in, their evangelization. Once they are evangelized, the prayer component and giving of our talent become even more important. They realize the treasure part is the least important. The hardest part is being able to give of ourselves. The part that is most critical is giving one's will to God in prayer.

As I indicated on the parish's stewardship calendar, each month we also hold a smaller, less elaborate ministry fair during our regular coffee and donut Sunday. This is another opportunity for ministries to promote their activities and to encourage more parishioners to become involved in the many opportunities available in the parish.

Volunteer Appreciation

"Just so, your light must shine before others, that they may see your good deeds and glorify your heavenly Father" (Mt 5:16).

WE GENERALLY HOLD A VOLUNTEER appreciation party on the second Friday after Easter. When this was begun in 1988, parishioners were very suspicious of why then pastor, Father Michael Walsh, wanted to bring them to a party. They thought he wanted to get some money from them so only about a hundred came. Many had such a good time, however, that everyone talked about the party later. Now many hundreds of parishioners come to a party which is planned around a variety of themes and featured entertainment, and is prepared in its entirety by the paid staff. Because of our number of volunteers, we usually do not publicize this event other than the invitation sent to all volunteers.

Although many volunteers are happy just to have the opportunity to serve God through their ministries in the parish, they, too, appreciate and are honored to be recognized in a special way.

During our "St. Thomas More Day" in June, we distribute at Mass the "Pastor's Annual Award" to outstanding volunteers who receive a statue of the Blessed Mother. We publish their accomplishments in the parish newsletter. In this way they can be seen as role models for others.

Tracking

NOWADAYS IT IS A LOT easier to keep track of our volunteers and the ministries in which they are involved. With our large numbers, it is important that we are able to find the volunteers for a particular ministry. This is how we are able to make an estimate of the monetary value of our volunteers. (Just think how much all those hours of service would cost the parish if that work was not done by volunteers!) This list is also important for us when we send invitations to the volunteer appreciation party. We generally begin updating the database in January so we're ready to mail invitations a few weeks before the party.

One discouraging factor regarding volunteer recruitment is the failure to followup with those who have signed up. For example, someone has filled out a sheet but doesn't get contacted. It is very important that everyone is contacted, either by a visit, a phone call, or a postcard in order to acknowledge their interest. They want to participate in parish life and need to feel wanted. With computers, it is so much easier than ever before to do the tracking.

Please note too that with the spate of the sexual-abuse scandal in the Church, we have taken seriously the safeguarding of our children. We have, therefore, a special section in our time and talent sheet regarding this sensitive issue. Our database is able to track volunteers who have complied with our requirements to protect our children.

STEWARDSHIP OF FAITH

"The desire for God is written in the human heart, because man is created by God and for God" (CCC 27).

FAITH IS A GIFT ROOTED in God. It is a supernatural manifestation of the Holy Spirit. In Hebrews 11:1, St. Paul describes faith as "the realization of what is hoped for and evidence of things not seen." In the same chapter, he offers examples of faith including, Abel, Abraham, Joseph, and Moses, and many other heroes of our faith, who performed difficult duties, endured severe trials, and obtained very important blessings because of their faith in God.

Faith is also one of the three theological virtues — faith, hope, and love — all supernatural gifts impossible for us to acquire on our own. Although St. Paul writes that the greatest of these virtues is love, it is impossible to love without faith. Peter Kreeft, a Catholic apologist and professor of philosophy at Boston College, once said, "Faith is the root, hope is the stem, and love is the flower on a single plant." If faith then is the root, it must be watered and nourished to keep the stem healthy and for the flower to bloom. Faith is a gift we can nurture; it is one that can grow.

In stewardship spirituality, we teach that we are to receive all our gifts with thanks. And as with our talents, we need to nourish and develop our God-given gift of faith. At St. Thomas More we offer many opportunities to develop and increase our faith. That is why we added the stewardship of faith to our program. This weekend is usually associated with the catechetical Sunday, around the third Sunday of September. At Mass, the celebrant reminds our parishioners that parents are their children's primary teachers of the faith. The weekend also involves recognizing and commissioning all catechists at all Masses. More importantly, throughout the year all parish commissions have a responsibility to incorporate nourishing of the faith in their programs, especially the faith and academic formation commission which includes the office of catechesis, parish school, and youth ministry.

To help our parishioners nourish their faith, we started a special literature rack featuring different topics such as:

1. What the Church teaches
2. Eucharistic Adoration
3. Questions Catholics are asked
4. How to make a good confession
5. How to forgive the Church
6. The Eucharist, sacrament of unity, a timeless invitation for holiness
7. How to celebrate Sunday as a Catholic

We added a CD kiosk of various talks by renowned Catholic speakers, theologians and spiritual directors (both clergy and laity), including for example Scott Hahn, Blessed Teresa of Calcutta, and Pope John Paul II.

During the stewardship of faith weekend, we ask parishioners to make a commitment of time to nourish their faith. As with other stewardship programs, the cards used are perforated. One part is turned in during an "altar call" and another kept for record keeping. This card also has a stewardship prayer on the back. With the stewardship of faith, we ask parishioners to make a commitment on how they will nurture their own faith and how they will share their faith with others.

(See *Sample Commitment Form: "Stewardship of Faith"* on next page.)

STEWARDSHIP OF TREASURE

"Do not store up for yourselves treasures on earth, where moth and decay destroys, and thieves break in and steal. But store up treasures in heaven, where neither moth nor decay destroys, nor thieves break in and steal. For where your treasure is, there also will your heart be" (Mt 6:19-21).

We have a five-week stewardship of treasure renewal process I will describe in detail later. As mentioned, we also handle the Archbishop's Catholic Appeal (ACA), which funds diocesan programs. The stewardship of treasure component of our program also coordinates the building fund campaigns after the fund-raising company leaves the premises. In 1994, we built a new school and shortly after, expanded it. The project cost close to $13 million. Our fund raiser brought in $1.1 million and the office of stewardship raised another $1.5 million by a combined effort with our stewardship of treasure weekends. However, we paid off the new school mostly through the offertory collection.

In 2006 we embarked on another $13 million capital fund campaign, using the principles of stewardship and the jubilee gift. Father Andrew had used this jubilee-gift method very effectively in his previous parish, which practiced stewardship as a way of life for decades.

Sample Commitment Form: "Stewardship of Faith"

Stewardship of
Faith
Commitment

Keep this copy for your records.

(Please indicate what you will do to strengthen and renew your faith.)

- ☐ Participate in one or more of the following:
  - ☐ Advent / Lenten series
  - ☐ Catholic Biblical School
  - ☐ Catechism Class
  - ☐ Family Program
  - ☐ Parish Mission
  - ☐ Stations of the Cross (Lent)
  - ☐ Sponsor RCIA
- ☐ Attend a Catechetical Conference.
- ☐ Attend Mass weekly, daily. (Circle one or both.)
- ☐ Attend a retreat.
- ☐ Help those in need: family/friends/neighbors.
- ☐ Join a Small Christian community.
- ☐ Join a Bible Study.
- ☐ Listen attentively to the homily on Sundays and discuss with family after Mass.
- ☐ Make a 15 minute visit per week to the Adoration Chapel.
- ☐ Pray each day—at least 15 minutes.
- ☐ Pray Grace before/after meals.
- ☐ Pray the Rosary daily/weekly.
- ☐ Read Spiritual books.
- ☐ Receive the Sacrament of Reconciliation 3 times per year or more often
- ☐ Read the following on a regular basis: STM bulletin, Denver Catholic Register, papal documents, *Grace in Action*.
- ☐ Share your faith story with a friend/ family member.
- ☐ Spend one hour per week in the Adoration Chapel.
- ☐ Read Scripture each day—15 minutes or more.

Stewardship of
Faith
Commitment

Please return this copy to the parish.

(Please indicate what you will do to strengthen and renew your faith.)

- ☐ Participate in one or more of the following:
  - ☐ Advent / Lenten series
  - ☐ Catholic Biblical School
  - ☐ Catechism Class
  - ☐ Family Program
  - ☐ Parish Mission
  - ☐ Stations of the Cross (Lent)
  - ☐ Sponsor RCIA
- ☐ Attend a Catechetical Conference.
- ☐ Attend Mass weekly, daily. (Circle one or both.)
- ☐ Attend a retreat.
- ☐ Help those in need: family/friends/neighbors.
- ☐ Join a Small Christian community.
- ☐ Join a Bible Study.
- ☐ Listen attentively to the homily on Sundays and discuss with family after Mass.
- ☐ Make a 15 minute visit per week to the Adoration Chapel.
- ☐ Pray each day—at least 15 minutes.
- ☐ Pray Grace before/after meals.
- ☐ Pray the Rosary daily/weekly.
- ☐ Read Spiritual books.
- ☐ Receive the Sacrament of Reconciliation 3 times per year or more often
- ☐ Read the following on a regular basis: STM bulletin, Denver Catholic Register, papal documents, *Grace in Action*.
- ☐ Share your faith story with a friend/ family member.
- ☐ Spend one hour per week in the Adoration Chapel.
- ☐ Read Scripture each day—15 minutes or more.

Stewardship of Faith

Keep this copy for your records.

Please check the things you will do to strengthen and renew your faith.

Faith is a spiritual gift that helps us believe in God and trust that the Lord loves us. Like other gifts, faith requires care.

HOW WILL YOU STEWARD YOUR FAITH?

- ☐ Dress modestly.
- ☐ Learn your Catholic prayers. *(Ask your parents to help you.)*
- ☐ Go to Mass each week on Sunday and on Holy Days. *(Parents will take you.)*
- ☐ Say a decade of the Rosary each day. *(Great to do in the car!)*
- ☐ Read your Bible—a passage each day or every other day.
- ☐ Study the life of your patron saint. How can you follow your patron saint's example?
- ☐ Celebrate the true spirit of holidays, especially Christmas and Easter.
- ☐ Keep the Fourth Commandment: Honor thy father and mother.
- ☐ Play a Bible game or Catechism game. *(Check them out from our parish library!)*
- ☐ Watch a video about the Bible or a saint.
- ☐ Pray for your family and friends each day.
- ☐ Go to Religion class/youth group each week.
- ☐ Go to the Sacrament of Reconciliation at least 3 times a year. *(More often is better!)*
- ☐ Pray to your Guardian Angel. *(Your parents can teach you the prayer.)*
- ☐ Help with chores around the house.
- ☐ Do your homework.
- ☐ Respect your parish priests, your teachers, your neighbors and friends.
- ☐ Say Grace before and after meals, thanking God for your food.
- ☐ Wear a crucifix, scapular medal or other jewelry that symbolizes your Catholic faith.
- ☐ Live the Beatitudes.
- ☐ When cruising the Internet, visit our website or another Catholic page.

Stewardship of Faith

Return this copy to the parish.

Please check the things you will do to strengthen and renew your faith.

Faith is a spiritual gift that helps us believe in God and trust that the Lord loves us. Like other gifts, faith requires care.

HOW WILL YOU STEWARD YOUR FAITH?

- ☐ Dress modestly.
- ☐ Learn your Catholic prayers. *(Ask your parents to help you.)*
- ☐ Go to Mass each week on Sunday and on Holy Days. *(Parents will take you.)*
- ☐ Say a decade of the Rosary each day. *(Great to do in the car!)*
- ☐ Read your Bible—a passage each day or every other day.
- ☐ Study the life of your patron saint. How can you follow your patron saint's example?
- ☐ Celebrate the true spirit of holidays, especially Christmas and Easter.
- ☐ Keep the Fourth Commandment: Honor thy father and mother.
- ☐ Play a Bible game or Catechism game. *(Check them out from our parish library!)*
- ☐ Watch a video about the Bible or a saint.
- ☐ Pray for your family and friends each day.
- ☐ Go to Religion class/youth group each week.
- ☐ Go to the Sacrament of Reconciliation at least 3 times a year. *(More often is better!)*
- ☐ Pray to your Guardian Angel. *(Your parents can teach you the prayer.)*
- ☐ Help with chores around the house.
- ☐ Do your homework.
- ☐ Respect your parish priests, your teachers, your neighbors and friends.
- ☐ Say Grace before and after meals, thanking God for your food.
- ☐ Wear a crucifix, scapular medal or other jewelry that symbolizes your Catholic faith.
- ☐ Live the Beatitudes.
- ☐ When cruising the Internet, visit our website or another Catholic page.

We have touched on this earlier in the book but it's worth going into more detail here. What is a jubilee gift? The word "jubilee" is a biblical word. It is found in the Book of Leviticus (chapters 25 and 27) and once in the Book of Numbers (36:4). In Isaiah 61:1-2, the jubilee year is the "a year of favor from the LORD." The word refers to the sacred practices that are still observed every fifty years. Jubilee is used in the Bible in a tithing and stewardship sense. In Leviticus, God tells us that once a week there should be a day of rest. One of every seven days is the Sabbath. God also commands the Israelites that there should be a Sabbath year. Every seven years they are to let their fields rest. The jubilee year signifies seven years of Sabbath years. Seven times seven is forty-nine; so, in the fiftieth year we are to have a "super Sabbath year": the jubilee year, which means freedom for slaves, rest for the land, and release of debts of the poor.

When we ask people to make a commitment, we encourage them to start with a small amount first. If they never made a commitment before, we ask them to start with one or two percent of their annual income. Then we ask those who made any kind of commitment to make half of a tithe or five percent. At the renewal, we ask those who made half a tithe to make a full tithe. Some people found out that they weren't worse off, but in fact, were even better off so they made a full tithe. We emphasize that the giving is out of gratitude for the many blessings from God. That is the motivation.

We don't usually publish the weekly collection amounts to avoid attracting robbers. We publish the results of our pledges in the bulletin and thank all participants. For example, we might say that twenty percent have already pledged some amount. Then we ask others to pledge, reminding them that they still have time to make a commitment to support the parish. Newcomers receive pledge forms in the newcomer packet.

We monitor the level of giving and number of participants during the entire campaign so that we are able to compare our progress from year to year. (Again, as mentioned earlier, some parishes do not monitor the commitment cards. Rather they are kept in a receptacle in full view of parishioners all year long, until their next annual renewal.)

Let's look at the five-week active phase of commitment renewal of stewardship of treasure.

WEEK 1

The first letter is sent to all parishioners. The pastor preaches at all Masses.

The stewardship committee or office needs to decide whether to send letters and other information before commitment Sunday. Keep in mind that the goal is to help parishioners examine their priorities in life in light of the Gospel message. Of the six phases of stewardship, we only send personalized letters for the annual renewal for treasure.

In the beginning of our program we used to send brochures or other inserts on stewardship. We enclosed professionally, preprinted stewardship materials about the spirituality of tithing and stewardship. For parishes in the beginning stages of stewardship we recommend ordering stewardship materials at least one month in advance. As our stewardship education program began to develop as an ongoing, year-round effort, we realized that keeping letters simple and to the point was very effective. (And keeping stewardship material simple is a way of showing the practice of good stewardship of the parish resources!)

The first letter announces the beginning of the stewardship of treasure renewal weekends (see sample letter on page 190). This letter talks about the stewardship season, which starts in August with the stewardship of prayer, followed by time and talent, and then the stewardship of faith. The pastor also thanks parishioners for their support of the parish in time, talent, and treasure.

The letter might include the following:

1. You can ask them to make a commitment to God in thanksgiving for what God has done for them.
2. Remember to stay positive and be upbeat. No apologies.
3. Describe the three weekends that are approaching. On commitment Sunday they will be asked to make a commitment in church.

Sample: First Letter

Dear John and Jane,

As a priest, I am privileged to hear about conversions. Some of these are miraculous stories. A miracle is over and above the working of nature and is beyond chance. There is no other explanation that can be given except to believe in the direct working of God. When it comes to stewardship, I have heard many miracle stories. The conversion that some people experience demonstrates how God directly works in their lives.

We, at St. Thomas More, continue our season of stewardship. We renewed our Time and Talent in August. In the next few weeks we will renew our Treasure. Since stewardship is the whole parish's responsibility, I am asking everybody to participate.

I would like to thank you for your involvement in our parish. Please review your blessings and be prepared to thank God by giving a portion back in thanksgiving for what God has given you. This portion is called the "tithe." The Bible tells us that we are to thank God by tithing. God in His part will work in your life in a way that is nothing short of a miracle. Please have enough faith to give a tithe to God.

On the weekend of October 14th and 15th, I will preach at all the Masses about the Spirituality of Stewardship and tithing. Then on the following weekend, October 21st and 22nd, we will have lay witness talks. On the weekend of October 28th and 29th, we will make our treasure commitments to God in church. In preparation for the final weekend, you will receive a letter from me with a commitment card.

I look forward to everyone's participation. I hope you look forward to a miracle! Let the grace of God work in your life in a way that brings a conversion of heart.

Sincerely in Christ,
Very Rev. Andrew Kemberling, V.F.
Pastor

We send the pastor's first letter (using first-class postage) for the stewardship of treasure renewal on the Wednesday prior to week one so parishioners receive them before the weekend.

For the stewardship of treasure renewal weekend, the beginning of Mass should include introductions with a stewardship theme. For instance, the lector could say, "Today is the thirtieth Sunday in Ordinary Time. Today we begin our stewardship of treasure weekends." Prayers of the faithful should include stewardship petitions. The Sunday bulletin has a blurb about stewardship or tithing two weeks before the weekend and during these three weeks. Those items emphasize stewardship as a way of life and our need to give.

It is important for the pastor to take a leadership role in asking for money and so he preaches twice: on the first and third annual renewal weekends.

SAMPLE HOMILY: TREASURE

"Getting Our Priorities Straight"

When I was staying with a family in Grand Junction, the twelve-year-old son was reading golf jokes from a golf magazine. I told him that I thought I had heard every golf joke from the time I was a little boy.

I explained to him and his mom that my dad, being a doctor, got Thursdays off. Most Thursdays Dad went golfing. When he came home I could tell if he had won because he came in whistling. If not, he only did OK. In the kitchen he would recount how things went and he would tell all the golf jokes he had heard that day.

My dad couldn't tell a joke, so he would tell the joke badly. Mom would quickly step in (since she had heard them all before) and retell it correctly, and we would all laugh. This happened almost every week.

The joke was that there was a man who was wondering if there was golf in heaven. He had heard about a holy priest in the monastery that had a reputation for talking with God.

The man tracked down the holy priest and said, "Would you ask God if there is golf in heaven?" The priest said he couldn't guarantee an answer, but if he received word he would call him.

About a week later, the man got a call from the holy priest. The man said, "So, Father, is there golf in heaven?"

The holy priest said, "I have good news and I have bad news. The good news is yes, there's golf in heaven. The bad news is that you're playing there today."

Today is the eighteenth Sunday in Ordinary Time. We hear today's Gospel reading from the twelfth chapter of St. Luke's Gospel. Jesus tells a story and the punch line of the story is: "You fool, this very night your life will be demanded of you, and these things you have prepared, to whom will they belong? Thus it will be for all who store up treasure for themselves but are not rich in what matters to God."

Both stories focus upon what's really important in life: one was worried about golf, the other about his possessions. Both were mistaken.

In stewardship spirituality we work on getting our priorities in proper order. People are more important than things, and the most important person in our life is God. God gives us all that we need. He gives us what we need to take care of our persons: to feed us, clothe us, house us and provide for appropriate recreation, like golf. God gives us what we need so we can help others. Remember, Jesus tells us that the poor will always be with us, so we have the need to give. The extras we have are not solely for our benefit.

You see, God gives us the extra portion that we are going to give away. That portion has a biblical foundation and it is called a tithe. The first tenth of what we earn belongs to God. It is not ours. When we use it as God intends we grow in what matters to God. When we widen our storehouse to take what was to be given away and store it for ourselves, it is foolishness.

Now, before we start judging others by looking at what they have — looking to see who is wealthier, who has more things — let us not be fooled by appearances. One of the greatest paradoxes or ironies of stewardship spirituality is that the good steward does not end up with less, but with more. The good steward begins to realize that the material goods in our possession are only a means to an end, and not an end unto themselves. (Remember persons are more important than things.) The ends of God are to uphold the human person and to better the human person, to respect the life and dignity of the human person. God gives us what we need both to take care of our own needs and to care for the needs of others.

So what does that mean to us?

Let us examine how we own the things in our possession. Do we set a portion aside from what we earn and give it back to God in thanksgiving for what God has given us? Is this the first portion of what we earn or is it what's left over? If we do this, we can have assurance that we are growing rich in what matters to God. If we are not, remember the punch line of Jesus' story: "You fool, this night your life will be demanded, and these things you have prepared, to whom shall they go?" Thus it will be for all who store up treasure for themselves but are not rich in what matters to God.

So what do we take with us this eighteenth Sunday in Ordinary Time?

1. Let us remember that people are more important than things and that the most important person in our life is God.
2. Let us be good stewards, so that we come to realize our material goods are a means to an end, and not the end itself.
3. May we realize God's end, the upholding of the dignity of the human person. That is what matters to God.

WEEK 2

Weekend for Lay Witnesses

The lay witness speakers give testimony to how stewardship has worked in their lives. For the benefit of those who had not been at Mass that weekend, their talk appears in the following issue of the newsletter. (As I have mentioned, Appendix 1 has samples of lay witness talks.)

The liturgy introduction must have a stewardship theme. The prayers of the faithful must include stewardship petitions. The bulletin has an article about tithing and stewardship.

Meanwhile, the second letter, which includes a commitment card and envelope, is mailed this week. Everyone is encouraged to come to Mass prepared to make a commitment in thanksgiving for God's many blessings and in fulfillment of their responsibility as Christian stewards. Parishioners are asked to bring their completed cards to Mass. People are encouraged to use the commitment card they were sent because it already has their name, address, and envelope number on it and that makes it much more efficient for us in data entry.

Sample: Second Letter
Sent Wednesday before Commitment Sunday

Dear John and Jane,

A pig said to the chicken, "What shall we have for breakfast?" The chicken suggested, "Let's have ham and eggs." The pig responded, "No way! For you the eggs are a donation. The ham is a commitment for me!"

We, as a parish, will make treasure commitments on the weekend of October 28th and 29th. Enclosed you will find a commitment card that we ask you to bring to church that weekend.

Let us not forget that Jesus laid his life down for us and became food for us in the Eucharist. Jesus did not make a donation but a commitment. At every Mass, we are asked to make a gift of ourselves when the collection is taken up. Our contribution is taken to the altar and in return we receive from the altar the body and blood of Christ in communion. It is up to us to determine whether or not our gift to God is a donation. Please know that God's gift to us is a commitment.

Please come prepared to make a treasure commitment in thanksgiving for God's many blessings, and in fulfillment of our responsibility as Christian stewards. Let us make a gift of ourselves to God.

Sincerely in Christ,

Very Rev. Andrew Kemberling, V.F.

Pastor

SAMPLE LAY WITNESS TALK

"A Stewardship Journey — Partnership with God"

By Jim and Jan Zapapas,
and daughters Laura and Michelle

Jan:

My name is Jan Zapapas and this is my husband, Jim. We have been married for twenty-four years and have been parishioners of St. Thomas More for twenty-one years. We have four daughters, and one of our children (Laura or Michelle) has joined us up here today as we talk to you about stewardship, and, in particular, the stewardship of treasure.

First of all, it might be helpful to share with you what the word stewardship means to us. Plain and simple, stewardship is living out Christ's instruction to "love one another as I have loved you." It's the actions behind the words "I believe." It's the realization that we truly are Christ's hands and feet.

Stewardship is a way of life; a way of thanking God for all of his blessings by being his caretaker, by being one hundred percent accountable for these gifts he has given us. Taken to its fullest, being a Christian steward is a tall order, one that's impossible for us to fill. Trust me. We would be the last ones up here talking about stewardship if it were a final destination, since we would have a long way to go. Stewardship is a journey; a journey that's a partnership with God, since we acknowledge there is nothing we do by ourselves. At the end of that journey, our greatest hope would be to someday hear Our Lord speak the words "Well done, good and faithful servant."

So today we want to share with you a little of our journey. Our first experience in stewardship actually was in the stewardship of treasure. It started back when I was a senior in college (a long time ago). I had just returned to campus at Purdue University. My bank account was flush with my earnings from my summer job, but those earnings needed to last me the entire school year. The homily one of those first fall weekends was on stewardship. I decided to take the plunge so before the offertory basket came around, I quietly calculated my summer's earnings, and wrote a check out for a 10 percent tithe. I felt good about it, and then quickly forgot about it until a few weeks later. I was informed by the head of the engineering school that I had just been awarded a scholarship that I had never applied for — a scholarship that would more than cover the cost of my tuition and books that entire senior year. Now you never give with the intention of receiving, but to this day, I think it was God's way to make a lasting impression on a young person's heart that God really can't be outdone in his generosity. I was overwhelmed at the thought of this awesome God.

Jim:

So when Jan and I married, we decided to make that same financial commitment to stewardship as a family. That's the journey we've taken ever since. Over the years, we've realized that God was asking us to step beyond our stewardship of treasure, and to begin giving back more in the areas of prayer, time, and talent. With four kids and both of us working, our time became the precious resource.

In retrospect, a key step for us was joining a small Christian community several years ago, similar to the RENEW groups which happen to be re-launching this coming week in our parish. By meeting regularly with other couples, we challenged each other to live out our faith in our everyday lives. More recently, God has led us into other ministries such as teaching confirmation and being an extraordinary minister of the Eucharist for the sick. But in each of these ministries, God still proves to us that he can't be outdone in his generosity. We still receive far more than it seems we give.

But to focus again on treasure, let me tell you what stewardship of treasure is not. It is not a get-rich scheme. It is not a guarantee that you'll never lose your job. We know. Just ask us. It is not a technique to avoid ever making unlucky stock picks or investment decisions. Again, just ask us. We know. Stewardship is not about giving because God needs the money.

But it is a way to ensure that greed and envy never find a home in your heart. It is a way, for the most part, to make money a "non-issue" in your life. It is a way to keep you focused on the fact that you have what you have because of God's generosity, not because you "earned it." And it's a way to realize that our need for God and our need to "give back" to God is stronger than God's need to receive.

For each of us, stewardship will be a different level of commitment and a different combination of our prayer, time, talent, and treasure. And in striving to live the life of a Christian steward, we follow the example of others before us, and set an example for those who follow.

Laura/Michelle:

I want to encourage young people to not wait *all* the way to your college years before embracing stewardship like my parents did. There are so many ways to give back of your time, talent, and treasure.

Around six years ago, with our parents' help, my sister Laura/Michelle and I began sponsoring a needy child through the Christian Foundation for Children and Aging. Once we were old enough to start making the fifteen-dollar monthly payments ourselves, we took over. Receiving letters and pictures from our little girl in Colombia is a reward in itself as we hear about her schooling, her family life, and her growth with God. In one of the letters, her mother writes, "We want to thank you very much for the generous help you give to my child through the good Franciscan nuns. The nuns made a Christmas party for all the children. In your name they gave her a very beautiful gift of dresses and shoes. She was so happy because it was the only gift she received this Christmas." Letters like these remind us how lucky we are to live where we live, even as we take so much for granted.

Since our freshmen year in high school, Laura/Michelle and I have been involved with the high school youth group, Breakaway, and we joined the choir a year later. Through these ministries, we have experienced the joy of sharing our time and talent with the Lord by helping to lead the congregation in song; helping others grow in their faith life; and through various service projects within the youth group. There are many opportunities for youth to be as much a part of stewardship as, oh, say, the older generations. In all seriousness, giving back to God should not be reserved for adults. Why wait until you're older when your life can be blessed now?

Jan:

One final note: In our stewardship journey, we are asked to decide what organizations, among so many wonderful causes and charities, to give our treasure to. Each individual and family should carefully take this matter up in prayer.

For us, we've determined that our faith is the most critical aspect of our lives, for without faith and without God, what would we really have? We are too often reminded of what a culture looks like that fails to put God first, or even put him anywhere near the top. For our family, there is no greater need than spreading the Good News. Our giving reflects the high priority we place on our church community, both locally at St. Thomas More, and to our larger church, the Archdiocese of Denver. This "Body of Christ" is the community we gather with on Sundays and throughout the week, encouraging and sustaining us and so many others on our journey.

Our personal giving also acknowledges the great work being done by many other organizations — from the Christian radio station that plays throughout our home and cars; to agencies helping those in need such as Catholic Charities, Samaritan House, and Seeds of Hope; to the schools that served us and now our children. We humbly remind ourselves that the need for these organizations to receive our gifts may be great, but it pales compared to our need to give.

Jim:

We want to thank you for this opportunity to share with you today some of our thoughts and experiences of stewardship. We know that we have benefited from the wonderful example of love and service which so many people live out in this community. Our lives and the lives of our children have been deeply touched by the generosity of others. Thank you for being our parish family over these last twenty-one years. May God help each of us gathered here to truly be his hands and feet to the world. Thank you.

Commitment Sunday

WEEK 3

Again, the liturgy introduction must include a stewardship theme. The intentions must include stewardship petitions. The bulletin will have an article about making a commitment. Everyone's involvement is requested.

Meanwhile, the pastor preaches at all Masses and gives instructions on completing the commitment form. A special or "bangtail" envelope with the commitment form attached is made available in the pews. Using the bangtail envelope is more practical. There aren't too many items in the pews, especially because there's a commitment envelope for adults and another one for children. (Again: All of the children's offertory goes to the charity account, and is distributed to various charities upon the request of the children and youth.) Once the commitment cards are completed, the pastor invites everyone to come forward to the altar as a symbol of their offering their commitment to God.

The pastor gives a talk on stewardship at all the Masses. Items include:

1. God asks a tithe in thanksgiving for what God has given.
2. A tithe is the *first* tenth of income (gross, not net) and not what is "leftover."
3. The tithe is the sole source of income for the parish. There will be no other charitable collections taken and therefore *no second collections.*
4. A tithe includes all of your charitable giving, but at least half your tithe should go to the parish. For example the Archbishops' Catholic Appeal is a part of one's tithe (five percent to parish, one percent to ACA, and four percent to other charities). Catholic school parents are encouraged to make a half tithe.

In encouraging people to tithe, Father Andrew suggests they just take the plunge and start. He often says, "Make a commitment and stick to it — a part tithe or a half tithe." He usually reminds parishioners that their commitment begins January 1 although they may start their new pledge immediately following commitment weekend.

At the end of each homily, the pastor leads the faithful in filling out the commitment cards. He asks everyone to pick up a commitment card and pencil placed in the pews. When everybody has done so, he leads the congregation in praying the stewardship prayer printed on the back of the commitment card. When finished praying, he has the people fill in their name, address, and phone number; and mark how much and how often they will give (each week, once a month or annually); and then sign their commitment. Of course there will be some who are not comfortable making a commitment. That's all right! Perhaps they will some other time as we continue to educate the parish on the spirituality of stewardship. The pastor then reminds the congregation that commitments begin January 1. Everyone inclined then brings up the card to the altar and gives them to the pastor, deacon or altar servers, while some soft music is played. The cards are then placed in a basket at the altar as a sign of their sacrificial gift to God.

The pastor also reminds the congregation that the parish tithes or gives ten percent of the offertory to a charity account for distribution to charitable organizations outside of St. Thomas More. This is our commitment of solidarity with the poor.

Sample Commitment Card: "Stewardship of Treasure"

St. Thomas More Catholic Church
Stewardship of Treasure Commitment

Envelope Number

Name

Address

City Zip Code

Parishioner's Signature Date

In thanksgiving for God's blessings and in support of my parish

Please choose one:

I will give $________ Weekly

I will give $________ Monthly

I will give $________ Yearly

☐ Please take me off your mailing list for envelopes.

☐ Please delete me from your parish.

Reason

To register, please stop by the Parish Office.

STM
STEWARDSHIP PRAYER

O God, our loving creator and giver of all good gifts, bless our parish and the archdiocese, strengthen our faith and grant us the spirit of Christian Stewardship so that we may give generously of our Time, Talent and Treasure to the spreading of your Kingdom here at St. Thomas More and throughout the world. we ask this through our Lord Jesus, your Son, who lives and reigns with you and the Holy Spirit, one God forever and ever. Amen.

Giving Guideline

Yearly Income	Half Tithe — 5%	Tithe —10%
$ 18, 000.00	$ 900.00	$ 1,800.00
24,000.00	1,200.00	2,400.00
30,000.00	1,500.00	3,000.00
36,000.00	1,800.00	3,600.00
42,000.00	2,100.00	4,200.00
48,000.00	2,400.00	4,800.00
60,000.00	3,000.00	6,000.00
75,000.00	3,750.00	7,500.00
100,000.00	5,000.00	10,000.00

Sample: Children's Commitment Card

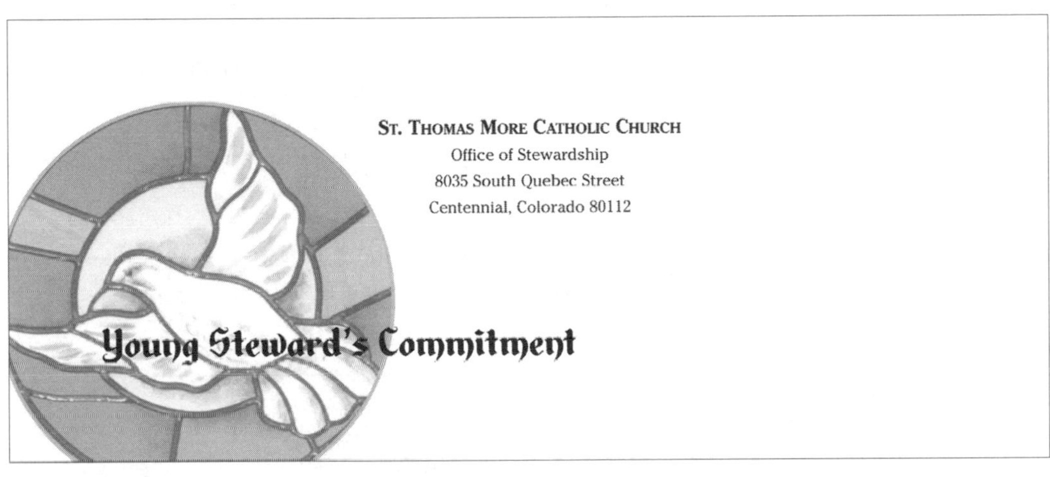

ST. THOMAS MORE CATHOLIC CHURCH
Office of Stewardship
8035 South Quebec Street
Centennial, Colorado 80112
Young Steward's Commitment

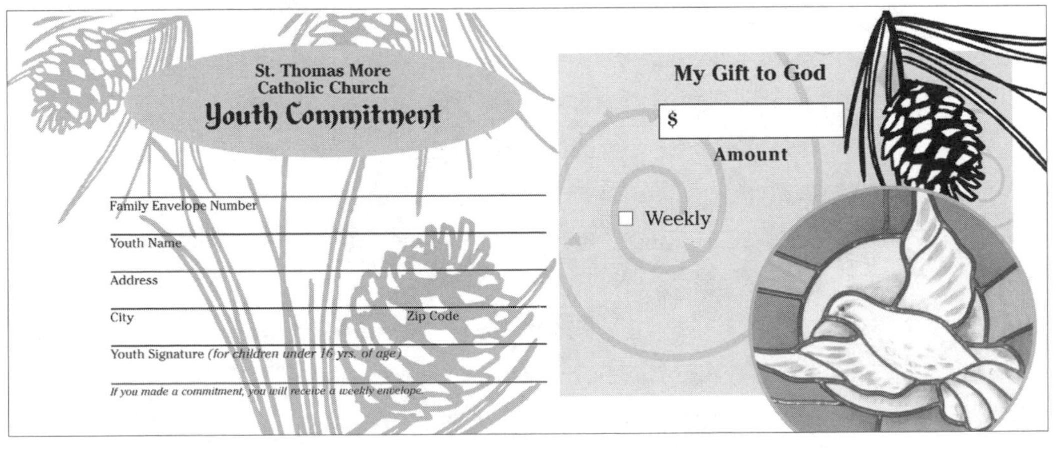
St. Thomas More
Catholic Church
Youth Commitment

Family Envelope Number ____________________

Youth Name ____________________

Address ____________________

City ____________________ Zip Code ____________

Youth Signature *(for children under 16 yrs. of age)* ____________________

If you made a commitment, you will receive a weekly envelope.

My Gift to God

$ ____________

Amount

☐ Weekly

Sample: Children's Commitment Card (continued)

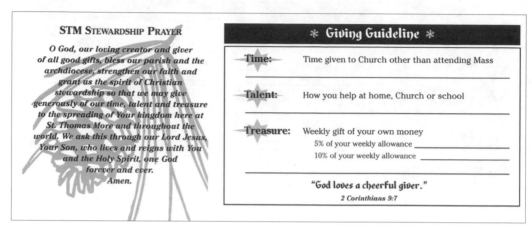

STM STEWARDSHIP PRAYER

O God, our loving creator and giver of all good gifts, bless our parish and the archdiocese, strengthen our faith and grant us the spirit of Christian stewardship so that we may give generously of our time, talent and treasure to the spreading of Your kingdom here at St. Thomas More and throughout the world. We ask this through our Lord Jesus, Your Son, who lives and reigns with You and the Holy Spirit, one God forever and ever. Amen.

✻ Giving Guideline ✻

Time: Time given to Church other than attending Mass

Talent: How you help at home, Church or school

Treasure: Weekly gift of your own money
5% of your weekly allowance ______
10% of your weekly allowance ______

"God loves a cheerful giver."
2 Corinthians 9:7

SAMPLE HOMILY: TREASURE

"The Year 2000, at the End of 'Hearts on Fire'"

There was a very stingy man who wanted to buy his niece a gift for her college graduation. Everything he saw was too expensive. However, he noticed that there was an exquisite vase that was drastically reduced in price because it had a broken handle.

"Aha!" he thought. He had an idea. "I'll have it shipped by mail. My niece will think it got broken in the shipping. But she'll still be impressed by the quality of the gift." He bought the vase and then had the merchant ship it by mail. Well, she was impressed all right. Two weeks later he received a thank you note from the niece, who loved the vase. She added, "It was so nice of you to wrap the broken handle separately."

Today is the twenty-ninth Sunday in ordinary time. This weekend we are concluding our stewardship renewal by making a commitment of our treasure.

Today's Gospel from the tenth chapter of Mark tells us that the Son of Man did not come to be served but to serve, and to give his life as a ransom for many. Yes, Jesus teaches us how to give. He doesn't give second best or halfhearted efforts. He gives his all.

This weekend we are being asked to make a commitment on how much we will give this coming year. Please take into consideration that whatever is given to this parish, part of it is shared with the diocese for the fifth and final year of "Hearts on Fire." Our archbishop is a stewardship bishop. Being a good steward, he is participating in "Hearts on Fire."

In my letter to all of you this week, I quoted from the third chapter of the book of the prophet Malachi where God dares us to tithe. God backs his dare with a promise. "Try me in this, says the LORD of hosts: Shall I not open for you the floodgates of heaven, to pour down blessing upon you without measure?" The phrase "try me in this" is the theme we used in the helpful monthly statement sent to all who make a commitment.

Just as God asks each of us individually to tithe, as a parish we also tithe. That means in addition to the portion we send to the archdiocese we take 10 percent off the top of the collection to be given to the poor and other worthy causes. By giving to the parish your tithe, I will do my best to eliminate other fund raisers that compete for your money. The sixteen mandated second collections will be handled by our tithing ten percent of what is found in the collection.

God does not expect us to gamble in our ways of finding the money to run his church. We find that money by realizing our need to be good stewards and realizing that everything is a gift from God.

Now, I need everyone to cooperate. I'd like each one to take a deep breath and hold it, 1-2-3. Take a breath — hold it. OK, for those that followed, that next breath you took is a gift from God! We on our part are asked to give a gift to him in return. We can give it directly or send it in the mail. Don't expect God to be fooled into believing we are being generous when we are not! Remember the stingy uncle?

Please pick up a commitment card. If you brought yours from home, please check to see that your address is correct. Please mark the amount you will give and the frequency of that amount. We will send you your envelopes each month with a statement that reminds us, "Try me in this." If you have never filled out a commitment card before, today is the day to take the leap of faith. Call to mind the lay witness talk. They did not wait for things to improve. They tithed and then watched things improve in their lives. It is as God says, "Try me in this."

Please come up as you would to Communion, so the commitments can be put on the altar.

Who's in the Pews?

Father Andrew often talks about five types of parishioners usually present at Mass. These types are:

1. Those who have never given anything in the past and probably will never give in the future. Usually these people are angry with the priest, the pope, or the entire Church. Father would often say, "I am praying for you, so that you will begin to forgive and get rid of your anger."
2. Those who throw a dollar or two into the offertory basket, and did not plan their giving to the church.
3. Those who will make a commitment for the first time.
4. Those who will make a tithe for the first time.
5. Those who have been tithers.

Sample Letter: Thank-You Letter

Dear John and Jane,

On the tombstone of her husband's grave, a Southern mountain woman has chiseled in rough uneven letters this epitaph: "He always appreciated."

Surely God appreciates the generosity of his faithful. Thank you for making a commitment to God through St. Thomas More Parish. I truly appreciate your annual stewardship commitment of $_________ of your treasure. Yes, when we encounter the judgment seat of God, we will be judged in terms of stewardship. If we manage our affairs well, then God will say, "Well done, good and faithful servant.... Come receive your master's joy" (Mt 25:21).

Each month, we will send you envelopes so that you will be able to honor the privilege of giving back to God what he has provided you. We will enclose a monthly statement for your convenience so you can better track your pattern of giving.

My ministry as a priest never ceases to be enriched, as I am impressed with the generosity and witness of faithful parishioners like you. May God bless you abundantly, for God cannot be outdone in generosity.

Sincerely in Christ,

Very Rev. Andrew Kemberling, V.F.

Pastor

WEEK 4

Follow-up weekend

The bulletin reminds those who didn't make a commitment to make a commitment *today*. Pencils and commitment cards are placed in the pews to give people another opportunity to make a commitment. At the beginning of Mass the celebrant asks those who have yet to make a commitment to please do so, and to place the cards in the collection basket along with their regular Sunday contribution.

We remind parishioners about making a commitment by an announcement at the beginning of the Mass, such as "Today is the thirtieth Sunday in ordinary time. We continue our commitment renewal weekend. If you have not made a commitment, and would like to do so today, place your commitment envelopes in the offertory basket along with your regular offertory envelope." We also make sure there's an announcement in the bulletin. Those who have not made a commitment are asked to give serious consideration to give back to God in thanksgiving for all the blessings they have received.

WEEK 5

Final active follow-up weekend

It is sufficient to have pulpit and bulletin announcements in connection with the liturgy. Commitment bangtail envelopes are no longer distributed in the pews. This week the commitments have already been entered in the database, making it possible to start sending thank-you letters until everyone who has made a commitment is acknowledged. In addition, a follow-up letter is mailed to those who have not made a commitment. The follow-up phase continues through December.

After this active phase there should be an ongoing follow-up year-round. In the bulletin, there's a stewardship section which includes Scripture passages, prayers for vocations, and various reflections and activities on practicing stewardship as a way of life. Another section, called "Stewardship at Work," lists how St. Thomas More lives out stewardship as a parish. For instance, when the pastor and the stewardship committee approve a donation of such and such amount for a particular mission in the developing countries, that news is published

Sample Letter: Follow-up

Dear John and Jane,

The feelings we feel when we are left out are similar to the feelings of missing someone. The parties involved usually have the same goal. They want to make things right. The person left out wants to be included. Those who notice the absence of the other want to see them involved. The same is true for us at the parish.

Recently, we as a parish made treasure commitments at the weekend Masses. For whatever reason, we missed your commitment. We know that many people travel and are away from the parish. Who knows? You might be feeling left out right about now. Don't worry, we can make things right. Enclosed is a commitment card. Please fill it out or drop it in the basket during the collection the next time you attend Mass.

As good stewards, we are asked to follow the example of Jesus. Since everybody is invited, in conscience, we want everyone to be included. At every Mass, we are asked to make a gift of ourselves when the collection is taken up. Our contribution is taken to the altar. In return we receive from the altar the body and blood of Christ in Communion. Our communion would not be complete without you.

If you have received this letter in error, please accept our apologies. Thank you for your commitment. Please know that God appreciates your generosity as does the Church.

Sincerely in Christ,

Very Rev. Andrew Kemberling, V.F.

Pastor

in the Sunday bulletin. This shows people their money is being used wisely and that the parish is a good steward.

After data entry is complete, a follow-up letter is sent to those who did not make a commitment. As we said earlier, we outsource all our mailings, but this can be done in-house in smaller parishes. If you use the latter, volunteers are more than willing to do this task. Thus you might want to have a mailing committee as part of your time and talent form. The task may include the following:

1. Print name labels
2. Pull out labels for each card responding
3. Place remaining labels on the envelopes to be mailed with a letter from the pastor and another commitment card

In the letter, give parishioners the benefit of the doubt that they were traveling but missed a commitment. Remind them that it would save time and postage if everyone makes a commitment even if it is zero. Therefore, they need to fill out a commitment card *today*.

A Word about Collection Baskets

It is said that on average the giving level is higher when people have to handle the basket instead of having it "waved" in their direction. Commitments are honored when they actually have to hold the basket. By waving the basket in the direction of the non-givers we effectively make it painless for them to be ungrateful. Separate baskets could easily be done here. Two baskets per section would be ideal. One basket would start in the back and one in the front, with them meeting in the middle. Ushers are needed to help pass on the baskets where there are gaps, and to gather the baskets that meet in the middle. Giving will increase.

It is also important within the spirituality of tithing and stewardship to bring the offertory collection up to the altar as a symbol of the sacrificial gift. The baskets are placed near the altar as a reminder that their gift is offered along with the bread and wine.

STEWARDSHIP OF VOCATIONS

"The harvest is abundant, but the laborers are few"(Lk 10:2).

When Father Andrew came to St. Thomas More, the archbishop told him he wanted him to promote vocations. As a result, we decided to include vocations as a part of our stewardship program, seeing it as stewardship issue. We plan one or two weeks in November for vocations, using a "Called by Name" program.

The first weekend, the presiding cleric preaches about his own vocation. The priest then asks parishioners to think of someone whom they think may have a vocation and to plan on nominating that person the next weekend. That means they identify some young man or woman, or even a young person twelve years or older, who could start studying for the priesthood or religious life.

The following week, the priest gives another homily on vocations. As with other stewardship renewals, the priest asks parishioners to pick up a card in the pews and pray the stewardship prayer for vocations.

Since 2001, we have received an average of one hundred fifty names per year. They usually receive at least two letters from Father Andrew. The first letter informs them they have been nominated as a person who might consider a vocation. Some people feel honored by this. The second letter informs them of upcoming diocesan events. We also send a magazine or brochure on vocations.

Father Andrew says, "We ask them to give us a call, but I personally get very few phone calls because they're afraid of what I may say to them. What happens is moms and dads, brothers and sisters, teachers or youth ministers talk about vocations. Vocations then become an open issue. When everyone talks vocation, vocation no longer seems like a dirty word."

Working on vocations takes time; two, three, or four years of this. Imagine, here's an eighteen-year-old boy who's been nominated four times and here comes the fifth nomination. He's wondering what he's going to do with his life, and he thinks, "God is calling me again?" He needs to check it out. He then phones the vocation director. It works!

We actually get the most response for our diaconate program. Many men have been identified as permanent deacons through this program. A particular young man had dropped out of the program and then he got nominated. As a result, he thought of giving it another try and re-entered the formation to be a permanent deacon. He was ordained in 2005. "Then there's another young man who is twenty," said Father Andrew. "I see him once in a while. The last time I saw him I asked if he got my letter. He said he's thinking about it. He recently was instituted as a reader. It's our job to cultivate vocations."

One of the things we started in 2001 was "Clergy and Religious Appreciation Day" on the last weekend before Ash Wednesday. We organize a party for all the religious and clergy, even those who are retired and residing in the parish. The children and youth make posters and write letters to each of our clergy and religious expressing appreciation for their giving their lives to God. This is a good time for them to learn about vocations to the priesthood or to the religious life.

In addition, the parish remembers them at Christmas and Easter, on their birthdays, and on the anniversaries of their ordination or profession of vows. We have a regular column in the Sunday bulletin that lists the birthdays and special days of our clergy and religious so the parish can be aware of those special dates. We remind our parishioners to pray for our clergy, religious, and seminarians, as well as all the seminarians of the Archdiocese of Denver included on this list.

This gives credibility to the men and women who are going to talk about stewardship. It helps people appreciate that when they give their life to the service of the Church, they are not alone. Being called Brother, Sister, or Father clearly denotes that we are family. The church family's role in our vocation is to recognize and remember important anniversaries such as ordinations or professions as you would do with any family member on their special days. By encouraging this, it emphasizes that having a religious vocation is a good thing. When children see parents pick up a card to give to a priest or a nun, they can see the appreciation. They see it's worthwhile to have a vocation and are left with a positive image of the clergy.

We also promote vocations throughout the year especially following the Church liturgical celebrations such as the World Day of Prayer for Vocations as well as the "Pastor's Appreciation Day" in October.

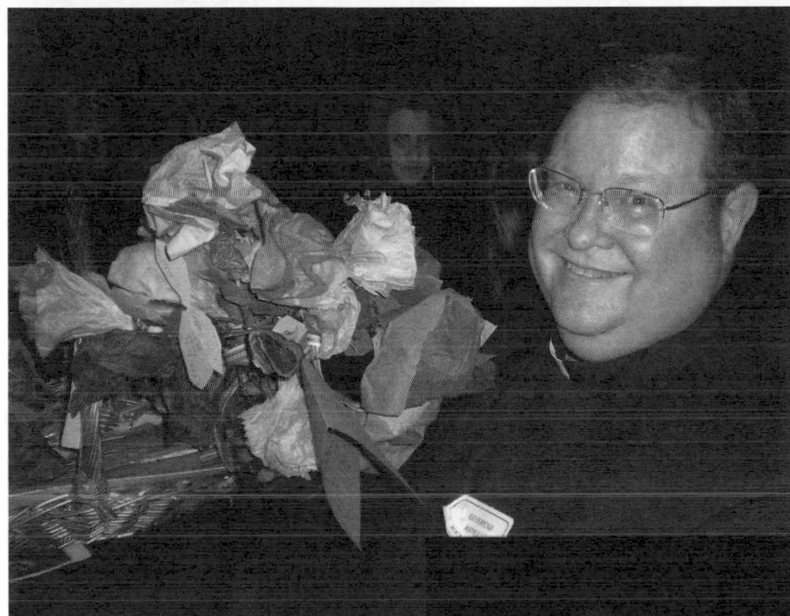

STEWARDSHIP OF THE EARTH

"In the beginning, when God created the heavens and the earth" (Gn 1:1).

"Then, God said, 'Let us make man in our image, after our likeness. Let them have dominion over the fish of the sea, the birds of the air, and the cattle, and over all the wild animals and all the creatures that crawl on the ground'" (Gn 1:26).

"Be fertile and multiply; fill the earth and subdue it. Have dominion over the fish of the sea, the birds of the air, and all the living things that move on the earth" (Gn 1:28).

"The LORD God then took the man and settled him in the garden of Eden, to cultivate and care for it" (Gen 2:15).

"In the beginning God entrusted the earth and its resources to the common stewardship of mankind to take care of them, master them by labor, and enjoy their fruits. The goods of creation are destined for the whole human race. However, the earth is divided up among men to assure the security of their lives, endangered by poverty and threatened by violence. The appropriation of property is legitimate for guaranteeing the freedom and dignity of persons and for helping each of them to meet his basic needs and the needs of those in his charge. It should allow for a natural solidarity to develop between men" (CCC 2402).

The Bible and the *Catechism* clearly show that God gave us the moral responsibility of taking care of the earth. As God's stewards or caretakers of the earth, we are to responsibly use his creation in the service of God and humankind rather than waste, exploit or abuse it.

We are to take care of his creation, not as hired help, but as children of God made in his own image and likeness. In the end we will all be accountable to God for our stewardship of the earth.

Indeed, God has given us the mandate to be his collaborators in the work of creation. In other words we are to work with God in building up the world and, ultimately, the Kingdom of God. As the USCCB said, "Work is a partnership with God — our share in a divine human collaboration in creation. It occupies a central place in our lives as Christian stewards."

Furthermore, in their pastoral letter on stewardship, the bishops said that caring for, and cultivating, the world involves:

1. Joyful appreciation for the God-given beauty and wonder of nature
2. Protection and preservation of the environment, which would be the stewardship of ecological concern
3. Respect for human life — shielding life from threat and assault, doing everything that can be done to enhance the gift and make life flourish
4. Development of this world through noble human effort — physical labor, the trades and professions, the arts and sciences

Here at St. Thomas More we have a very active and visible respect life committee that handles year-round all aspects of the gift of life. As the U.S. bishops said in their pastoral letter on stewardship, we are "collaborators in creation." This means having a "profound reverence for the great gift of life, their own lives and the lives of others, along with the readiness to spend themselves in serving all that preserves and enhances life" (*Stewardship: A Disciple's Response*).

The stewardship of the earth phase at St. Thomas More is dedicated to ecology, "to cultivate and care for" creation (Gn 2:15). As the bishops said, "The stewardship of the world is expressed by jubilant appreciation of nature, whose God-given beauty not even exploitation and abuse have destroyed."

We are still developing this program to include all aspects of cultivating and caring for creation and instilling a deep sense of human

Sample Commitment Card: "Stewardship of the Earth"

Adult Stewardship of Earth Commitment

Please return this copy to the parish.

(Please indicate what you will do to care for God's creation.)

- □ Recycle newspaper, paper, cardboard,glass, tin and aluminum.
- □ Wash clothes in cold water and air dry when possible.
- □ Use old clothes and cloth for cleaning, instead of paper towels.
- □ Reduce use of disposable products, or, if you must buy disposable, buy paper or glass products instead of plastic.
- □ Recycle engine oil.
- □ Invest your money in environmentally and socially conscious businesses.
- □ When purchasing a car, select an energy-efficient model.
- □ Avoid buying aerosol cans and Styrofoam products.
- □ Purchase products made from recycled materials.
- □ Ask candidates for office what they are prepared to do to pursue environmental justice.
- □ Go to the Catholic Relief Services website at www.catholicrelief.org and get involved in an international relief campaign.
- □ Go to the Bread for the World website at www.breadfortheworld.org and help fight world hunger.
- □ Consider purchasing fair-trade coffee. Go to www.cafecampesino.com and learn more about fairly traded, shade grown coffee.

Adult Stewardship of Earth Commitment

Keep this copy for your records.

(Please indicate what you will do to care for God's creation.)

- □ Recycle newspaper, paper, cardboard,glass, tin and aluminum.
- □ Wash clothes in cold water and air dry when possible.
- □ Use old clothes and cloth for cleaning, instead of paper towels.
- □ Reduce use of disposable products, or, if you must buy disposable, buy paper or glass products instead of plastic.
- □ Recycle engine oil.
- □ Invest your money in environmentally and socially conscious businesses.
- □ When purchasing a car, select an energy-efficient model.
- □ Avoid buying aerosol cans and Styrofoam products.
- □ Purchase products made from recycled materials.
- □ Ask candidates for office what they are prepared to do to pursue environmental justice.
- □ Go to the Catholic Relief Services website at www.catholicrelief.org and get involved in an international relief campaign.
- □ Go to the Bread for the World website at www.breadfortheworld.org and help fight world hunger.
- □ Consider purchasing fair-trade coffee. Go to www.cafecampesino.com and learn more about fairly traded, shade grown coffee.

beings as "collaborators in the work of creation, redemption and sanctification" (*Stewardship: A Disciple's Response*). This means including the values of work as well as "a heightened sense of human interdependence and solidarity."

Usually, we celebrate this around Earth Day. We use this time to encourage parishioners to take care of the earth — to plant flowers and trees and to promote the three "R's" (reduce, reuse, and recycle) of stewardship of the earth. We have a recycling program with a company that picks up all our recycling material.

The stewardship of the earth commitment card reflects some ways to care for God's creation at home and abroad, perhaps living a simpler life to do so.

Educational Plans: Year-round Education

Parishes have ample opportunity to educate parishioners regarding stewardship other than during Mass. The regular faith and academic formation classes are excellent ways of promoting stewardship as a way of life. The Sunday bulletin, newsletters, the Web site, e-mails, and other communication tools are often available inexpensively for this purpose. They often reflect stewardship as lived in the parish. There's no need to start everything from scratch. There are currently many sources of educational material on stewardship that come from publishers. It is important to give credit where credit is due. Although we have a communications office, which can easily produce educational materials, we find that it's more effective to use those already available.

For instance, Sharon Hueckel's *Stewardship by the Book* gives weekly Gospel reflections on stewardship. Our Sunday Visitor's *Grace in Action* is published in standard size or in a size that can be inserted in the monthly offertory envelope. If you are a member of the

International Catholic Stewardship Council (ICSC), you will receive many examples of stewardship practices shared by hundreds of parishes.

We use all of the above in our education efforts. Father Andrew also sometimes writes about stewardship in his weekly pastor's message. The Sunday bulletin includes a stewardship section that features some gospel reflection on stewardship; a list of seminarians, clergy and religious to pray for; and a list of charity grants.

In addition, our bimonthly newsletter publishes many accounts of how parishioners live the life of a Christian steward to serve, as reflected in Matthew 5:16: "Just so, your light must shine before others, that they may see your good deeds and glorify your heavenly Father."

Web Sites

WEB SITES ARE POWERFUL TOOLS for timely dissemination of information, stewardship activities and literature. Although the Web site might be an expensive medium to start, it is also a powerful form of evangelization. Many parishioners are now cyberspace savvy and could help with creation, monitoring, and maintenance. With the latest trend on Facebook, Twitter, and YouTube, it might be worthwhile to create a Web site that is interactive.

Newcomers' Welcome Packet

AT ST. THOMAS MORE, NEW parishioners receive a "welcome packet" when they register. It contains a booklet on the parish and a couple of stewardship handbooks — one for adults and another for children and youth — on opportunities to practice stewardship as a way of life. When stewardship forms are returned, the time and talent information is routed to chair people and leaders of committees or ministries so they can contact potential members. Returned commitments are entered immediately into the database and are included in the following month's mailing.

Newcomers' Welcome Dinners

St. Thomas More registers at least twenty-five families a month. After trying several options to welcome newcomers, we finally settled on welcome dinners on the third Saturday of the month. The newcomers' welcome committee organizes and coordinates this monthly event. A simple postcard serves as an invitation. Babysitting is provided. The pastor, staff, and parish leaders usually attend, and the program includes a video presentation on the parish. A question-and-answer period usually ends the evening.

Sample: Newcomers' Welcome Packet

Sample: Sunday Bulletin and Newsletter

STEWARDSHIP *a way of life*

Prayer/Time ◆ Ministry/Talent ◆ Faith ◆ Treasure ◆ Vocations ◆ Earth

Stewardship of the Earth

by Very Rev. Andrew Kemberling, V.F.

The Catholic of the Catholic Church uses the word stewardship in terms of the earth. The Bible tells us that God gave us the earth to use wisely for our generation and the next. We need to use the resources to support human life. If we overuse the resources, we are stealing from the next generation. We need to be good stewards of what God has given to us. We don't own them. We share them with the next generation. This means it is our responsibility to steward it, to use and create resources that are renewable. It's our responsibility to make sure that those resources are available to them. We need to do what we can to renew resources, rather than waste them. Like it or not, we are in it together when it comes to stewardship issues. If we inherit problems caused by other people, our job is to be responsible in lessening the harm that any problem has caused in the world – pollution or the misuse of resources and environmental damage. We need to take care of the world that God has given to us to take care of for the next generation.

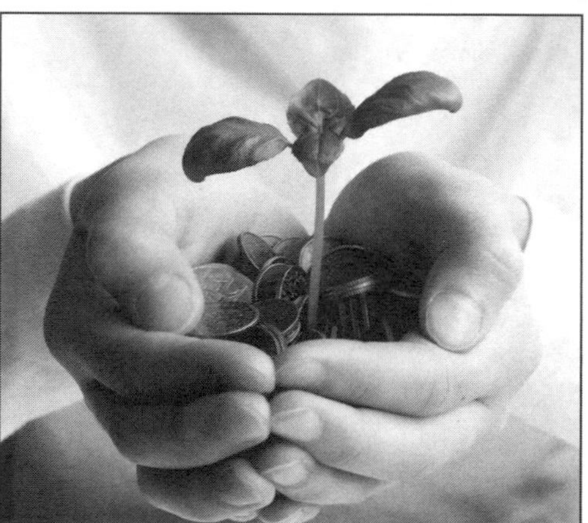

Design: Liturgical Publications Inc. Photography from bigstockphoto.com.

At St. Thomas More we encourage our people to thank God for the resources that they have received from God, and to remember the three R's – reduce, reuse and recycle. For instance, we ask our people to wash their clothes in cold water and to air dry if possible. We ask them to purchase products made from recycled products and to recycle engine oil.

The secular view of "going green" is actually compatible with our Spirituality of Stewardship of the Earth. The problem is some of the secular movements see humanity as the disease on the earth. We do not agree. God has given us dominion over the earth, but we have to be responsible. When it comes to animals, animals don't have rights. God did not give rights to animals. We are not just an animal among animals. We are humans and we have rights that have been given to us by God. Humans have primacy over animals. Human beings want to give animals rights. That is an offense to God. When we're good stewards of animals, we are responsible for them. We have to be good stewards as to how animals are used for meat, for material goods such as leather and clothing. We have to do it in a way that is responsible and not cruel and allows for future generations to continue using these animals for the benefit of humanity.

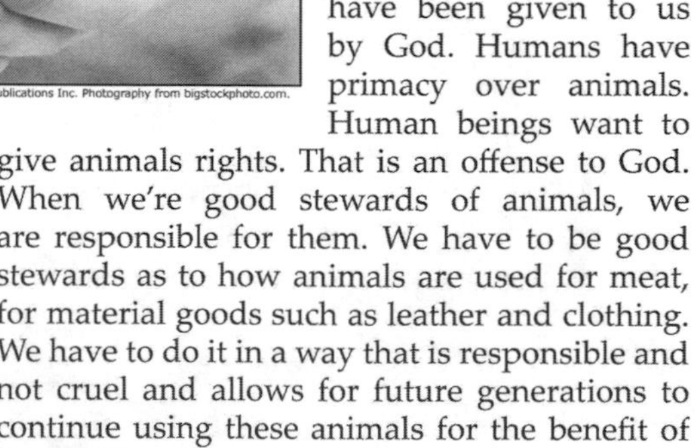

We are not only responsible for the earth, we are accountable for it.

MORE Informed 36

July 26, 2009, Seventeenth Sunday of Ordinary Time

Stewardship

prayer/time talent/ministry faith treasure vocations earth

Stewardship... A Way of Life

"A generous man will prosper; he who refreshes others will himself be refreshed." Proverbs:11:25

Stewardship of Vocations

Daily Prayer Intentions for Vocations Archdiocese of Denver and in celebration of the Year for Priests

July and August

27. Rev. Bernard Schmitz
    Maurizio Pietrolungo
28. Rev. Blaine Burkey, O.F.M. Cap.
    Nicholas Larkin
    (SJV College Seminary, St. Paul, MN)
29. Rev. Brian Morrow
    Joseph Foss
30. Rev. Carlos Bello
    Sr. Kristina McBride
    (Abbey of St. Walburga)
31. Rev. Charles Albanese, O.C.S.O.
    Dcn. Tim Kenny *•
    ReJune Cytaki
    (Sisters of Charity of Leavenworth)
1. Vocations to the priesthood
    Ryan Balke
    (SJV College Seminary, St. Paul, MN)
2. Rev. Charles Anedo
    Elias Espinoza

** Designates Birthday*
• Designates Parishioner

Prayer Chalice for Vocations

August Parishioners

August 2-8: Maggie Donnegan
August 9-15: Brett & Maria Ammerman
August 16-22: Jean Finegan
August 23-29: Tim & Sheri Jeske

Please pray for an increase in vocations to the priesthood and religious life.

We welcome our newest Parishioners

Edie Aberle
Jack & Ann Anderson
Brooke Barickman
Todd & Michele Bradbury & Family
Chris & Ellen Case & Family
Adam Gerk
Holly Green
Bill & Maribeth Hanzlik
Ryan & Nikki Schroeder
Susan Tomazin

Stewardship of Treasure at Work

On behalf of our parishioners, a donation was made of:

$365 Catholic Biblical School for tuition and book financial assistance
$800 Endow to support Catholic professional women's programs
$5,000 Centro San Juan Diego to support educational services

Only $9,000 To Go!

Can you help complete the $50,000 Matching Gift Fund? We are thankful for the 6 new pledges totalling $7,000! We are only $9,000 away from matching the $50,000. The date was extended to July 31 to accommodate those of you that were on vacation.

Please consider donating to Phase 2 and help finish our remodel. Phase 2 includes a new rectory for our current and future priests, remodeling of the church gym, the Padre, replacing the equipment in the Padre kitchen and updating the Youth Center for our high school students. *If you have any questions, please contact Mila Glodava at 303-221-9240*

Our Jubilee Vision Phase 2

as of July 20, 2009

We thank the 1109 families who have pledged for Phase 2.

Goal: $5,000,000
Pledges to Date: $2,972,000
Pledges Still Needed: $2,028,000

A wedding lasts just a day, but a marriage lasts a lifetime.

Mike and Sandi Green ~ 40 years

Please e-mail Maryanne Carter at maryannec@stthomasmore.org two weeks before your anniversary date.

Retrouvaille

Retrouvaille is a program for married couples that feel bored, frustrated, or angry in their marriage. Most don't know how to change the situation or even communicate with their spouse. This program has helped couples experiencing marital difficulty at all levels including disillusionment and deep misery.

For confidential information or to register for the September 25-27 program, please call Bill and Arlene Newlin at 1-800-470 2230 or visit www.retrouvaille.org.

www.stthomasmore.org *St. Thomas More Catholic Church, Centennial, CO* 5

Program and Ministries Directory

THIS IS A VALUABLE TOOL to distribute to inform parishioners of the many opportunities available in the parish to give of their time and talent. This booklet should include pertinent information about the parish such as its mission, goals, and objectives as well as information on staff and parish leaders who those interested in any given program might want to contact. It also contains a description of each program and ministry available in the parish as well as information on meetings and activities associated with the program or ministry.

Kiosk

A PARISH THE SIZE OF ST. Thomas More can be intimidating. Therefore, we have installed a kiosk (a computer) which lists all activities of the parish, their locations, and map to get there. This kiosk may also play videos on how stewardship is lived in the parish.

Sunday Bulletin and Newsletter

THE SUNDAY BULLETIN AND A regular newsletter are important sources of information and media on stewardship education. At St. Thomas More we have a section or a page on stewardship activities and education. All of our phases of stewardship are reflected on most of the pages of the Sunday Bulletin. Thus our Stewardship of Prayer message involves praying for the sick, the deceased, and other special intentions. The Stewardship of Faith involves all faith and academic formation for the young and old. On the Stewardship of Vocations page we pray for our clergy, religious, and seminarians as well as for our families and marriages. The bi-monthly newsletter at St. Thomas More is mailed to all registered parishioners. It is a great tool for evangelization and a valuable tool to showcase how stewardship is lived in the parish. The articles, which are written by a host of volunteer writers and edited by staff and a couple of volunteer editors, can be a source of inspiration for inactive parishioners to participate in parish life and for the homebound to feel connected to the parish.

Conclusion

In this section, we attempted to give you a model that has worked for us over the years. We hope that you have identified some practices that may work for you and your parish. As we mentioned earlier, the model can easily be adapted to fit the style and the culture of any parish. You and your parish will have to determine what will and will not work for you.

Certainly some would not work for you. Remember, copying another parish's program in the early years of our program, we asked our parishioners to make a commitment of their time, talent, and treasure all at one time. It did not work for us. So we had to try other ways of doing things. Do not be afraid to change and to find out what is the right program for your parish.

More importantly, remember that stewardship is only a means to an end. It is only a means to evangelization. Once again, in the words of the U.S bishops: "The practice of authentic stewardship inevitably leads to evangelization."

NOTES, REFLECTIONS, & POINTS TO REMEMBER

For Part V: Six-Phase Program of Stewardship

NOTES, REFLECTIONS, & POINTS TO REMEMBER

For Part V: Six-Phase Program of Stewardship

NOTES, REFLECTIONS, & POINTS TO REMEMBER

For Part V: Six-Phase Program of Stewardship

APPENDIX 1

Sample Lay Witness Talks

"I CAN'T BELIEVE I WAITED SO LONG TO BEGIN TITHING!"

By Jean Harper

It seemed like I never had any money to spare whenever the collection basket came around at church. Selfishness was not the reason my purse remained closed, but as a young college student on a limited income, I had barely enough cash to cover minimal necessities. Besides, at that time in my life I had exciting goals and aspirations that seemed to take up all my energy and attention.

Ever since I was a little girl I had wanted to be an airline pilot, and all along I knew it would take a lot of education and flying experience. So there I was, fifteen years later, a licensed pilot and flight instructor studying toward my aviation degree. But the various part-time piloting jobs I held paid very poorly, and after graduation, I accepted a position with an aircraft insurance company because I needed more than just a subsistence income.

Shortly after I moved to my new job in Chicago, I went to visit my younger sister. She had recently begun working as a secretary for a salary of four hundred dollars a month.

"Helen," I said, "how can you live on that?" She smiled and told me that she was not only getting by — she was *tithing* on her income! I was shocked and my face must have shown it. She quickly explained that she had recently experienced a great spiritual rebirth, and dedicating her life entirely to Christ included following the biblical commands regarding tithing — the giving of ten percent of one's income to the Church.

"But... even before you pay your bills and buy food?" Certainly her gesture reflected noble intentions, but I thought it was foolhardy and financially irresponsible.

"Oh, that's not how I see it," she said.

Pulling out her Bible she read a passage from Malachi about the Lord opening up the windows of heaven and pouring out blessings on his followers who offered their tithes — the first and the best of everything they had — to him.

I did not find this very convincing, and saw little evidence of abundance in her lifestyle and tiny efficiency apartment. I felt troubled during the drive back to Chicago. Upon returning home, I found that a pilot's position was immediately available at O'Hare Field — and I gladly quit my insurance job to take it. Unfortunately, the flying paid only four hundred dollars a month! One year later, my poor eating habits and too-long days caught up with me and I hit rock bottom physically and financially. I had no more credit and no money to pay my bills. I felt like a hypocrite considering prayer as a last resort — but where else could I turn?

My reply came quickly and with unmistakable clarity.

"Are you ready to follow me now?"

For a moment, I was confused by God's gentle query until I remembered my sister gladly tithing on her small income. That was when I realized with great shame that I had been putting God in last place in my life — after personal ambition, earthly goals, and real and imagined responsibilities. Somehow I sensed that he wanted the best for me as much as I did, but there was something standing in his way — me.

"OK, Lord," I said, "you know how broke I am but if you will help me find a job I can live on, I promise I'll do things your way — and I'll start by tithing."

It might sound a little unbelievable if I say that everything took a turn for the better from that day on — but that's exactly what happened. In less than a week, I was hired by an air freight company in Memphis to fly DC-3s, and for once I actually had enough money to live on. The job was challenging and enjoyable, the employees and other pilots treated me like family, and I met a wonderful man whom I got to know and eventually fell in love with. And before that year had ended, I got three major airline interviews and was hired as a pilot by United Airlines. Three years later (after all my old bills were paid!) my boyfriend Victor and I were married. Now that is what I call a pouring out of blessings!

Some amazing things happened as a result of tithing — the first being similar to the miracle of the loaves and fishes. It seemed that once the tithe had been paid, there was always enough money left over for everything we needed —and that held true even during the six months that Vic and I were laid off from our jobs. It seemed that the more we gave, the more would come our way in both material and spiritual gifts. The initial nervousness of giving (actually a lack of faith that God would really provide) was quickly replaced by joy and trust in his endless bounty. Money itself became less and less important as our attention and interest was redirected to God, and as our willingness to let him lead our lives completely grew stronger.

My sister Helen — the one whose fine example of giving I had found so disturbing — now has three children and they live in a large home west of Chicago. She told me that she couldn't ever remember a time when there hadn't been enough. Now that I have experienced the gracious abundance God is waiting to pour out for those who love and trust him — I can't believe I waited so long to begin tithing!

THERE'S MORE TO LIFE THAN BEING A CPA

By Steve Corder and his daughter, Stephanie

Steve

Thank you, Father. Hello, everyone. My name is Steve Corder and this is my daughter, Stephanie. My family was asked a short time ago by Father Andrew and Mila to speak at the Masses this weekend about stewardship. At first, I admit, I was very hesitant to speak as I know of other more deserving people who do much more than I do here at St. Thomas More Parish. However, after reflecting on Father and Mila's request I realized what an opportunity this would be for me to share with others my enjoyable experiences that have resulted from volunteering here at the church and to lay witness to what Christ has meant in my life.

First of all, I have been a parishioner here since 1975 and was always either too afraid, or lazy, or naïve to get involved at my parish. I also thought that being a CPA, I already had a pretty exciting and fulfilling life! It was not until 1991 — some sixteen years after joining the parish — that I finally began sharing my time at STM. And it all began with the encouragement of a fellow parishioner and dear friend of mine, Don Smith, who suggested I help out with the Cadillac raffle committee. The experience was personally rewarding in that I made a few new friends, learned much more about the parish, and (most importantly) I had fun (even if I didn't win the Cadillac that night!). This big parish of mine soon became less intimidating and more spiritually fulfilling. I learned that sharing Mass with people who I know is much more satisfying, especially compared to my old habit of only coming to STM for Mass, sitting in the last pew, and then immediately leaving Mass after having received Communion.

Well, after my first volunteer experience I decided I could, and even wanted to, do more so I soon joined the lector ministry, then the finance council, and eventually some other STM school committees. I even learned to regularly donate blood, thanks to the Booth family! Because of volunteering here at STM, I have been truly blessed. For example, my wife, Pat, and I were able to see the pope twice during World Youth Day, I have been able to work side by side with numerous talented and devoted Catholics (including my favorite priest, Father Andrew), and to see first hand, the Holy Spirit at work. And if you doubt me about feeling the Holy Spirit's presence, just listen to the poignant stories of volunteers who deliver angel tree Christmas gifts to the families of prisoners.

You see, I have also learned that (incredibly enough) there is more to life than just being a CPA!

My family has also heard the calling to be more involved at our parish. For example, Pat helps head up the angel tree project, assists in the Helping Hands program, and even finds time for Bible study each week at the parish. Now Stephanie is going to tell you about some of her volunteer experiences.

Stephanie

Hello, my name is Stephanie Corder and I am a freshman at Arapahoe High School. I began volunteering at church in fourth grade when I became an altar server. Serving allowed me to better understand the Mass and to be able to work closely with my favorite priest, Father Andrew. After starting with altar serving, I learned to enjoy donating my time at the parish by joining the STM School Beta Club and student council, and now I have fun being involved in youth group, youth choir and Breakaway. There are many opportunities to volunteer here at STM even as young as I am. I have learned that just going to school and spending time with my friends and family is important, but not enough. I also need to spend time being with and helping others.

Steve

Perhaps the most meaningful aspect of volunteering my time and talent at church has been strengthening my faith life. Not only do I feel a closer relationship with God, I also see my family's spiritual life getting stronger.

I now invite you to join me and all the other members of our parish to become a volunteer today by completing the forms in the pew. If you have completed the form sent to you in the mail, please feel free to place your completed form in the large brown basket in front of the altar. This act symbolizes your offering of your gifts of time and talent to the Lord. Those who did not get a chance to complete it ahead of time, please take the time to do it now.

One final thought about volunteering: If I can do it, you can do it!

"TITHING: CHOOSING GOD'S PLAN OVER THE WORLD'S PLAN"

By Rodge and Colleen Goffredi

Rodge

A few weeks ago, John Longo talked to us about sharing our time and talent in some type of ministry in our church. He challenged us to live our faith by giving our time in some apostolic way and using our God-given talents to help and to serve God's people. Then last week, Father Solan began challenging us to look at our treasure — our money — and he challenged us to give out of love so we can build

God's kingdom here on earth. Today, Colleen and I have been asked to continue talking about stewardship of our treasure and about how much of it we give back to the One who has given us everything.

Colleen

About thirteen years ago, I heard at Mass about how we can give back to God by tithing (giving ten percent of our gross income). Five percent would go to our parish collection and the other five percent would be divided among other charities and ministries. I was intrigued by this idea, but I thought that Rodge would never go for it. He had always seemed so stingy — I mean thrifty — with our money. Anyway, he was out of town at the time, and I hesitated to bring it up when he got home. But when I did, he actually agreed. It was so amazing to me that he also thought we should tithe, and I knew it was the Holy Spirit confirming that this is what we should do. Ever since then, we've been giving back five percent of our income to St. Thomas More. We've seen how our gifts have helped build our church and evangelization center, have helped educate the children of the parish in the Catholic faith, and have supported various other programs in the parish.

And with the other five percent, we've been able to give regularly to the homeless and hungry at the Samaritan House. We've given to Mary's Choice, a shelter for young pregnant women who refuse to have an abortion and need a home. We've regularly sent funds to help train young Filipino seminarians for the priesthood. Out of the five percent, we also pledge to the archbishop's annual campaign. Each month, we sit down and decide how God is calling us to help his people, and it's kind of fun deciding where our gifts will go.

Rodge

Once when we had some extra income, we took the kids shopping and spent the tithed portion for items to give to the Samaritan House. Our whole family then went down there for a tour and to drop off what we had purchased. Our kids have also pitched in at Christmas time to purchase cardigans for senior citizens living at Mullen Home, and they've helped to serve meals to the needy on Thanksgiving day.

I think this gives our children a sense of gratitude for the home that we have, and their need to give to those who have less than they have.

Giving significantly to various charities fills us with joy and a sense of self-worth. But the joy of giving is only half the story. Ever since we started tithing, God has blessed us in more ways than we could ever tell. This is because, as you've heard before, God will not be outdone in generosity. He has given back to us a hundredfold. We have good health; our marriage is strong; our relationships with our parents and children are good — well most of the time; my job is great, with a super boss and coworkers. And we've been able to take care of our needs financially.

Colleen

God has given us so much. He has provided all that we need for our family, even during a time of unemployment. He also gave our children the luxury of a parent at home full-time.

Before we began tithing, we just put in a few dollars each week during the collection. Looking back on that time, we see us with our hands clenched tightly around our money, not really willing to share what we had, what God had given to us. When he went to bless us with extra graces, he couldn't put them into our hands — they were closed.

But now, we are opening our hands to give our treasure back to him by helping others, and because our hands are open in giving, God can put all sorts of blessings back in them. As the prophet Malachi wrote: "Bring the whole tithe into the storehouse, that there may be food in my house, and try me in this, says the LORD of hosts: shall I not open for you the floodgates of heaven, to pour down blessing upon you without measure?"

The first time I sat down to pay our bills and wrote out the tithing checks first, it seemed like such a large amount, I almost didn't want to let it go. Now, when I pay the bills, it wouldn't feel right if I *didn't* give it away. I write out the tithing checks first, because God deserves the first fruits, not the leftovers. That's what we were doing before we started tithing: throwing the few dollars we had left into the basket — giving God the dregs after we had spent everything else on us.

We have encouraged our children to tithe as well. When our older girls put ten percent of their paychecks in the collection basket, I am delighted this value has been passed down to the next generation. I have even seen our kids tithe from their birthday money.

Rodge

What are the obstacles to practicing stewardship as a way of life? Well, the first one may be how we think about "being successful." After watching television and reading newspapers and magazines, it's easy to buy into the mind-set that to be successful we have to own new and expensive cars, a large and costly house, belong to certain clubs, and we have to have lots of nice clothes and furniture. Well, what do you think would impress God more, buying a new sport utility vehicle or helping the homeless have a bed to sleep in? Having an expensive home or feeding the needy? Having one-hundred-twenty-five dollar tennis shoes to wear, or helping take care of elderly priests and nuns?

We have only sixty, seventy, maybe eighty years in this life — less than a blink of an eye compared to the eternity that awaits us after we die. The decisions we make now determine whether we spend that eternity with, or without, God. When we pass on and our particular day of judgment comes, what questions will we be asked? We're pretty sure that we're not going to be asked "What kind of car did we drive?" or "What kind of house did we have?" Instead, we think we're only going to be asked one question: "How much did we love?"

In God's plan, the definition of success is loving God, our family, and our fellow brothers and sisters as much as we can. A large part of that love is using what God has given us, our time, talents, and treasure, to help further his works on earth.

Colleen

Another obstacle is thinking about how much money ten percent of our gross income is — it's a lot. When you write a check out to charity, it's a big check! You may think to yourselves that you can't possibly afford that. Well, we can assure you that you can, because God will not be outdone in generosity. I can assure you that no one in our family has ever gone without three meals a day; we have a nice home, and we've taken our kids on wonderful vacations.

Honestly, there may be some areas in your present lifestyle that you will have to change once you start practicing stewardship as a way of life. You might have to brown bag it once in a while instead of going out to lunch. You might get a different car model, rather than the most expensive one. You alone can decide what your lifestyle changes will be, but God will bless you in many other ways.

Rodge

Being a Catholic Christian is much more than just showing up for Mass once a week. It is a lifestyle, it is a decision. It also means being good stewards of all that God has given, of our time, talents, and treasure.

Spend some time thinking about the gifts God has given you and how you can follow his example by giving some of your treasure to others. Listen to the Holy Spirit, that little voice that whispers to you when you least expect it. Let the Spirit guide you as you reflect on how you will begin to practice stewardship as a way of life. Let this year, the year of the Holy Spirit, be the year you take the plunge — the year that you open your hands to give more than you have ever before, and also be ready to receive more than you ever thought possible!

"YOU CAN GIVE OF YOUR TIME AND TALENT IN MANY WAYS"

By John and Laurie Christian

Laurie

Six and a half years ago I was discussing with a business associate how John and I were struggling with our faith. I was worried about John returning to his Catholic roots and mentioned how I had no intention of ever raising our children Catholic let alone becoming one myself. She listened to my dilemma and reached into her desk to hand me a tape. She said it might be interesting for me to listen to. It took me several weeks to get around to listening to it and to my surprise it was a tape of Scott Hahn's conversion story.

There is a long story between my listening to that tape and us standing here before you which we don't have enough time to cover. I think, though, that it is an example of stewardship in its simplest form. I didn't even know this woman was Catholic, but she started us on a path that led us to come together in our faith. You can give of your time and talent in many ways. This woman has no idea of the impact she eventually had on our lives nor does she know how many more people she has touched through us. This weekend the Church is asking all of us to consider what we might give in time and talent. The Church offers many different ways to do this which you can see at the fair just outside the doors.

John

Two of the ways we've shared our time and talent over the last couple of years is in the hospital Eucharistic ministry and in spending an hour a week in the adoration chapel. In the hospital ministry, I take Communion to Catholics at Swedish Hospital one day a month. I've sometimes pondered how absurd it seems that God, the all-powerful, all-knowing creator of the universe, makes use of a little, insignificant pip-squeak like me to deliver himself to these poor sick and injured people. I am always deeply touched by how grateful most of them are to receive him in Holy Eucharist, compared to how at times a lot of us take it for granted. This is one ministry where I always feel that I receive much more than I give.

Another ministry with that same benefit is adoration. Think about it: How often can you go sit down for an hour with the mayor, the governor, the president, or even our very own parish administrator? Yet in the adoration chapel, that same all-powerful, all-knowing creator of the universe waits patiently for us to come to him, and spend just one hour with him.

I usually say the rosary during the hour, and since it is on Friday night, I almost always say the sorrowful mysteries. While meditating on these mysteries a few weeks ago, it suddenly struck me, more forcefully than it ever had before, what Christ did for all of us on the cross, dying for us, paying the price for our sins (another thing we more often than not take for granted). We've all probably seen a movie or cartoon where someone saves somebody's life, and the person saved is so grateful that they will do anything for the other person. Usually the saved is so anxious to help out and do good things for the saver that they become almost an annoying pest. I wondered, am I making a pest of myself with God? How many of us are making a pest of ourselves with God?

Well here's your chance to make a pest of yourself with God. Take out the forms in the pews and...

APPENDIX 2

Sample Stewardship Homilies

By Father Andrew Kemberling

"A COMMITMENT OF LOVE"

Two young men were sharing their concerns about marriage. The first said, "You know, it's odd — but now that I am engaged I'm starting to get nervous about being married!" The other said, "I know what you are thinking. It's only natural to be nervous. Marriage is a big commitment. Seven or eight years can be a long time!"

Those who are married can laugh at the short-sightedness of such a dialogue. Marriage means making a commitment and sticking to it. Sadly, many marriages today only last a little over a handful of years. When we allow our commitment to be conditional, we devalue the meaning of love. When couples stop giving of themselves, their marriage suffers. The sacrament of marriage means so much to all of us. Sadly, the sacrament of marriage loses it meaning when we put conditions on how and when we love. Stewardship requires a commitment of love, as does marriage. Love and charity are, after all, the same idea. Both require the giving of oneself. Both require a commitment.

At St. Thomas More we have entered our season of stewardship renewal. I am thankful for the commitments people have made in our renewal of time and talent. Now in the month of October, we are asking parishioners to make a commitment of their treasure.

The stewardship and communication commission has chosen as their objective to increase the number of families making a treasure commitment. Currently, out of 5,946 registered families, only 1,882 have filled out a treasure commitment. That means that only thirty-one percent of our parish families are honoring a treasure commitment in thanksgiving for what God has done. There are however, 3,325 families with a gift record to date. That means that fifty-six percent of our parish families are giving. These numbers can be higher.

Just as the sacrament of marriage suffers when we put conditions on how and when we love, the same is true when we put conditions on our financial giving to God and his Church. One of the reasons why people don't give to the Church is because they are angry and hurt. I pray that God will heal their hurt and calm their anger. When married people are angry and hurt they don't stop loving each other. They continue to give even if it hurts. They know that the suffering they feel purifies their marriage. They know that acceptance and forgiveness triumphs over anger and resentment. Love never fails.

I believe the same is true in a parish. When parishioners are angry and hurt because of the parish, they cannot stop loving the Church. Some try to punish the Church by not giving. That only hurts them and others. Resentments like these are like taking poison and expecting the other person to die.

Thankfully, there are others who allow love to never fail. They give even if it hurts because they know that in suffering they are purified. They know from their marriages that acceptance and forgiveness triumph over anger and resentment. I call upon those who know the deeper of meaning of charity, because of their marriage, to set an example to the rest of the parish and make a stewardship commitment of their treasure. They know what it means to make a commitment and stick to it.

Please make a stewardship commitment of your treasure this year, especially those who have not made one before. Our parish can do better than thirty-one percent participation. I am sure there are many good marriages in our parish that can set an example and give to God and his Church through a commitment of their treasure.

Some people do not give because they don't think that the parish needs it. Some say that we are a rich parish. I like to describe ourselves as a generous parish. We tithe on the tithe, on the Sunday offerings, and we are making efforts to expand our giving to exceed our tithe.

Once we realize our obligation to give out of love, we will not be tricked into making excuses not to give. If, as parishioners, we are looking for excuses not to give, the devil will tempt us with hundreds of reasons. All of these will be filled with logical reasons to withhold funding, all filled with righteousness, and all of them wrong. Each of them will have a trapdoor that causes us to fall. Don't fall for the tricks the devil can play when it comes to our contributions. It's a trick. Don't fall for it. Please learn we have a need to give and have an obligation to give.

Does the parish have needs? Oh, indeed we do. The need to increase our collections is great. Our parish has felt the financial downturn of our economy but we weathered it because our parishioners have embraced their need to give. We as a parish have been setting an example of good stewardship by paying our staff living wages. Justice demands this before we begin to tithe. We have met this obligation, but rising health-care costs have put greater demands upon our operating budget. We did not want to lay off employees. So we instituted cuts to budgets across the board.

If your particular area got cut, please don't try and retaliate by not giving. It's a trick with which the devil loves to tempt us good Catholics. The temptation of righteous anger is a trap that hurts us and hurts others. We need all parishioners to contribute especially if they benefit from the parish ministries. Most of us benefit from the evangelization center, the catacombs, and the parish school buildings. These buildings are not paid off yet. We are counting on the Sunday collection to make the interest and principal payments on these loans. Yes, we have needs, but don't ever forget our need to give.

Stewardship requires a commitment as does marriage. Just as marriages fail when conditions are put on love, so too does the parish get hurt when people put conditions upon their financial giving. As we continue our stewardship renewal of treasure, I hope that everyone makes a treasure commitment this year. I certainly hope that we surpass the thirty-one percent level that we are at now.

I am particularly counting upon our married people, as those who know the meaning of love, to demonstrate their capacity to love by committing to the same kind of love for God and his Church. Let's not be tricked with self-righteous excuses but be inspired to accept humbly our need to give. I invite everyone to pray for those who feel hurt and angry. Let us pray that God will let them know that acceptance and forgiveness triumphs over anger and resentments. Love never fails. I pray that our financial commitment to God will lead us to his all-powerful love.

People will then want to know: "How do I take these four values of identity, trust, gratitude, and love, pull them all together, and make it a spirituality within my parish?

HOMILY ONE ON TIME

Please pray together with me: "Glory be to the Father and to the Son and to the Holy Spirit, as it was in the beginning is now and ever shall be world without end. Amen."

This prayer, which is quite familiar, speaks about the central biblical image of God's timelessness. The Bible repeatedly reminds us that there is no time for God. "As it was in the beginning, is now and ever shall be world without end. Amen."

Today, we begin our stewardship renewal of time, talent, and treasure. Some places prefer to promote stewardship and all they talk about is treasure, treasure, treasure. Stewardship is first and foremost a *spirituality*. Today we will only talk about time. Next week we will talk about talent and in October we will talk about treasure.

Now let's talk about time. As we pray the Glory Be, we say, "world without end." Yes, God's "world" is not like our world. Time is a creation of God, a creation for our world. Perhaps time has been created solely for our human benefit, which is a staggering thought in the light of the millions, the billions, of years that have passed before our human experience. Perhaps so much time was created so the phrase "in the fullness of time, God sent his only son to be our Redeemer" would take on an even greater meaning in comparison to the vast amount of time that has passed, compared to the relatively short time since Christ first came. "This is the time of fulfillment; the kingdom of God is at hand."

Yes, time is a gift from God — a gift to be used in this world because it is not used in the next. I suspect that absence makes the heart grow fonder. We, in the timelessness of eternity, will be able to look back at how we *spent* our time and how we *prioritized* our time. When we no longer have it, we will realize the profound gift that time was for us. We will then relish the fact that we "made time" for God.

In the beginning, God took six days to create and on the seventh day he rested. As a reminder, these are divine days, not earth days. The "earth day" is created on the fourth day, when God creates the sun and the moon. An earth day is marked by our relation to the sun. Whatever these divine days mean to God, who has no time, he took the seventh day and made it holy.

We, too, in imitation of God, have seven days in our week. Sunday is our day set aside for rest, in imitation of God. Six of these days may be considered ours but Sunday belongs to God. That's why it's called the Lord's Day. The main reason for the prohibition of work is so we will have the time to pray. Remember the days when to miss Mass on Sunday was a sin? It still is! Sunday is our primary day to pray.

The good steward knows that the portion given back is called a tithe. The first ten percent is given back to God. What does that mean in relation to time? How do we tithe our time? I recommend that an important part of stewardship spirituality is to tithe the time of one day, one day a week. The best day is the Lord's Day, Sunday. What does that mean? Well, in a twenty-four-hour day broken down into minutes, a tithe of time is two hours and twenty-four minutes. We already spend one hour at Mass. That leaves another hour and twenty-four minutes that can be broken up in the morning, or in the evening. Perhaps we could pray a family rosary, or spend an hour in front of the Blessed Sacrament in our twenty-four-hour adoration chapel.

If I asked us to take two hours and twenty-four minutes watching television, I think few would find it difficult (depending upon which channel we have to watch). Can't we spend this much time in prayer as a gift back to God in thanksgiving for what God has given us?

Please pick up a card. We are all going to pray the prayer on the back of the card.

Today's responsorial psalm is a prayer — a prayer in time of need, a psalm paired up with today's first reading from the thirty-fifth chapter of the book of the prophet Jeremiah, who was in trouble and may have prayed this very prayer.

Now turn the card over and look at the various ways in which we can pray privately and publicly. Please make a commitment to pray as a gift back to God.

HOMILY TWO ON TIME

During the lunch hour, the president of a large factory wanted to talk to his company's manager about an urgent matter, but the manager's secretary said, "He is in conference, as he is every day at this time."

"But," said the impatient official, "tell him the president wants to see him." She firmly replied, "I have strict orders not to disturb him when he is in conference."

Angrily he brushed the secretary aside and opened the door to the manager's private office. After one quick look, he backed out, gently shut the door, and said, "I'm sorry, I didn't understand. Is this a daily occurrence?"

"Yes. Every day he spends fifteen minutes in such a conference."

The president had found the manager on his knees before an open Bible. You see, his fifteen-minute daily conference was with God.

Today is the Twentieth Sunday in Ordinary Time. In today's second reading from the fifth chapter of Paul's letter to the Ephesians, we hear that we should address one another in "psalms and hymns and spiritual songs, singing and playing to the Lord in our hearts, giving thanks always and for everything, in the name of our Lord Jesus Christ to God the Father." Just as the factory manager scheduled time with God each day, we are asked in today's reading to take the time to pray.

This fits in nicely with the fact that our parish, this weekend and next, is focusing upon our stewardship renewal of time and talent. Our renewal of treasure will happen in October.

Stewardship is first and foremost a spirituality. It is not a gimmick to get more volunteers and to raise the collection. Stewardship is a conversion of heart in that place where we stand alone before God. It is to the deep within the heart of each and everyone here today, that this homily is addressed. It is within the heart that this spirituality continues to grow. Please, let us open our hearts to hear and receive God's grace.

Our time and talent come from God. They are not our own. It *seems* like they belong to us. They're always with us and are a part of us, but we ourselves are not our own; we belong to God. If *we* don't belong to ourselves, then our time and talent are not our own either. They have been given to us by God. We don't own them. We steward them. We manage them.

God is like the president of the company and we are the manager: our factory involves time and talent and God expects us to manage our time and talent well. We are to give a portion back to God of our time and talent, in thanksgiving for what God has given to us. This portion is called a tithe, which is ten percent or one tenth.

Time and talent are often linked together because when we give of our talent we naturally have to give of our time. Next weekend we will ask everybody to review what gifts of talent we have that we can share with the community of St. Thomas More. We will have lay witness talks and an in-pew sign-up on our time and talent sheets.

But giving time alone to God is a part of the spirituality of stewardship. Giving time alone to God, of course, is giving time to God in prayer. Just as the factory manager scheduled a fifteen-minute conference with God each day, we are asked to "schedule" time with God. Why? Well, one of the motivations of prayer is gratitude.

Today's second reading says that we are to give thanks always and for everything in the name of Jesus Christ to God the Father. We thank God for the gifts of time, talent, and treasure. We take the time to think about, and to list, all that God has done in our lives. We take the time to think about, and list, all that we have done for God. As we think and pray about what we are doing for God we naturally set, and perhaps recognize, our priorities. So how we spend our time is consistent with how important God is to us. One way to show that God is important to us is to tithe our time to God one day a week.

Think about it! What would it entail? Well, there are twenty-four hours in a day. If we convert that into minutes, we get one thousand four hundred forty. Ten percent of one thousand four hundred forty minutes is one hundred forty minutes or two hours and twenty-four minutes. Sunday is the natural day of the week to set aside to tithe the day.

Walk this through with me. This would mean one hour in prayer at the Sunday Mass. That would leave an hour and twenty-four minutes. We can pray first thing in the morning. We can pray before Mass in preparation, then spend some time in prayer two other times such as in the evening and before going to bed. In doing this we would sanctify the whole day. Sunday would live up to its name of being called a holiday, which is short for holy day. That's what holy day means.

As good stewards we remind ourselves that stewardship is, first and foremost, a spirituality, a way of getting closer to God. The more we pray, the more we tithe our time one day a week. The other disciplines of spirituality of stewardship become easier and much more meaningful. The conversion within our hearts changes our attitudes, and draws us closer to God. The meaning of life changes, our priorities change. Life becomes better.

So what do we take with us today as we begin our stewardship renewal of time and talent?

1. Well, let us remember that stewardship is first and foremost a spirituality, a spirituality that requires us to "schedule" time with God in prayer.
2. Let us thank God for our gifts of time and talent and be prepared to make a commitment to God of our time and talent in thanksgiving for what God has done for us.
3. And may we do something for God in return as good stewards. Perhaps we can accept the challenge to give to God ten percent of a day, one day a week, a tithe of a day — Sunday.

May our hearts be filled with God's grace to accept this challenge as we renew our commitment of time and talent.

HOMILY ON TALENT

"Being a Good Servant"

There was a political leader in Washington, D.C., who was in his living room and asked his wife, "My dear, do you know how many truly great men there are in the world today?" Without missing a beat, she replied, "No, I don't, but I do know there is one less than you think there is."

Being ego-centered causes us to miss the point of stewardship. Being a good steward is to recognize God's greatness, not our own. Having a good self-identity is the start of stewardship. Being a steward means that we think of ourselves as managers who are to be responsible and accountable for what we have. There is one greater than us who gives us what we manage, and, of course, that one is God. God is the boss, not us. That means we are all in middle-management. That also means that there are those who look to us to find out what should be done. When we get comfortable being in charge of our own affairs as well as the affairs of others, there is the temptation to forget who the boss is. We are not the boss. God is the one who is great and he gives us all we have.

Mila Glodava is our parish's director of stewardship and communications. She recently gave a workshop on stewardship in the Philippines. She discovered that because of cultural differences, good stewards identify best with a spousal image. I believe this image can work in our culture as well.

Looking at stewardship from a spousal relationship begs the question of greatness. Marriage is a mutual and lasting loving relationship. Being ego-centered will cause spouses to lose their focus. In this case we must understand that we, as a Church, are married to God. If we focus on ourselves, we cannot focus on God. Our greatness does not come from ourselves but from God. Great things are expected of us by virtue of us being wedded to God. God is the husband and the Church is his faithful wife.

It is important to recall that the Church has often been called our mother. This is to reassure us, who are called God's children, of God's love for us. Children grow up. If we keep only the mother image of Church, then we might expect the Church always to do for us, rather than for us to do for the Church. Stewardship expects a certain maturity and asks us to see ourselves as the Church. We are the Church. God is the husband and the Church is his faithful wife.

This faithfulness, this fidelity means that things do not get in the way of our love for our spouses. Loving God alone means we cannot have other gods before him. Money is a false god. Loving money more than God would be an offense against fidelity.

The wedding rite says: "for richer or poorer" which means people are more important than things. The love relationship anticipates the needs of the other but understands that material needs are subordinate to the emotional or spiritual needs of the spouse. By caring and sharing we place an emphasis upon persons and not on things. Self-giving is the goal of marriage. It takes humility to give of oneself. God has demonstrated his humility through Jesus Christ's love. We are to imitate the humility of our God. Giving is a requirement of spouses. God gives to us and we are to give to God. No matter what our state in life, we must give because giving is the requirement of the love relationship. Giving is the requirement of the Christian life.

Giving God our skill and our wealth without giving of ourselves is meaningless. If a man showers his wife with gifts but does not love her, his gestures are empty. If a wife loves the gifts more than the husband, her actions are also empty. Stewardship is truly a spirituality. When a stewardship commitment is made of our time, talent, or treasure, we are first of all giving ourselves. We are giving of our love and devotion to God. We are sharing with God what God, out of love, has shared with us.

A good steward can identify with being a manager or a spouse. A manager remembers who the boss is and a spouse knows that love is mutual. Each sees the folly of being self-centered, and recognizes that greatness comes from God. Let us remember that stewardship is a spirituality that allows us to grow in our love for God. May our gifts of time, talent, and treasure be symbols of that love.

HOMILY ONE ON TREASURE

(Note: This homily was given shortly after September 11, 2001.)

How do we preach stewardship in the light of the terrorists' attack upon our society? The Holy Spirit led me to preach stewardship in a different way — something new for me.

When I was studying for the priesthood in 1985, I spent a semester living in Jerusalem. It was there I had some important conversations with people of the Islamic faith. It was the first time I understood why the United States was called the "Great Satan" — the devil. Us, the devil? Why? Well, the Islamic people put God (their understanding of God is not completely different from our understanding) into every aspect of their lives. They make no distinction between religious life and secular life; they are one and the same. God is part of their work, their schools, and their government. To take God out of these things would be wrong. Their perspective of us is that we have taken God out of our lives, out of our work, out of our schools, and out of our government. With God moved out, the devil has moved in.

From this perspective we, the United States of America, are the "Great Satan" because we have a secular life.

In reflecting upon that assessment of American life, we as Catholics have a similar concern. Don't we also decry the removal of religious values from our society, our schools, our workplace? The lack of morality on television and in movies and the media is shocking. We, as a Church, decry materialism and consumerism where a concern for material goods pushes God out of our lives. Greed breeds contempt for the poor, makes us self-centered and elitist.

Today is the Twenty-sixth Sunday in Ordinary Time and the renewal of our stewardship of treasure. This is a good place to bring in today's reading from the sixth chapter of Amos and today's Gospel from the sixteenth chapter of St. Luke. Amos condemns the rich for allowing the poor to suffer in their midst. In the Gospel, Jesus tells the parable of the rich man and Lazarus. The *Catechism of the Catholic Church* tells us that when we pray the Our Father, and say, "Give us this day our daily bread," we are to reflect upon the Parable of the Rich Man and Lazarus.

Yes, God gives us everything. He gives us everything on which to live. Yes, God gives the "daily bread" to Lazarus. The problem is Lazarus didn't receive it. Why? Because the rich man did not deliver it.

From a larger perspective, the world looks upon America as the rich man and if you have at all traveled outside of America, it is easy to see why. We do look rich in comparison. When we sing, "God bless America," God has indeed answered our prayers. We have been richly blessed. But if this is true, then the Parable of the Rich Man and Lazarus is a warning to us. The rich man is condemned, not for being rich, but because he was indifferent to the poverty of Lazarus.

From a stewardship perspective he was a bad steward. He took the tithe, the first tenth of what he earned and he spent it on himself instead of giving it away. The great irony is that the rich man would not have had less. He would have had more. In the end he would have attained eternal life. He, too, would have rested in the arms of Father Abraham. Will we?

As we renew stewardship in the light of the terrorist attacks (even if they think we are the "Great Satan") on America, we, as Americans, have to do some soul searching. We must bring these people to justice. But we must review our lack of God in our society. I was very pleased to see politicians in the news appealing to God for help. The song *God Bless America* is being sung openly. Thank God that we see God being put back into our secular lives, but we cannot stop there!

The freedom of religion in America is *not* the freedom *from* religion. It is not the *absence* of religion. Freedom of religion is the tolerance of religion. It allows us to put God into all parts of our lives — including the financial parts of our lives. We, as Catholic Christians, must seize this opportunity to see what we have, what we earn, what we work for, as gifts from God, which they really are. Our material wealth is evidence that God has blessed Americans, has blessed you and me. Lazarus is waiting for us around the world to deliver the "daily bread" that God has given to us to give away. This is precisely what tithing and stewardship teach. God wants us to tithe. He has blessed us. He blesses us and wants us to tithe!

"Even if one should rise from the dead"— we have the risen Christ in us. We are to convince our brothers and sisters to be good stewards. We will prove the terrorists wrong.

For every ten dollars given in the collection, one dollar goes to charity. On behalf of the St. Thomas More parishioners, we give thousands of dollars each week to the poor, the elderly, the victims of terror in New York and Washington, and the churches of the Philippines, Nicaragua, Africa. Yes, Lazarus receives his "daily bread" each time we share a portion or a tithe given as a gift at this sacrifice of the Eucharist.

If every person in the Church gave, we would ask, "What poor?"

If every person in the U.S. gave, we would ask, "What poor?"

Stewardship conversion: Malachi's word prophesizes "You ain't seen nothing yet!" When we pray, "God bless America," watch out, He keeps his promises! What are you waiting for? A vision? An opportunity? We have stewardship parables. We have God and the prophets. We have the Risen Christ.

So what do we take with us from this Twenty-sixth Sunday and the stewardship renewal of treasure?

1. When we pray "Give us this day our daily bread," let it be a stewardship reminder of the gifts God has given us and our need to give.
2. May we realize the need to put God back into our secular lives, especially in our materialistic and consumerist world.
3. And let us ponder how much God has richly blessed us when we pray "God bless America." God cannot be outdone in generosity.

HOMILY TWO ON TREASURE

When I was in college, I remember telling my brothers why I attended daily Mass. I used the analogy of life insurance. I said people pay life insurance on a regular schedule. In the end, they hope to reap a number of benefits: peace of mind and the security of knowing everything will be OK when they die, that those after them won't be burdened by their choices in life.

Well, I likened my going to Mass to a part of my payment of eternal life insurance. I spoke of it as being the best policy. In the end I hoped to reap a number of benefits: peace of mind, security, the knowledge that everything will be OK when I die and that those after me will not be burdened by my choices.

Today we begin our stewardship renewal of treasure. I'm preaching at all of the weekend Masses here at St. Thomas More about the spirituality of stewardship. The spiritual reasons for giving are not the same as the practical reasons for giving. The practical reasons focus upon giving to a need. We have plenty of needs that I won't go into now. The spiritual reasons for giving focus upon the need to give. The spiritual reasons for giving take care of our practical reasons for giving, and leave the person with the feeling of giving for the right reasons. These may be peace of mind, the security that everything will be OK, and that when we die, our choices won't be a burden to others.

Today's three readings on this Twenty-eighth Sunday in Ordinary Time give us some insight for our stewardship renewal of treasure. The first reading from the twenty-fifth chapter of the book of the prophet Isaiah says, "On this Holy Mountain, the Lord of Hosts will provide for all peoples, a feast of rich food, and pure, choice wines."

This passage has been interpreted to mean that God would give us the gift of the Eucharist — bread and wine that become the Body and Blood of Jesus Christ. It can also be interpreted at a symbolic level. God gives us what we need; the food on which to live and shelter for security. God does save us.

Today's second reading is from the fourth chapter of Paul's letter to the Philippians. Paul talks about living with plenty and living without. The passage ends with, "My God will fully supply whatever you need in accord with his glorious riches in Christ Jesus."

Yes, again we hear God will give us what we need.

In the Gospel from the twenty-second chapter of St. Matthew we hear of the parable of the king who gives a wedding feast. The original guests refused to come, occupied with worldly affairs. The king grows angry and invites strangers to fill his hall. This parable is too deep to go into all the details, but again God gives us what we need.

The king is God. The original guests were the Jewish people of Jesus' day. The strangers are those of us who eat at the Eucharistic banquet. Being properly disposed to receive the Eucharist can be seen in the strangers who came dressed properly.

Being prepared and properly disposed is more than just saying an act of contrition before Mass. It includes the disposition in our lives. Stewardship helps us with how we take care of the gifts God has given us. Do we remember our role as good stewards? Do we act as if know

God gives us everything we need? Do we trust? Do we know he gives us food and shelter?

I am aware of the difficult times that we have in the Denver area. It is precisely during the difficult times when we are glad to have insurance. Do we have spiritual life insurance? The good stewards know what peace of mind and security are all about. They trust in God in good times and in bad. God takes care of them.

If you think, "Well, now is not a good time to give," I would beg to differ, for now is the perfect time to give and to trust in God.

How we live demonstrates how disposed we are to trust in God. A good example is car insurance. You pay regularly and you hope you may not have to use it. Do we trust God more than our car insurance agent? When something goes wrong, do we have more faith in God than in the insurance agent?

What are the spiritual reasons for giving? How much should I give? God gave us the tithe. He gave it to us as a guideline. Tithe means ten percent, not of what's leftover, but of the first of our treasure, the first and the best. You may want to start with a quarter of a tithe, or maybe half of a tithe.

I like to say that you would want to give God more than you give for car insurance. If not, wouldn't you be trusting your car insurance agent more than you would be trusting God?

What do we take away with us?

1. Let us remember that the practical reasons for giving have us giving to a need, while the spiritual reason for giving is that we have a need to give.
2. Let us remember that the security and peace of mind we get from life insurance is like the security and peace of mind we get from being a good steward.
3. Let us trust that God will provide for all our needs, especially here at the Eucharist. Let us all be properly disposed by being good stewards.

HOMILY THREE ON TREASURE

During the Great Depression there was a man named John Griffith who was a railroad drawbridge operator across the Mississippi River. One summer day in 1937 he invited his eight-year-old son Greg to come to work so they could have lunch together. After the drawbridge was raised up so ships could pass, they enjoyed a leisurely lunch and time slipped away.

Suddenly John Griffith was startled by the shriek of a train whistle. It was the 107 Memphis Express with four hundred passengers. He scrambled to the control tower and was about to lower the bridge when he caught sight of his young son caught in the great rear wheels of the drawbridge. His mind raced for a solution when suddenly the train whistle shrieked again, louder, closer. He knew he had to make a decision to lower the bridge or four hundred passengers would die, but that was his son down there. He knew what he had to do. He lowered the bridge just in time for the train to pass by effortlessly, as tears streamed down his face knowing that his son was now dead.

He looked into the windows of the passing train and saw people casually unaware of the tragedy that took place. He cried out: "I sacrificed my son for you. Don't you even care?"

Today is the Thirty-second Sunday in Ordinary Time. Our three readings today can be interpreted to bring out a deeper meaning of the word "sacrifice." In today's first reading from the seventeenth chapter of the first book of Kings, the widow of Zaraphath makes a sacrifice of all she and her son had to live on so that Elijah, the prophet, could live. In today's Gospel from the twelfth chapter of Mark's Gospel, again a widow makes a sacrifice of all she had to live on to show her love for God.

Our story of John Griffith recounts a modern-day sacrifice, but we have a greater sacrifice in Jesus Christ.

Just recently I asked everyone in this parish to make a commitment of tithing treasure as a way of accepting the challenge of sacrificial giving, and as part of our stewardship renewal. I thank everyone who made a commitment. It is my hope to bring out the spiritual meaning of our giving by helping explain the meaning of sacrifice. Tithing is often called sacrificial giving. What is this sacrifice in our giving?

Our readings today give us deeper insight, especially the first reading from the ninth chapter of the letter to the Hebrews. Let's take a closer look.

I like to recount that "letter to the Hebrews" is contradictory in terms. It's not a letter like one of Paul's other letters. It may not even be by Paul. It's more of a theological position paper. It's not to the Hebrews but to groups of Jewish Christians who wanted to understand their Jewish roots. Hence, the "letter to the Hebrews."

In the Old Testament, the Jewish practice of an annual sacrifice was a regular part of worship. Now with Jesus Christ, we don't sacrifice *annually* anymore, because Jesus is the sacrifice offered *once for all.* Now, some might mistakenly think, "Well, since we don't offer annual sacrifices anymore, I don't need to make a sacrifice!" Not at all! That's not what we teach, nor is that what our readings are telling us today.

We still need to offer sacrifice, but there has been a shift in our thinking in three ways.

1. *Disposition.* The inner disposition of the giver is so important that the disposition is based on trust. Today's first reading and the Gospel tell us a double story of widows, people who are basically helpless and vulnerable. They need all the help they can get. Yet, they are not free from the need to sacrifice. When they do, God doesn't let them down. They are rewarded for their trust in God's word and are praised for giving examples to follow.

2. *External circumstances.* Surrendering our sacrifice has been replaced by a simpler form of giving of ourselves and what we possess. We don't slaughter a lamb. We make a commitment of time, talent, and treasure as a sacrifice. We don't have to come to the temple. We can offer our sacrifice to God at home and at work, but it is always fitting when we come to church. We are prepared to offer our hearts, humbled and not weighed

down by worldly cares. We are to let go of our material goods, for the sake of God.

3. *Sacrifice.* We identify our sacrifice with Christ's perfect gift. We are not doing this on our own. There is a common misperception in Catholic thought that "we" are somehow working our way to heaven. We do not work our way to heaven. Salvation is a gift given to us to receive. We receive the gift by participation in the offer to take up our cross, and following in his footsteps. In other words, we participate in Christ's sacrifice by joining our sacrifice to "Christ living in me, and I living in Christ." We do this mainly by our prayers. Our prayers join together at this Eucharist as a "sacrifice of praise." Our prayers cannot be empty words. If all we ever do is talk about sacrifice without sacrificing, what good is that? We are like a noisy gong or a clanging cymbal.

The sacrifice that Christ represents is that of the paschal lamb — the lamb that was sacrificed and whose blood was placed on the doors of the Israelites so the Angel of Death would *pass over.* The paschal lamb was selected with the same standard one used for offering a tithe. It had to be pure and spotless and without blemish.

Jesus is truly "the Lamb of God who takes away the sins of the world; happy are those who are called to his supper."

God gives us the best he has and we are to imitate him. We give the first tenth of what we have. The *best* of what we have. Like the widow who placed her gift in the collection box, we put our first and best in the collection. It is placed by the altar where God has given his first and his best.

So what do we take with us today this Thirty-second Sunday in Ordinary Time?

1. Let us make sure that our sacrificial giving is meaningful by remembering our need to make a sacrifice.
2. Let our inner disposition be one of trust. God can and will provide for us if we let him.

3. May we remember we don't work our way to heaven. Salvation is a gift, Christ living in me and I living in Christ. I unite my sacrifice to the perfect sacrifice at his Eucharist.

APPENDIX 3

"The Stewardship Way of the Cross"

By Father Andrew Kemberling

An English proverb says, "No cross, no crown." This is a deft way of saying that the glory of Christ as King comes from the fact that he died for us on the cross. We, too, must die to ourselves if we are to receive the crown of glory. "The Way of the Cross" is normally seen as a Lenten devotion, but during Advent and Christmas it teaches us some important lessons, especially as we bring to conclusion our season of stewardship renewal. I have composed "The Stewardship Way of the Cross." I'd like to share it with you:

Prelude: Jesus in his dying and rising to new life gave us salvation as a gift. He gives us his life and asks us to do the same by picking up our cross and following him. How well we respond to God's gifts is the task of the good steward. "The Stewardship Way of the Cross" focuses upon the gifts of time, talent, and treasure. We also explore the values of identity, trust, gratitude, and love.

The First Station: Jesus is condemned to death. Jesus is falsely judged. Do we fall into the trap of judging people as being rich or poor? The hidden generosity of others cannot be known by outward appearances. Have we been victims of false judgment? Jesus bears with being falsely judged with endurance and patience.

The Second Station: Jesus carries the cross. Jesus' burden does not interfere with his trust in the Father. When bad things happen, do we fail to trust God? Do we give hope to those who are burdened by sharing our trust in God? Jesus carries the cross which becomes our gift.

The Third Station: Jesus falls the first time. Pride precedes the fall of humanity. Jesus in his humanity undoes our pride with humility. We fall each time we are too proud to accept God's will for us. Are we humbled by our lack of possessions? Are we sinfully proud of what we have? Jesus falls and rises as we are expected to do.

The Fourth Station: Jesus meets his afflicted mother. Our parents are among the first gifts that God gives us. These people have been entrusted to take care of us when we are vulnerable. Children are a gift that parents steward. Mary has been given to our Church as a gift. Do we meet the needs of our elderly parents? Are we good parents? Do we entrust ourselves to the motherly care of Mary when we carry our burdens?

The Fifth Station: Simon of Cyrene helps Jesus carry his cross. Are we resentful when we volunteer and others do not? Does it bother us to carry the financial burden of the parish when others who could, refuse? We see in Simon, who may have been a reluctant volunteer, a man whose good deed is remembered in his favor for generations. Our good deeds can have a lasting effect as well.

The Sixth Station: Veronica wipes the face of Jesus. Do we know how to receive the kindness of others? Jesus did in his humility. Learning to give is matched by our ability to receive. Are we grateful for the kindness of others even as we are grateful for the kindness of God in our lives? Do we help those in need? Do we see Jesus in the least of our brothers and sisters?

The Seventh Station: Jesus falls the second time. Greed causes many people to fall. Jesus rises from his fall, as we are to rise from our sins of greed. Does our greed teach others to fall? Avarice is a capital sin along with pride and envy. Greed causes us to create other sins such as sins against justice and charity. Does our preoccupation with material goods blind us to the reality of God?

The Eighth Station: Jesus meets the women of Jerusalem. Jerusalem, as a location, can cause us to think of the whole world. Are we good stewards of the earth? Do we steal from future generations the resources they will need? Do we respect the property rights of others? We are stewards for providence which means that we need to share our benefits with others, especially with the poor of our own locality and beyond.

The Ninth Station: Jesus falls the third time. Envy causes people to fall. Jesus always put people before things. We can rise from our envy by putting people first. Covetous desires place more importance upon our neighbors' goods than upon the dignity of individuals. Do we have the poverty of heart as shown by Jesus? Jesus celebrates the joy of the poor to whom the kingdom already belongs.

The Tenth Station: Jesus is stripped of his clothes. Jesus shows us how to give it all away, even the clothes off his back. Private property must not be gained by theft or coercion. Commutative justice demands respecting the rights of others and making reparation for injustice. Jesus stands here as a victim of injustice, naked and humiliated. Do we defend the rights of the vulnerable?

The Eleventh Station: Jesus is nailed to the cross. Jesus shows that suffering does not have to be meaningless. Christ is living in me, I am living in Christ. He suffers in my place as a gift to satisfy justice. Do I consider offering my suffering for the reparation of sin? Do I encourage others to find meaning in their suffering so they may offer it as a gift to God?

The Twelfth Station: Jesus dies on the cross. Jesus gives us the gift of his death. We are to imitate him. That means that our own death may be offered as a gift to others when we offer it up to God. We only receive one death and in return we may offer it for the reparation of sin. Do we encourage others to find hope in dying? Have we refused to find meaning in death? Have we prepared for our own death?

The Thirteenth Station: The body of Jesus is taken down from the cross. Jesus' cross stands empty as an invitation to pick up the cross and follow him. The cross is a gift to us. We are to pick it up and to receive it as a gift. Adversity can be the best teacher. Do we learn from our crosses? Have we thanked God for the lessons that we have learned through suffering?

The Fourteenth Station: Jesus is laid in the tomb. Corporal works of mercy are an obligation of a good steward. Joseph of Arimathea's giving of his tomb for Christ symbolizes the charity we are to show to others. Gifts given to the grieving are signs of our love for the living and the dead. Are we charitable to the sorrowing?

Closing: The Resurrection of Jesus. The revelation of the Resurrection is a gift. Do we cherish the Resurrection as the gift that it is? Gratitude for this victory is shown in how we live our lives. We cannot just say we are thankful; we have to show that we are thankful in deed. Do we give back to God a portion of what we receive in thanksgiving for what God has given us?

APPENDIX 4

References to Stewardship in the Bible

Leviticus 27:30: All tithes of the land, whether in grain from the fields or in fruit from the trees, belong to the Lord, as sacred to him.

Deuteronomy 14:22: Each year you shall tithe all the produce that grows in the field you have sown.

Deuteronomy 14:28: At the end of every third year you shall bring out all the tithes of your produce for that year and deposit them in community stores.

Deuteronomy 16:10: You shall then keep the feast of Weeks in honor of the Lord, your God, and the measure of your own freewill offering shall be in proportion to the blessing the Lord, your God, has bestowed on you.

Deuteronomy 16:16-17: Three times a year, then, every male among you shall appear before the Lord, your God, in the place which he chooses: at the feast of Unleavened Bread, at the feast of Weeks, and at the feast of Booths. No one shall appear before the Lord empty-handed, but each of you with as much as he can give, in proportion to the blessings which the Lord, your God, has bestowed on you.

Deuteronomy 26:2: You shall take some first fruits of the various products of the soil which you harvest from the land which the Lord, your God, gives you, and putting them in a basket, you shall go to the place which the Lord, your God, chooses for the dwelling place of his name.

1 Chronicles 29:14: But who am I, and who are my people, that we should have the means to contribute so freely? For everything is from you, and we only give you what we have received from you.

Proverbs 3:9-10: Honor the LORD with your wealth, with first fruits of all your produce; Then will your barns be filled with grain, with new wine your vats will overflow.

Proverbs 11:25: He who confers benefits will be amply enriched, and he who refreshes others will himself be refreshed.

Sirach 35:6-10: The just man's sacrifice is most pleasing, nor will it ever be forgotten. In generous spirit pay homage to the LORD, be not sparing of freewill gifts. With each contribution show a cheerful countenance, and pay your tithes in a spirit of joy. Give to the Most High as he has given to you, generously, according to your means. For the LORD is one who always repays, and he will give back to you sevenfold.

Malachi 3:8, 10: Dare a man rob God? Yet you are robbing me! And you say, "How do we rob you?" In tithes and in offerings!... Bring the whole tithe into the storehouse, That there may be food in my house, and try me in this, says the LORD of hosts: Shall I not open for you the floodgates of heaven, to pour down blessing upon you without measure?

New Testament

Matthew 5:3-12: The Beatitudes

Blessed are the poor in spirit, for theirs is the kingdom of heaven.
Blessed are they who mourn, for they will be comforted.
Blessed are the meek, for they will inherit the land.
Blessed are they who hunger and thirst for righteousness, for they will be satisfied.
Blessed are the merciful, for they will be shown mercy.
Blessed are the clean of heart, for they will see God.
Blessed are the peacemakers, for they will be called children of God.

Blessed are they who are persecuted for the sake of
righteousness, for theirs is the kingdom of heaven.
Blessed are you when they insult you and persecute you and
utter every kind of evil against you (falsely) because of me.
Rejoice and be glad, for your reward will be great in heaven.
Thus they persecuted the prophets who were before you.

Matthew 5:16: Just so, your light must shine before others, that they may see your good deeds and glorify your heavenly Father.

Matthew 5:42: Give to the one who asks of you, and do not turn your back on one who wants to borrow.

Matthew 6:24: No one can serve two masters. He will either hate one and love the other, or be devoted to one and despise the other. You cannot serve God and mammon.

Matthew 10:8: Without cost you have received; without cost you are to give.

Matthew 10:42: And whoever gives only a cup of cold water to one of these little ones to drink because he is a disciple — amen, I say to you, he will surely not lose his reward.

Matthew 13:3-9: The Parable of the Sower

Matthew 13:31-32: The Parable of the Mustard Seed

Matthew 13:33: The Parable of the Yeast

Matthew 14:19-21: Taking the five loaves and the two fish, and looking up to heaven, he said the blessing, broke the loaves, and gave them to the disciples, who in turn gave them to the crowds. They all ate and were satisfied, and they picked up the fragments left over — twelve wicker baskets full. Those who ate were about five thousand men, not counting women and children.

Matthew 16:27: For the Son of Man will come with his angels in his Father's glory, and then he will repay everyone according to his conduct.

Matthew 22:37-39: He said to him, "You shall love the Lord, your God, with all your heart, with all your soul, and with all your mind. This is the greatest and the first commandment. The second is like it. You shall love your neighbor as yourself."

Matthew 25:14-30: Parable of the Talents

Mark 10:21: Go, sell what you have, and give to (the) poor and you will have treasure in heaven; then come, follow me.

Mark 10:43-45: Whoever wishes to be great among you will be your servant; whoever wishes to be first among you will be the slave of all. For the Son of Man did not come to be served but to serve and to give his life as a ransom for many.

Mark 12:42-44: A poor widow also came and put in two small coins worth a few cents. Calling his disciples to himself, he said to them, "Amen, I say to you, this poor widow put in more than all the other contributors to the treasury. For they have all contributed from their surplus wealth, but she, from her poverty, has contributed all she had, her whole livelihood."

Mark 13:34: It is like a man traveling abroad. He leaves home and places his servants in charge, each with his work, and orders the gatekeeper to be on the watch.

Luke 3:11: Whoever has two cloaks should share with the person who has none. And whoever has food should do likewise.

Luke 6:38: Give and gifts will be given to you; a good measure, packed together, shaken down, and overflowing, will be poured into your lap. For the measure with which you measure will in return be measured out to you.

Luke 6:43-45: A good tree does not bear rotten fruit, nor does a rotten tree bear good fruit. For every tree is known by its own fruit. For people do not pick figs from thornbushes, nor do they gather grapes from brambles. A good person out of the store of goodness in his heart produces good, but an evil person out of a store of evil produces evil; for from the fullness of the heart the mouth speaks.

Luke 10:29-37: Parable of the Good Samaritan

Luke 11:5-8: [Teaching on perseverance in prayer]

Luke 11:9-13: And I tell you, ask and you will receive; seek and you will find; knock and the door will be opened to you. For everyone who asks, receives; and the one who seeks, finds; and to the one who knocks, the door will be opened. What father among you would hand his son a snake when he asks for a fish? Or hand him a scorpion when he asks for an egg? If you then, who are wicked, know how to give good gifts to your children, how much more will the Father in heaven give the holy Spirit to those who ask him?

Luke 11:42: Woe to you Pharisees! You pay tithes of mint and of rue and of every garden herb, but you pay no attention to judgment and to love for God. These you should have done, without overlooking the others.

Luke 12:34: For where your treasure is, there also will your heart be.

Luke 12:48: Much will be required of the person entrusted with much, and still more will be demanded of the person entrusted with more.

Luke 14:33: In the same way, everyone of you who does not renounce all his possessions cannot be my disciple.

Luke 16:10-13: The person who is trustworthy in very small matters is also trustworthy in great ones; and the person who is dishonest in very small matters is also dishonest in great ones. If, therefore, you are not trustworthy with dishonest wealth, who will trust you with true wealth? If you are not trustworthy with what belongs to another, who will give you what is yours? No servant can serve two masters. He will either hate one and love the other, or be devoted to one and despise the other. You cannot serve God and mammon.

Luke 16:19-31: Parable of the Rich Man and Lazarus

Luke 19:8: But Zacchaeus stood there and said to the Lord, "Behold, half of my possessions, Lord, I shall give to the poor, and if I have extorted anything from anyone I shall repay it four times over."

John 6:27: Do not work for food that perishes but for the food that endures for eternal life, which the Son of Man will give you.

John 9:4-5: We have to do the works of the one who sent me while it is day. Night is coming when no one can work. While I am in the world, I am the light of the world.

John 12:26: Whoever serves me must follow me, and where I am, there also will my servant be. The Father will honor whoever serves me.

John 14:21: Whoever has my commandments and observes them is the one who loves me. And whoever loves me will be loved by my Father, and I will love him and reveal myself to him.

John 15:12-13: This is my commandment: love one another as I love you. No one has greater love than this, to lay down one's life for one's friends.

John 15:16-17: It was not you who chose me, but I who chose you and appointed you to go and bear fruit that will remain, so that whatever you ask the Father in my name he may give you. This I command you: love one another.

John 20:21: As the Father has sent me, so I send you.

John 21:17: (Jesus) said to him [Peter], "Feed my sheep."

Acts 2:44-45: All who believed were together and had all things in common; they would sell their property and possessions and divide them among all according to each one's need.

Acts 4:34-35: There was no needy person among them, for those who owned property or houses would sell them, bring the proceeds of the sale, and put them at the feet of the apostles, and they were distributed to each according to need.

Acts 20:24-35: You know well that these very hands have served my needs and my companions. In every way I have shown you that by hard work of that sort we must help the weak, and keep in mind the words of the Lord Jesus who himself said, "It is more blessed to give than to receive."

Romans 12:6-8: Since we have gifts that differ according to the grace given to us, let us exercise them: if prophecy, in proportion to the faith; if ministry, in ministering; if one is a teacher, in teaching; if one exhorts, in exhortation; if one contributes, in generosity; if one is over others, with diligence; if one does acts of mercy, with cheerfulness.

1 Corinthians 4:1-2: Thus should one regard us: as servants of Christ and stewards of the mysteries of God. Now it is of course required of stewards that they be found trustworthy.

1 Corinthians 16:2: On the first day of the week each of you should set aside and save whatever one can afford, so that collections will not be going on when I come.

2 Corinthians 8: [Paul's encouragement to be generous]

2 Corinthians 9:6: Consider this: whoever sows sparingly will also reap sparingly, and whoever sows bountifully will also reap bountifully.

2 Corinthians 9:7: Each must do as already determined, without sadness or compulsion, for God loves a cheerful giver.

2 Corinthians 9:8-9: Moreover, God is able to make every grace abundant for you, so that in all things, always having all you need, you may have an abundance for every good work. As it is written: "He scatters abroad, he gives to the poor; his righteousness endures forever."

1 Timothy 6:7: For we brought nothing into the world, just as we shall not be able to take anything out of it.

1 Timothy 6:18-19: Tell them to do good, to be rich in good works, to be generous, ready to share, thus accumulating as treasure a good foundation for the future, so as to win the life that is true life.

Titus 3:14: But let our people, too, learn to devote themselves to good works to supply urgent needs, so that they may not be unproductive.

Hebrews 13:16: Do not neglect to do good and to share what you have; God is pleased by sacrifices of that kind.

James 2:15-17: If a brother or sister has nothing to wear and has no food for the day, and one of you says to them, "Go in peace, keep warm, and eat well," but you do not give them the necessities of the body, what good is it? So also faith of itself, if it does not have works, is dead.

James 4:3: You ask but do not receive, because you ask wrongly, to spend it on your passions.

1 Peter 4:10: As each one has received a gift, use it to serve one another as good stewards of God's varied grace.

APPENDIX 5

References to Stewardship in the *Catechism of the Catholic Church*

Time

1021 final destiny
1042 end of time
1165 today
1166 the Lord's day
2174 Sunday
2606 the Resurrection
2659 Word of the Lord
2660 everyday situations
2836 every day

Talent

893 bishops and priests
898 laity
899 initiative of lay Christians
900 duty
910 called
1734 voluntary
1913 participation
1914 taking charge
1915 public life
1916 ethical obligation
1917 authority
2239 service

Treasure

1351 gifts
2113 temptation
2172 the Sabbath
2402 resources
2404 external goods
2414 seventh commandment
2415 dominion
2416 animals
2417 entrusted
2426 economic activity
2439 rich nations
2534 tenth commandment
2536 greed
2538 envy
2539 immoderate desire
2545 perfect charity
2547 blessed are the poor

Identity

355 image of God
357 dignity
2156 baptism
2157 Sign of the Cross
2158 name is sacred
2159 unique character
2258 human life
2784 adoption
2829 "Give us"

Trust

227 God is enough
2464 eighth commandment
2734 filial trust
2785 humble heart
2828 trust of children
2837 daily

Gratitude

1360 Eucharist
2637 thanksgiving
2638 offering of thanksgiving

Love

1939 solidarity
1940 goods and work
1941 socio-economic problems
1942 beyond material goods
2093 God's love
2094 sin against God's love
2196 first of the commandments
2831 hunger

APPENDIX 6

Data Analysis

I. HOW TO CALCULATE THE EFFECTS OF INFLATION

Inflation works this way mathematically:

I = Inflation rate
R = Nominal Return (the apparent return before inflation)
Rr = Real Return after inflation

To obtain a ball park estimate of Rr:

$$R\text{-}I \approx Rr$$

More precisely:

$$[1 + R \div 1 + I] - 1 = Rr$$

To measure the nominal return of our case study, we use a financial calculator. Suppose a large parish in New York had these figures:

Offertory 2000 value = $3,043,731
Offertory 2008 value = $4,352,872
t = 8 years
R = 4.57%
Inflation = 2.78%

So:

$$[1.0457 \div 1.0278] - 1 = .0221 = 1.74\% = \text{Real return}$$

So stewardship grew the offertory at 1.74% a year on average. We can also double check using our formula R-I ≈ Rr:

$$4.57\% - 2.78\% = 1.79\% \approx 1.74\%$$

Recall inflation rate was about 2.8%. The offertory was increasing. During that time parish expenses were also increasing at 2.8%. Therefore if the parish did absolutely "nothing" it is still reasonable to expect the offertory to rise to $3.8 million in 8 years simply due to the effects of inflation. Inflation doesn't sleep. It doesn't rest. It is always eating away at your money.

Our case study parish managed to grow the offertory from $3.0 million to $4.4 million in 8 years with stewardship. They *beat* inflation. Over time, they enjoyed a nominal offertory increase of 4.57% per annum and a real increase after inflation of 1.74% annually. You don't have to memorize countless financial formulas. Just understand stewardship *does* work.

2. FORMULA FOR CALCULATING OFFERTORY GROWTH

Mathematically speaking, the offertory is a function of two variables: donors and gift size. Consider the following example.

A = number of donors
B = average gift
ΔA = percentage change in number of donors
ΔB = percentage change in average gift
T = Total Offertory
ΔT = percentage change in Total Offertory

And the formula to calculate the total is:

$$\Delta T = \Delta A + \Delta B + [(\Delta A) \times (\Delta B)]$$

So it is evident that to increase your offertory, you have to increase either the number of donors or the average size of donations, right? One can therefore increase the average size of donations by soliciting large gifts from a select few. How do you increase the number of donors? By asking for pledges!

In this example, suppose the average gift in any given year was $906. The number of pledged givers was 3,489. Do you believe 100% of parishioners were making a pledge? By no means! In fact, assume less than 50% of families were making a pledge in our example. If you are able to increase the number of families making a pledge by a mere

5% and they make an average gift, mathematically you can expect your offertory to increase 5%.

On the other hand, if you can increase the average gift 5%, you can also expect the offertory to increase 5%. If you increase *both* the number of families pledging *and* the size of the gift by 5% each, you can expect an offertory increase of about 10.25%!

In a hypothetical example using round numbers:

A = 3489 families donating
B = $906 average annual gift
T = A x B = Total Offertory = $3,161,034

ΔA = 5%
ΔB = 5%

ΔA(A) = 174 = (5% of 3489)
ΔB(B) = $45 = (5% of $906)

A1 = 3663 (new total of families donating as a result of stewardship)
B1 = $951 (new average gift as a result of stewardship)

To calculate the new offertory use:

T1 = [A1] x [B1] = $3,483,513
T1-T = $322,479

ΔT = T1-T ÷ T = $322,479 ÷ $3,161,034 = 10.21%

INDEX

STEWARDSHIP RESOURCES

Our Sunday Visitor (For a variety of stewardship materials, including books, periodicals, parish resources, and offering envelopes.)
200 Noll Plaza
Huntington, IN 46750
1-800-348-2886
www.osv.com
www.osvenvelopes.com

Veritas Financial Ministries (Phil Lenahan's ministry to equip people for personal financial management according to Catholic principles.)
P.O. Box 892425
Temecula, CA 92589-2425
951-541-9522
www.veritasfinancialministries.com

International Catholic Stewardship Council
1275 K Street, NW, Suite 880
Washington, DC 20005-4077
202-289-1093
www.catholicstewardship.org

United States Conference of Catholic Bishops
USCCB Publishing
3211 Fourth Street NE
Washington, DC 20017-1194
1-800-235-8722
www.usccb.org

Books

Best Practices in Parish Stewardship
by Charles E. Zech
Our Sunday Visitor Publishing Division (200 Noll Plaza, Huntington, IN 46750, 1-800-348-2886, www.osv.com)

The Bible

Catechism of the Catholic Church
United States Conference of Catholic Bishops (USCCB Publishing, 3211 Fourth Street NE, Washington, DC 20017-1194, 1-800-235-8722, www.usccb.org)

Called To Be Stewards: Bringing New Life to Catholic Parishes
by Patrick McNamara
The Liturgical Press (Saint John's Abbey, P.O. Box 7500, Collegeville, MN 56321-7500, 1-800-445-5899, www.litpress.org)

Catholic Stewardship: Sharing God's Gifts
by Colleen Smith
Our Sunday Visitor Publishing Division (200 Noll Plaza, Huntington, IN 46750, 1-800-348-2886, www.osv.com)

Creating a Stewardship Council
by Marilyn Judd
The Liturgical Press (Saint John's Abbey, P.O. Box 7500, Collegeville, MN 56321-7500, 1-800-445-5899, www.litpress.org)

Making Stewardship a Way of Life: A Complete Guide for Catholic Parishes
by Fr. Andrew Kemberling and Mila Glodava
Our Sunday Visitor Publishing Division (200 Noll Plaza, Huntington, IN 46750, 1-800-348-2886, www.osv.com)

More Than Silver or Gold: Homilies of a Stewardship Priest
by Daniel J. Mahan
Saint Catherine of Siena Press (4812 North Park Ave., Indianapolis, IN 46205, 1-888-232-1492, www.saintcatherineofsienapress.com)

Nurturing Sacrificial Giving: Practical Steps for Its Renewal and Growth
by Rev. Joseph M. Champlin
The Liturgical Press (Saint John's Abbey, P.O. Box 7500, Collegeville, MN 56321-7500, 1-800-445-5899, www.litpress.org)

7 Steps to Becoming Financially Free: A Catholic Guide to Managing Your Money
by Phil Lenahan
Our Sunday Visitor Publishing Division (200 Noll Plaza, Huntington, IN 46750, 1-800-348-2886, www.osv.com)

Sharing Gifts: A Spirituality of Time, Talent, and Treasure
By Rev. Joseph M. Champlin
The Liturgical Press (Saint John's Abbey, P.O. Box 7500, Collegeville, MN 56321-7500, 1-800-445-5899, www.litpress.org)

Stewardship: Disciples Respond — A Practical Guide for Pastoral Leaders
International Catholic Stewardship Council (1275 K Street, NW, Suite 880, Washington, DC 20005-4077, 202-289-1093, www.catholicstewardship.org)

Stewardship: A Parish Handbook
by C. Justin Clements
Liguori Publications (One Liguori Drive, Liguori, MO 63057, 1-800-325-9521, www.ligouri.org)

Time, Talent & Treasure: Reflections on the U.S. Bishops' Model for Parish Stewardship
Liguori Publications (One Liguori Drive, Liguori, MO 63057, 1-800-325-9521, www.ligouri.org)

Why Catholics Don't Give ... And What Can Be Done About It
by Charles E. Zech
Our Sunday Visitor Publishing Division (200 Noll Plaza, Huntington, IN 46750, 1-800-348-2886, www.osv.com)

Encyclicals and Pastoral Letters

Caritas in Veritate (Charity in Truth) — Encyclical of Pope Benedict XVI

Deus Caritas Est (God is Love) — Encyclical of Pope Benedict XVI

Spe Salvi (On Christian Hope) — Encyclical of Pope Benedict XVI

Stewardship: A Disciple's Response — A Pastoral Letter on Stewardship
United States Conference of Catholic Bishops

Other Media

Stewardship Spirituality — A DVD and accompanying workbook to assist in the education and formation of stewardship spirituality, from the Catholic Diocese of Wichita Office of Stewardship (424 North Broadway, Wichita, KS 67202, 316-269-3900, www.cdowk.org/offices/stewardship/index.htm).

Internet

Catholic Diocese of Wichita Office of Stewardship
www.cdowk.org/offices/stewardship/index.htm

International Catholic Stewardship Council
www.catholicstewardship.org

League of Stewardship Parishes
www.stewardshipleague.org

St. Thomas More Catholic Church
www.stthomasmore.org/stewardship

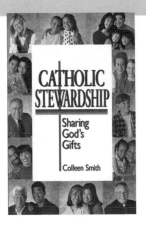

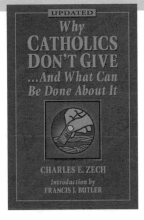

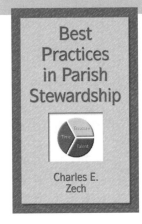

Offertory and Stewardship Solutions from Our Sunday Visitor

Build Offertory:

Stewardship envelopes

Reinforce the scriptural call to Catholic stewardship through OSV's offering envelopes. Biblical passages and images convey the concept of stewardship beyond the church into the homes of parishioners.

Mail-back envelopes

Increase parish revenue and help parishioners continue to give even in their absence by inserting a pre-addressed mail-back envelope into your periodic mailing packets.

R.E.A.C.H.- Renew. Educate. Announce. Connect. Heal.

Maximize your envelope mailing program with special messages and inserts to increase communication, promote events and stay connected with parishioners.

Loaves+Fishes™: A Process for Offertory Enhancement

Challenge parishioners' capacity to give and present them with the prayerful opportunity to increase their offertory gifts with this 10-week process.

Build Community:

Loaves+Fishes™: A Process for Stewardship Renewal

Encourage parishioner commitments of time, talent, and treasure. This process stands on its own as a stewardship mailing effort or as a follow up to *Loaves+Fishes™: A Process for Offertory Enhancement*.

Loaves+Fishes™ Webinars

Webinars are interactive web-based presentations designed to give practical techniques parishes can implement to enhance their ministries. An entire team of staff or committee members can participate for one low rate.

Inform! newsletters

Inform! is a newsletter design, print and mailing service that makes it easy to stay in touch with parishioners. Printed and mailed newsletters are an effective tool to keep both active and inactive members informed about parish life.

Get started today

For more information on any of these products or services, contact Our Sunday Visitor at 800.348.2886 or visit our website at www.osvoffertory.com.

Our Sunday Visitor serves millions of Catholics worldwide through its publishing, offertory and communication services. Established in 1912 by a local parish priest, Our Sunday Visitor has grown into the nation's largest supplier of offering envelopes, parish and diocesan mailings, books, periodicals, curriculum, address management and stewardship services. Our Sunday Visitor is a not-for-profit organization, returning a portion of net earnings back to the Catholic community through the OSV Institute.

OurSundayVisitor

Enriching Parishes...Enhancing Community

www.osvoffertory.com
800-348-2886

11/13/09